THE PASSION
OF
OUR LORD

Consisting of excerpts from
THE CITY OF GOD
By Venerable Mary of Agreda

Translated from the original Spanish
by FISCAR MARISON
(*Rev. George J. Blatter*)

AMI PRESS
Washington, N. J. 07882

First Printing
February 1980
Reprinted 1992

ISBN 0-911988-38-6

IMPRIMATUR

Santa Fe, New Mexico, February 9, 1949

I gladly give my "Imprimatur" as of today, to the new edition of the work, *"The City of God"* by Sister Mary of Jesus, to be reprinted from the original authorized Spanish edition of the year 1902 without change, and already bearing the Imprimatur of His Excellency, Most Reverend H. J. Alerding, Bishop of Fort Wayne.

†EDWIN V. BYRNE, D.D.,
Archbishop of Santa Fe

(NOTE: The above Imprimatur covers the complete four volume edition of the CITY OF GOD, from which the present volume is excerpted.)

— THE PUBLISHERS

CONTENTS

vi

THE CITY OF GOD
Historical Notes

THE MYSTICAL CITY OF GOD in four volumes, by Venerable Mary of Agreda, was translated into English from the original Spanish by Fr. George J. Blatter (under the *nom de plume* of *Fiscar Marison*), and published by him in 1912 under the aegis of the *Theopolitan Company* of Chicago, composed of Fr. Blatter, his brother and some friends, organized for the purpose of disseminating the book. In 1929, Mr. Louis W. Bernicken assumed publication of the four volumes, and in 1949 this work was taken over by Mr. Harry D. Corcoran of Albuquerque, N.M. under the name of the Corcoran Publishing Co. In 1971 the Blue Army (*AMI Press*) purchased publishing rights.

PREFACE

by JOHN M. HAFFERT

These revelations from Our Lady to the Venerable Sister Mary of Agreda have withstood the test of centuries. Literally thousands of devout persons (including many Bishops, Cardinals and saints) have read this book and found that its greatest proof of authenticity is its theological content.

It would seem impossible that any ordinary person could ever have imagined or fictionalized a work so evidently supernatural.

Sister Mary of Agreda has already been declared venerable by the Church, and there is now a growing movement for her canonization.

A devout layman, who prefers to be anonymous, was so deeply moved himself by this account of the Passion of Our Lord as revealed by Our Lady Herself to Venerable Mary of Agreda that he contributed $5,000 towards having this part of the four volumes of the revelations printed separately at a reasonable price, so that many persons could read it.

Therefore AMI Press printed double the number of copies which this gift made possible. Many were sent to convents and apostolic centers.

For the jacket of the book, and the opening fly leaf, we have chosen to reproduce part of the image of Our Lord which was left on the Holy Shroud at the moment of His resurrection.

In a sense, therefore, the reader is holding in hand a sort of "double miracle" of the Message of Our Lord's Passion: one the faithful reproduction of the battered and crucified body of Jesus as preserved for us on the Holy Shroud; the other the detailed account of His holy passion as revealed by His own Mother to the Venerable Mary of Agreda.

When we keep in mind that Jesus is God, and that therefore it is God Who suffered and died for us (O wonderful mystery!) we must be moved with the greatest love.

Our Lady offered to us Her Immaculate Heart at Fatima—but surrounded by thorns. She shows us a heart full of love, but surrounded by the memory of the great love shown to us by God in the Passion of Her Son.

We pray that all who read this book will be able to unite their hearts to the Sorrowful and Immaculate Heart of Mary and, in the light of Her own love, enter into the deep mystery of the great love God has shown for us as revealed on the Holy Shroud and in these pages....

PUBLISHER'S NOTE:

In the complete four volume edition of this work, paragraphs are numbered sequentially for easy reference. In this excerpted volume, the original paragraph numbers have been retained. It should be noted, however, that the paragraphs are numbered sequentially, beginning with 1, in each of the four volumes. All material for the present volume is excerpted from Volume 3, THE TRANSFIXION.

CHAPTER I .

445. Our Redeemer proceeded on his way to Jerusalem on the evening of the Thursday preceding his Passion and Death. During their conversation on the way, while he instructed them in the approaching mysteries, the Apostles proposed their doubts and difficulties, and He, as the Teacher of wisdom and as a loving Father answered them in words which sweetly penetrated into their very hearts. For, having always loved them, He, like a divine Swan, in these last hours of his life, manifested his love with so much the greater force of amiable sweetness in his voice and manner. The knowledge of his impending Passion and the prospect of his great torments, not only did not hinder Him in the manifestations of his love, but, just as fire is more concentrated by the frost, so his love broke forth with so much the greater force at the prospect of these sufferings. The conflagration of the love which burned in the heart of Jesus, issued forth to overpower by its penetrating activity, first those who were nearest about Him and then also those, who sought to extinguish it forever. Excepting Christ and His blessed Mother, the rest of us mortals are ordinarily roused to resentment by injury, or dismayed and disgusted by adversity, and we deem it a great thing not to revenge ourselves on those who offend us; but the love

1

of the divine Master was not daunted by the impending ignominies of his Passion, nor dampened by the ignorance of his Apostles and the disloyalty, which He was so soon to experience on their part.

446. The Apostle asked Him where He wished to celebrate the paschal supper (Matth. 26); for on that Thursday night the Jews were to partake of the lamb of the Pasch, a most notable and solemn national feast. Though of all their feasts, this eating of the paschal lamb was most prophetic and significant of the Messiah and of the mysteries connected with Him and his work, the Apostles were as yet scarcely aware of its intimate connection with Christ. The divine Master answered by sending saint Peter and saint John to Jerusalem to make arrangements for the paschal lamb. This was to be in a house, where they would see a servant enter with a jug of water, and whose master they were to request in Christ's name to prepare a room for his last Supper with his disciples. This man lived near to Jerusalem; rich and influential, he was at the same time devoted to the Savior and was one of those who had witnessed and had believed in his miracles and teachings. The Author of life rewarded his piety and devotion by choosing his house for the celebration of the great mystery, and thus consecrate it as a temple for the faithful of future times. The two Apostles immediately departed on their commission and following the instructions, they asked the owner of this house to entertain the Master of life for the solemn celebration of this feast of the unleavened bread.

447. The heart of this householder was enlightened by special grace and he readily offered his dwelling with all the necessary furniture for celebrating the supper according to the law. He assigned to them a very large

hall, appropriately tapestried and adorned for the mysteries which, unbeknown to him and the Apostles, the Lord was to celebrate therein. After due preparation had thus been made the Savior and the other Apostles arrived at this apartment. His most blessed Mother and the holy women in her company came soon after. Upon entering, the most humble Queen prostrated Herself on the floor and adored her divine Son as usual, asking his blessing and begging Him to let Her know what She was to do. He bade Her go to another room, where She would be able to see all that was done on this night according to the decrees of Providence, and where She was to console and instruct, as far as was proper, the holy women of her company. The great Lady obeyed and retired with her companions. She exhorted them to persevere in faith and prayer, while She, knowing that the hour of her holy Communion was at hand, continued to keep her interior vision riveted on the doings of her most holy Son and to prepare Herself for the worthy reception of his body and blood.

448. His most holy Mother having retired, our Lord and Master, Jesus, with his Apostles and disciples, took their places to celebrate the feast of the lamb. He observed all the ceremonies of the Law (Exodus 12, 3), as prescribed by Himself through Moses. During this last Supper He gave to the Apostles an understanding of all the ceremonies of the figurative law, as observed by the Patriarchs and Prophets. He showed them how beneath it was hidden the real truth, namely, all that He himself was to accomplish as Redeemer of the world. He made them understand, that now the law of Moses and its figurative meaning was evacuated by its real fulfillment; that, as the light of the new law of grace had begun to shine, the shadows were dispelled and the natural

law, which had been reconfirmed by the precepts of Moses, was now placed permanently upon its real foundation, ennobled and perfected by his own teachings; that the efficacy of the Sacraments of the new Law abrogated those of the old as being merely figurative and ineffectual. He told them that, by celebrating this Supper, He set an end to the rites and obligations of the old Law, which was only a preparation and a representation of what He was now about to accomplish, and hence having attained its end, had now become useless.

449. This instruction enlightened the Apostles concerning the deep mysteries of this last Supper. The other disciples that were present, did not understand these mysteries as thoroughly as the Apostles. Judas attended to and understood them least of all, yea, not at all; for he was completely under the spell of his avarice, thinking only of his prearranged treason and how he could execute it most secretly. The Lord revealed none of his secret treachery; for so it best served the designs and equity of his most high Providence. He did not wish to exclude him from the Supper and from the other mysteries, leaving it to his own wickedness to bring about his exclusion. The divine Master always treated him as his disciple, apostle and minister, and was careful of his honor. Thus He taught the children of the Church by his own example, with what veneration they should treat his ministers and priests, how they must guard their honor and avoid speaking of their sins and weaknesses still adhering to frail human nature in spite of their high office. None of them will ever be worse than Judas, as we can well assume; and not one of the faithful will ever be like Christ, our Lord and Savior, nor, as our faith teaches us, will anyone ever have his divine authority and power. Hence, as all men are of infinitely smaller con-

sideration than our Savior, let them accord to his ministers, who though wicked will ever be better than Judas, the same treatment as He condescended to accord to this most wicked disciple and Apostle. This duty toward priests is not less urgent even in superiors; for also Christ our Lord who bore with Judas and was so careful of his reputation was infinitely his superior.

450. On this occasion the Redeemer composed a new canticle by which He exalted the eternal Father for having in his Son fulfilled the figures of the old Law and for thus advancing the glory of his holy name. Prostrate upon the earth, He humiliated Himself in his humanity before God, confessing, adoring and praising the Divinity as infinitely superior to his humanity. Then addressing the eternal Father, He gave vent to the burning affection of his heart in the following sublime prayer.

451. "My eternal Father and infinite God, thy divine and eternal will resolved to create this my human nature in order that I may be the Head of all those that are predestined for thy glory and happiness and who are to attain their true blessedness by availing themselves of my works. For this purpose, and in order to redeem them from the fall of Adam, I have lived with them thirty-three years. Now, my Lord and Father, the opportune and acceptable hour for fulfilling thy eternal will has arrived, the greatness of thy holy name is about to be revealed to men and thy incomprehensible Divinity, through holy faith, is to be made known and exalted among all nations. It is time that the seven-sealed book be opened as Thou hast commissioned Me to do, and that the figures of old come to a happy solution (Apoc. 5, 7). The ancient sacrifices of animals, which prefigured the one I am now voluntarily to make of Myself for the children of Adam, for the members of my mysti-

cal body, for the sheep of thy flock, must now come to an end, and I beseech Thee in this hour to look down with an eye of mercy. If in the past thy anger has been placated by these ancient figures and sacrifices which I am now about to abrogate, let it now, my Father, be entirely extinguished, since I am ready to offer Myself in voluntary sacrifice to die for men on the Cross and give Myself as a holocaust of my love (Eph. 5, 2). Therefore, Lord, let the rigor of thy justice be relaxed and look upon the human race with eyes of mercy. Let Us institute a new law for men, by which they may throw down the bars of their disobedience and open for themselves the gates of heaven. Let them now find a free road and open portals for entering with Me upon the vision of thy Divinity, as many of them as will follow my footsteps and obey my law."

452. The eternal Father graciously received this prayer of our Redeemer and sent innumerable hosts of his angelic courtiers to assist at the wonderful works, which Christ was to perform in that place. While this happened in the Cenacle, most holy Mary in her retreat was raised to highest contemplation, in which She witnessed all that passed as if She were present. Thus She was enabled to co-operate and correspond as a most faithful Helpmate, enlightened by the highest wisdom. By heroic and celestial acts of virtue She imitated the doings of Christ, our Savior; for all of them awakened fitting resonance in her bosom and caused a mysterious and divine echo of like petitions and prayers in the sweetest Virgin. Moreover She composed new and admirable canticles of praise for all that the sacred humanity of Christ was now about to accomplish in obedience to the divine will and in accordance and in fulfillment of the figures of the old Law.

453. Very wonderful and worthy of all admiration

would it be for us, as it was for the holy angels and as it will be for all the blessed, if we could understand the divine harmony of the works and virtues in the heart of our great Queen, which like a heavenly chorus neither confused nor hindered each other in their superabundance on this occasion. Being filled with the intelligence of which I have spoken, She was sensible of the mysterious fulfillment and accomplishment of the ceremonies and figures of the old Law through the most noble and efficacious Sacraments of the new. She realized the vast fruits of the Redemption in the predestined; the ruin of the reprobate; the exaltation of the name of God and of the sacred humanity of Christ; the widespread knowledge and faith in the true God now beginning throughout the world. She fully understood, how the heavens had been closed for so many ages in order that now the children of Adam might enter through the establishment and progress of the new evangelical Church and its ministers; and how her divine Son was the most wonderful and skillful Artificer of all these blessings, exciting the admiration and praise of all the courtiers of heaven. For these magnificent results, without forgetting the least of them, She now blessed the eternal Father and gave Him ineffable thanks in the consolation and jubilee of her soul.

454. But also She reflected, that all these admirable works were to cost her divine Son the sorrow, ignominies, affronts and torments of his Passion, and at last the bitter death of the Cross, all of which He was to endure in the very humanity that He had received from Her; while at the same time, such a number of the children of Adam, for whom He suffered, would ungratefully waste the copious fruit of the Redemption. This knowledge filled with bitterest sorrow the purest heart of the loving

Mother. But as She was a living and faithful reproduction of her most holy Son, all these sentiments and operations found room in her magnanimous and expanded heart, and therefore She was not disturbed nor dismayed, nor did She fail to console and instruct her companions; but, without losing touch of her high intelligences, She descended to their level of thought in her words of consolation and of eternal life for their instruction. O admirable Instructress and superhuman example entirely to be followed and imitated! It is true, that in comparison with this sea of grace and light, our prerogatives dwindle into insignificance; but it is also true, that our sufferings and trials in comparison with hers are so to say only imaginary and not worthy to be even noticed, since She suffered more than all the children of Adam together. Yet neither in order to imitate Her, nor for our eternal welfare, can we be induced to suffer with patience even the least adversity. All of them excite and dismay us and take away our composure; we give vent to our passions, we angrily resist and are consumed with restless sorrow; in our stubbornness we lose our reason, give free reign to evil movements and hasten on toward the precipice. Even good fortune lures us to destruction, and so no reliance can be placed in our infected and spoiled nature. Let us be mindful of our heavenly Mistress on such occasions, in order that we may set ourselves right.

455. Having completed the Supper and fully instructed his disciples, Christ our Savior, as saint John tells us (John 13, 4), arose from the table in order to wash their feet. He first prostrated Himself before his eternal Father and addressed to Him another prayer of the same kind as that before the supper. It was not uttered in words, but was conceived interiorly, as follows: "Eternal Father,

Creator of the universe, I am thy image and the figure of thy substance, engendered by thy intellect (Heb. 1, 3). Having offered Myself for the Redemption of the world through my Passion and Death according to thy will, I now desire to enter upon these sacraments and mysteries by humiliating Myself to the dust, so that the pride of Lucifer may be confounded by the humility of thy Only-begotten. In order to leave an example of humility to my Apostles and to my Church, which must be built up on the secure foundation of this virtue, I desire, my Father, to wash the feet of my disciples, including the least of all of them, Judas, steeped in his own malice. I shall prostrate Myself before him in deepest and sincerest self-abasement to offer him my friendship and salvation. Though he is my greatest enemy among the mortals, I shall not refuse him pardon for his treachery, nor deny him kindest treatment, so that, if he shall decline to accept it, all the world may know, that I have opened up to him the arms of my mercy, and that he repelled my advances with obstinate contempt."

456. Such was the prayer of the Savior in preparing to wash the feet of his disciples. There are not words or similitudes in all creation which could properly express the divine impetus of the love with which He undertook and accomplished these works of mercy; for in comparison to it the activity of fire is but slow, the inflowing of the tide but weak, the tendency of a stone toward its center but tardy, and all the forces of the elements in the world that we can imagine in their united activity, but inadequate representations of the power of his love. But we cannot fail to perceive, that divine love and wisdom alone could ever conceive a humiliation, by which both the Divinity and his sacred humanity lowered themselves beneath the feet of mere creatures, and beneath the feet

of the worst of them, Judas, that He who is the Word of the eternal Father, the Holy of the holy, the essential Goodness, the Lord of lords and the King of kings, should prostrate Himself before the most wicked of men and touch the feet of this most impure and degraded of his creatures with his lips, and that He should do all this merely for the chance of justifying his wayward disciple and securing for him immeasurable blessings.

457. The Master arose from his prayer and, his countenance beaming with peace and serenity, commanded his disciples to seat themselves like persons of superior station, while He himself remained standing as if He were their servant. Then He laid aside the mantle, which He wore over the seamless garment and which covered all his Person except the feet. He wore sandals, which however He sometimes had dispensed with on his preaching tours, though at other times He had worn them ever since his most holy Mother had put them on his feet in Egypt. They grew in size with his feet as He advanced in age, as I have already remarked (Vol. II, 691). Having laid aside this mantle, which was the garment spoken of by the Evangelist (John 13, 4), He girded his body with one end of a large towel, permitting the other part to hang down free. Then He poured water into a basin for washing the feet of the Apostles, who were wonderingly observing the proceedings of their divine Master.

458. He first approached the head of the Apostle, saint Peter. But when this excitable Apostle saw prostrate at his feet the Lord, whom he had acknowledged and proclaimed as the Son of God, being again renewed and enlightened in his faith and overcome by humiliation at his own insignificance, he said: "Thou shalt never wash my feet!" The Author of life answered him with some earnestness: "Thou dost not know at present what I am

doing, but later on thou wilt understand it." This was the same as to say to him: obey now first my command and will, and do not prefer thy will unto mine, disturbing and perverting the order of virtues. Before all thou must yield captive thy understanding and believe that what I do is proper; then, having believed and obeyed, thou wilt understand the hidden mysteries of my doings, into the knowledge of which thou must enter by obedience. Without obedience thou canst not be truly humble, but only presumptuous. Nor can thy humility take preference of mine; I humiliated Myself unto the Death; and in order to thus humiliate Me, I sought the way of obedience; but thou, who art my disciple, dost not follow my doctrine. Under color of humility thou art disobedient, by thus perverting the right order thou stripst thyself as well of humility as of obedience, following thy own presumptuous judgment.

459. Saint Peter did not understand this doctrine contained in the first answer of our Lord; for though he belonged to his school, he had not yet experienced the divine effects of this washing and contact. Floundering in the errors of his indiscreet humility, he answered the Lord: "I will never consent that Thou wash my feet!" But the Lord of life answered with greater severity: "If I wash thee not, thou shalt have no part with Me." By this threatening answer the Lord sanctioned obedience forever as the secure way. According to human insight, saint Peter certainly had some excuse for being slow in permitting God to prostrate Himself before an earthly and sinful man as he was and to allow Him, whom he had so recently acknowledged and adored as his Creator, to perform such an unheard of act of self-abasement. But his opposition was not excusable in the eyes of the divine Master, who could not err in what He wished to do. For

whenever there is not an evident error in what is commanded, obedience must be blind and without evasion. In this mystery the Lord wished to repair the disobedience of our first parents, Adam and Eve, by which sin entered into the world; and because of the similarity and relation between it and the disobedience of saint Peter, our Lord threatened him with a similar punishment, telling him, that if he did not obey, he should have no part in Him; namely, that he should be excluded from the merits and fruits of the Redemption, by which alone we become worthy of his friendship and glory. He also threatened to deprive him of participation in his body and blood, which He was now about to perpetuate in the sacramental species of bread and wine. The Savior gave him to understand, that how ardently soever He desired to communicate Himself not only in part but in entirety, yet disobedience would certainly deprive even the Apostle of this blessing.

460. By this threat of our Lord Christ saint Peter was so chastened and instructed, that he immediately submitted from his whole heart and said: "Lord, not only my feet, but also my hands and my head." He wished to say: I offer my feet in order to walk in obedience, my hands in order to exercise it, and my head in order to surrender all of my own judgment, that may be contrary to its dictates. The Lord accepted this submission of saint Peter and said: "He that is washed, needs not but to wash his feet, but is clean wholly. And you are clean, but not all," for among them was seated the most unclean Judas. This Christ said, because the disciples (all except Judas), had been justified and cleaned by his doctrines; and they needed only to be cleansed from imperfections and venial sins, so that they might approach holy Communion with so much the more worthiness and better

preparation, such as is required in order to participate fully in its divine effects and receive its abundant graces with so much the greater efficacy and plenitude. For venial sins, distractions and lukewarmness hinder all these benefits very much. Thereupon the feet of saint Peter were washed, as also those of the other disciples, who permitted it in great astonishment and bathed in tears; for all of them were filled with new enlightenment and gifts of grace.

461. The divine Master then proceeded to wash also the feet of Judas, whose perfidious treason could not prevent the charity of Christ from secretly bestowing upon him tokens of even greater charity than upon the other Apostles. Without permitting it to be noticed by the others, He manifested his special love toward Judas in two ways. On the one hand, in the kind and caressing manner in which He approached Him, knelt at his feet, washed them, kissed them and pressed them to his bosom. On the other hand, by seeking to move his soul with inspirations proportionate to the dire depravity of his conscience; for the assistance offered to Judas was in itself much greater than that offered to the other Apostles. But as the disposition of this Apostle was most wicked, his vices deeply ingrown upon him, his understanding and his faculties much disturbed and weakened; as he had entirely forsaken God and given himself over to the devil, and, as he had enthroned the evil spirit in his heart; he resisted all the divine advances and inspirations connected with this washing of his feet. He was moreover harassed by the fear of breaking his contract with the scribes and pharisees. As the bodily presence of Christ and the interior urgency of his inspirations both bestormed his sense of right, there arose within his darkened soul a dreadful hurricane of conflicting thoughts, filling him with dismay

and bitterness, and fiercest anger, whirling him still farther away from his Savior and turning the divine balsam applied to his soul into deadly poison of hellish malice and total depravity.

462. Thus it came that the malice of Judas resisted the saving contact of those divine hands, in which the eternal Father had placed miraculous power to enrich all creatures with his blessings. Even if he had not received any other assistance except that naturally flowing from the visible and personal presence of the Author of life, the wickedness of this unhappy disciple would have been beyond all bounds. The outward aspect of Christ our Lord was most exquisitely charming and attractive; his countenance, serenely dignified, yet sweetly expressive and beautiful, was framed in abundant waves of golden chestnut hair, freely growing after the manner of the Nazarenes; his frank and open eyes beamed forth grace and majesty; his mouth, nose and all the features of his face exhibited the most perfect proportion and his whole Person was clothed in such entrancing loveliness, that He drew upon Himself the loving veneration of all who beheld Him without malice in their hearts. Over and above all this, the mere sight of Him caused in the beholders an interior joy and enlightenment, engendering heavenly thoughts and sentiments in the soul. This divine Personage, so lovable and venerable, Judas now saw at his feet, striving to please him by new tokens of affection and seeking to gain him by new impulses of love. But so great was the perversity of Judas, that nothing could move or soften his hardened heart; on the contrary, he was irritated by the gentleness of the Savior, and he refused to look upon his face or take notice of his actions; for from the time in which he had lost faith and grace, he was filled with hatred toward his Master and toward

his heavenly Mother and never looked Them in the face.
Greater, in a certain respect, was the terror of Lucifer
at the presence of Christ our Savior; for this demon,
having established himself in the heart of Judas, could
not bear the humility of the divine Master toward his
disciples and sought to escape from Judas and from the
Cenacle.   But the Lord detained him by his almighty
power in order that his pride might be crushed.   Yet
later on he was cast out from that place, filled with fury,
and with the suspicion, that Christ might after all be the
true God.

463. The Lord completed the washing of the feet, and
again assuming the upper garment, seated Himself in the
midst of his Apostles and began the discourse recorded by
saint John: "Know you what I have done to you?   You
call me Master, and Lord; and you say well; if then I,
being your Lord and Master, have washed your feet; you
also ought to wash one another's feet. For I have given
you an example, that as I have done to you, so you do
also. Amen, Amen, I say to you: The servant is not
greater than his lord; neither is the Apostle greater than
He that sent him" (John 13, 13).   Then the Lord proceeded to propound great mysteries and truths, which I
will not expatiate upon, but for which I refer the reader
to the Gospels. This discourse still further enlightened the
Apostles in the mysteries of the most blessed Trinity and
of the Incarnation, and prepared them by new graces for
the holy Eucharist, confirming them in their understanding of the vast significance of his doctrines and miracles.
Among them all saint Peter and saint John were most
fully enlightened; but each of the Apostles received more
or less insight according to his disposition and according
to the divine ordainment.   What saint John says about
his questioning the Lord concerning the traitor who was

to sell Him, and the answer of the Lord, all happened before at the Supper itself, when the beloved disciple reclined on the bosom of his divine Master. For saint Peter, in his fervent attachment to his Master and his outspoken love, was anxious to know who was the traitor, in order that he might avenge or prevent the treason. But saint John, though he recognized the traitor by the bread dipped into the sauce and handed to Judas, would not inform saint Peter. He alone knew the secret, but taught by the charity which he had acquired in the school of his divine Master, he buried the secret in his bosom.

464. While he thus reclined on the bosom of Jesus our Savior, saint John was privileged in many other ways; for there he was made to see many most exalted mysteries of the divine humanity and of the Queen of heaven, his most holy Mother. On this occasion also he was commissioned to take charge of Her; for on the Cross Christ did not say to him: She shall be thy Mother, nor, thou shalt be her son; but, behold thy Mother, because this was not a matter resolved upon at that time, but one which was then to be made manifest publicly as having been ordained and decreed beforehand. Of all these sacraments connected with the washing of the feet, of the words and discourses of her Son, his most pure Mother was minutely informed by interior vision, as I have stated at other times, and for all of them She gave thanks and glory to the Most High. And when afterwards the wonderful works of the Lord were accomplished, She beheld them not as one ignorant of them; but as one who saw fulfilled, what She had known before and what had been recorded in her heart like the law recorded on the tablets of Moses. She enlightened also her companions of all that was proper, reserving whatever they were not capable of understanding.

INSTRUCTIONS WHICH THE GREAT MISTRESS OF
THE WORLD, MOST HOLY MARY, GAVE ME.

465. My daughter, in three virtues mentioned by thee
in the foregoing chapter as especially practiced by my
Son and Lord, I wish that thou be particularly zealous
as his spouse and my beloved disciple. They are the
virtues of charity, humility and obedience in which Jesus
desired to signalize Himself toward the end of his life.
Without doubt He manifested his love for men during
his whole life, since He performed for them such admirable works from the very first instant of his conception
in my womb. But towards the end of his life, when He
established the evangelical law of the New Testament,
the fire of ardent love, that burned in his bosom, burst
out in more consuming flames. On this last occasion the
charity of the Savior for the children of Adam exerted
its full force, since it was urged on by the sorrows of
death that encompassed Him, and was spurred on from
the outside by the dislike of men for suffering, their self-
chosen misfortunes and their boundless ingratitude and
perversity in seeking to destroy the honor and the life
of Him, who was ready to sacrifice all for their eternal
happiness. By this conflict his love was inflamed to the
point at which it could not be extinguished (Cant. 8, 7);
and thus being now about to leave the earth, He was
driven to exercise all his ingenuity in attempting to prolong his benefactions and his intercourse with men, leaving among them, by his teachings, works and examples,
the sure means of participating in the effects of his
divine charity.

466. In this art of loving thy neighbor for God's sake
I wish that thou be very expert and zealous. This thou
wilt be, if the very injuries and sufferings with which

they afflict thee, shall waken in thee a greater love. Thou must remember, that then alone wilt thou be secure and unwavering, when neither benefits nor flatteries of men have any effect on thee. For to love those who do thee good, is a duty; but if thou art heedless, thou canst not know, whether in that case thou lovest them for God's sake, or for the sake of the benefits they confer, which would be loving thy own advantage or thyself rather than thy neighbor for God's sake. He who loves for other than God's sake or for vain complaisance merely, has not yet learned true charity; since he is yet taken up with the blind love of his own ease. But if thou love those who do not satisfy any of these cravings, thou art led on to love them for the Lord's sake as the principal motive and object of thy love, loving Him in his creatures, whoever they be. Thou must exercise thyself in both the corporal and the spiritual works of mercy; but as thou hast fewer occasions to exercise those of the body than those of the spirit, thou must continually extend thy spiritual works of charity, multiplying, according to the will of thy Savior, thy prayers, petitions, pious practices, accompanying them with prudent and holy admonitions and thus advancing the spiritual welfare of souls. Remember that my Lord and Son conferred no bodily blessings on any one, without accompanying them with spiritual, and it would have been derogatory to the divine perfection of his works, to perform them without this plenitude of goodness. From this thou wilt understand how much we must prefer the benefits of soul to those of the body; hence thou must always seek them in the first place, although earthly-minded men blindly prefer temporal blessings, forgetting the eternal ones and those tending toward the friendship and grace of the Most High.

467. The virtues of humility and obedience were highly

exalted by the conduct of my most holy Son in washing the feet of his Apostles. If by thy interior enlightenment concerning this extraordinary example thou dost not humble thyself to the dust, thy heart is indeed hardened and thou art very obtuse in the knowledge of the Lord. Let it then be understood henceforth, that thou never canst consider or profess thyself sufficiently humbled, even when thou findest thyself despised and trodden under foot by all men, sinners as they are; for they never can be as bad as Judas, or thou as good as thy Lord and Master. But to merit and to be honored by this virtue of humility, will give thee such perfection and worthiness, that thou wilt deserve the name of a spouse of Christ and make thyself somewhat like unto Him. Without this humility no soul can be raised to excellence and communication with the Lord; for the exalted must first be humbled and only the lowly ones can and should be exalted (Matth. 23, 12) ; and souls are always raised up by the Lord in proportion as they have humiliated themselves.

468. In order that thou mayest not lose this pearl of humility just at the time when thou thinkest thyself secure of it, remember that the exercise of it is not to be preferred to obedience, nor must thou practice it merely at thy own will, but in subjection to thy superiors; for if thou prefer thy own judgment to that of thy superiors even if thou do it under color of humility, thou art guilty of pride; for that would be not only refusing to seek the lowest place, but placing thyself above thy superior. Hence thou mayest understand the error of shrinking back, like saint Peter, from the favors and blessings of the Lord, depriving thee thereby not only of the gifts and treasures offered thee, but of the advantage of humility, which thou seekest and which is much preferable. Thou failest also in gratefully acknowledging the high ends and in striving

after the exaltation of his holy name, which the Lord
seeks in such works.   It is not thy business to enter into
the examination of his secret and exalted judgments, nor
to correct them by thy reasonings and thy objections on
account of which thou mightst think thyself unworthy of
his favors or incapable of performing the works enjoined.
All this is a seed of Lucifer's pride, covered up by apparent humility as he thus seeks to hinder the communica-
tions of the Lord, his gifts and his friendship, which thou
desirest so much. Let it then be to thee an inviolable rule,
that as soon as thy confessors and superiors approve of
certain favors and blessings as coming from the Lord,
thou accept them as such with due thanks and reverence.
Do not allow thyself to be led into new doubts and vacil-
lating fears, but correspond with the favors of the Lord
in humble fear and tranquil obedience.

CHAPTER II .

469. With great diffidence do I enter upon the treatment of the ineffable mystery of the holy Eucharist and of what happened at its institution; for, raising the eyes of my soul toward the light which encompasses and governs me in the performance of this work, the high intelligence given me of these vast wonders and sacraments reproaches me with my littleness in comparison with the greatness therein manifested. My faculties are disturbed and I cannot find words to explain what I see and conceive, although all these conceptions are far from the reality that is shown to my understanding. But, though ignorant of the terms and though very unfit for such discourse, I must speak, in order that I may continue this history and relate what part the great Lady of the world had in these wonders. If I do not speak as appropriately as the matter demands, let my amazement and my lowly condition be my excuse; for it is not easy to yield to the exactions of spoken words, when the will is so intent on supplying the defects of the understanding and on enjoying that, which it is hopeless and even unbecoming to manifest.

470. Christ had partaken of the prescribed supper with his disciples reclining on the floor around a table, which

was elevated from it little more than the distance of six or seven fingers; for such was the custom of the Jews. But after the washing of the feet He ordered another, higher table to be prepared, such as we now use for our meals. By this arrangement He wished to put an end to the legal suppers and to the lower and figurative law and establish the new Supper of the law of grace. From that time on He wished the sacred mysteries to be performed on the tables or altars, which are in use in the Catholic Church. The table was covered with a very rich cloth and upon it was placed a plate or salver and a large cup in the form of a chalice, capacious enough to hold the wine. All this was done in pursuance of the will of Christ our Savior, who by his divine power and wisdom directed all these particulars. The master of the house was inspired to offer these rich vessels, which were made of what seemed a precious stone like emerald. The Apostles often used it afterwards in consecrating, whenever the occasion permitted it. The Lord seated himself at this table with the Apostles and some of the other disciples, and then ordered some unleavened bread to be placed on the table and some wine to be brought, of which He took sufficient to prepare the chalice.

471. Then the Master of life spoke words of most endearing love to his Apostles, and, though his sayings were wont to penetrate to the inmost heart at all times, yet on this occasion they were like the flames of a great fire of charity, which consumed the souls of his hearers. He manifested to them anew the most exalted mysteries of his Divinity, humanity and of the works of the Redemption. He enjoined upon them peace and charity, of which He was now to leave a pledge in the mysteries about to be celebrated. He reminded them, that in loving one another, they would be loved by the eternal Father with

the same love in which He was beloved. He gave them an understanding of the fulfillment of this promise in having chosen them to found the new Church and the law of grace. He renewed in them the light concerning the supreme dignity, excellence and prerogatives of his most pure Virgin Mother. Among all the Apostles, saint John was most deeply enlightened in these mysteries on account of the office imposed upon him. The great Lady, from her retreat, beheld in divine contemplation all these doings of her Son in the Cenacle; and in her profound intelligence She entered more deeply into their meaning than the Apostles and the angels, who also were present in bodily forms, adoring their true Lord, Creator and King. By the hands of these angels Enoch and Elias were brought to the Cenacle from their place of abode; for the Lord wished that these Fathers of the natural and of the written Laws should be present at the establishment of the law of the Gospel, and that they should participate in its mysteries.

472. All these being present, awaiting full of wonder what the Author of life intended to do, there appeared also in the hall the person of the eternal Father and of the Holy Ghost as they had appeared at the baptism of Christ at the Jordan and at the Transfiguration on mount Tabor. Although all the Apostles and disciples felt this divine presence, yet only some of them really were favored with a vision of it; among these was especially saint John the evangelist, who was always gifted with eagle-sight into the divine mysteries. The entire heaven was transplanted to the Cenacle of Jerusalem; for of such great importance was the magnificence of this work, by which the new Church was founded, the law of grace established and eternal salvation made secure. For a better understanding of the doings of the incarnate Word, I must remind

the reader, that He possessed two natures in one Person, the divine and the human nature united in one divine Person of the Word; hence the proper activities of both natures are rightly attributed to one and the same Person, just as the same Person is called both God and man. Consequently, when I say that the incarnate Work spoke and prayed to the eternal Father, it must not be interpreted as meaning, that He prayed or spoke in as far as He was divine, since in Divinity He was equal to the Father; but in as far as He was human, inferior and composed of body and soul as we ourselves are. In this sense therefore Christ confessed and extolled the immensity and infinitude of the eternal Father, praying for the whole human race.

473. "My Father and eternal God, I confess, praise and exalt thy infinite essence and incomprehensible Deity, in which I am one with Thee and the Holy Ghost, engendered from all eternity by thy intellect, as the figure of thy substance and the image of thy individual nature (John 10, 30; Ps. 119, 3; Heb. 1, 3). In the same nature, which I have assumed in the virginal womb of my Mother, I wish to accomplish the Redemption of the human race with which Thou hast charged Me. I wish to restore to this human nature the highest perfection and the plenitude of thy divine complaisance; and then I wish to pass from this world to thy right hand, bearing with Me all those whom Thou hast given Me without losing a single one of them for want of willingness on our part to help them (John 17, 12). My delight is to be with the children of men (Prov. 8, 31) and as, in my absence, they will be left orphans, if I do not give them assistance, I wish, my Father, to furnish them with a sure and unfailing token of my inextinguishable love and a pledge of the eternal rewards, which Thou holdest

in reserve for them. I desire that they find in my merits an easy and powerful remedy for the effects of sin, to which they are subject on account of the disobedience of the first man, and I wish to restore copiously their right to the eternal happiness for which they are created."

474. "But since there will be few who will preserve themselves in this justice, they will need other assistance, so that they may reinstate themselves and strengthen themselves in the way of justification and sanctification by being continually furnished with new and exalted gifts and favors of thy clemency in their dangerous pilgrimage through life. It was our eternal decree, that they should have created existence and participate in our divine perfections and happiness for all eternity; and thy love, which caused Me to assume a nature able to suffer and welcome the humiliation of the cross (Philip 2, 8), would not rest satisfied, until it invented new means of communicating itself to men according to their capacity and our wisdom and power. These means shall consist in visible and sensible signs adapted to their condition as sentient beings and causing invisible effects in the spiritual and immaterial part of their natures."

475. "To advance these high ends for thy exaltation and glory, eternal Lord and Father, in my name and in that of all the poor and afflicted children of Adam, I ask the fiat of thy eternal will. If their sins call out for thy justice, their neediness and misery appeal to thy infinite mercy. At the same time I, on my part, interpose all the works of my humanity, which is indissolubly bound to my Divinity. I offer my obedience in accepting suffering unto death; my humility, in subjecting Myself to the depraved judgment of men; the poverty and labors of my life, the insults of my Passion and Death, and the love, which urges Me to undergo all this for the

advance of thy glory and for the spreading of thy knowledge and adoration among all creatures capable of thy grace and happiness. Thou, O eternal Lord and my Father, hast made Me the Brother and the Chief of men, and hast destined them to partake eternally of the joys of our Divinity (Colos. 1, 18). As thy children, they are to be heirs with Me of thy everlasting blessings (Rom. 8, 17), and as members of my body, they are to participate in the effects of my brotherly love (I Cor. 6, 15). Therefore, as far as depends upon Me, I desire to draw them on toward my friendship and to see them share in the goods of the Divinity, to which they were destined in their origin from their natural head, the first man."

476. "Impelled by this boundless love, Lord and Father, I ordain, that from now on men may re-enter into thy full friendship and grace through the sacrament of Baptism, and that they may do so as soon as they shall be born to daylight; and their desire of renascence into grace, which they cannot in their infancy manifest on their own account, shall, with thy permission, be manifested for them by their elders. Let them become immediate heirs of thy glory; let them be interiorly and indelibly marked as children of my Church; let them be freed from the stain of original sin; let them receive the gifts of faith, hope and charity, by which they may perform the works of thy children: knowing Thee, trusting in Thee, and loving Thee for thy own Self. Let them also receive the virtues by which they restrain and govern disorderly inclinations and be able to distinguish, without fail, the good from the evil. Let this Sacrament be the portal of my Church, and the one which makes men capable of receiving all the other favors and disposes them to new gifts and blessings of

grace. I ordain also, that besides this Sacrament, they may receive another, in which they shall be confirmed and rooted in the holy faith they have accepted, and become courageous in its defense as soon as they shall arrive at the use of reason. And because human frailty easily falls away from the observance of my law and since my charity will not permit Me to leave them without an easy and opportune remedy, I wish to provide the sacrament of Penance. Through it men, by acknowledging their faults and confessing them with sorrow, may be reinstated in justice and in the merits of glory promised to them. Thus shall Lucifer and his followers be prevented from boasting of having so soon deprived them of advantages of Baptism."

477. "By the justification of these Sacraments men shall become fit to share in the highest token of my love in the exile of this their mortal life; namely, to receive Me sacramentally under the species of bread and wine in an ineffable manner. Under the species of bread I shall leave my body, and under the species of wine, my blood. In each one of them I shall be present really and truly and I institute this mysterious sacrament of the Eucharist as a heavenly nourishment proportioned to their condition as wayfaring men; for their sake shall I work these miracles and remain with them until the end of the coming ages (Matth. 28, 20). For the strengthening and defense of those, who approach the end of their lives, I moreover appoint the sacrament of Extreme Unction, which shall at the same time be a certain pledge of the bodily resurrection of those thus anointed. In order that all may contribute proportionately to the sanctification of the members of the mystical body of the Church, in which by the most harmonious and orderly co-operation all must have their proper posi-

tion, I institute the sacrament of Ordination to distinguish and mark some of its members by a special degree of holiness and place them above the other faithful as fit ministers of the Sacraments and as my chosen priests. Although they derive all their powers from Me, I nevertheless wish that it should flow from Me through one of their number, who shall be my Vicar and the Chief, representing my Person and act as my high priest. Into his keeping I deposit the keys of heaven and him all upon earth shall obey. For the further perfection of my Church I also establish the last of the Sacraments, Matrimony, to sanctify the natural union of man and wife for the propagation of the human race. Thus shall all the grades of my Church be enriched and adorned by my infinite merits. This, eternal Father, is my last will, whereby I make all the mortals inheritors of my merits in the great storehouse of grace, my new Church."

478. This prayer Christ our Redeemer made in the presence of the Apostles, but without any exterior manifestation. The most blessed Mother, who from her retreat observed and followed Him, prostrated Herself upon the floor and, as his Mother, offered to the eternal Father the same petitions as her Son. Although She could not add anything to the merits of the works of her divine Son, nevertheless, as on other occasions, She, as his Helpmate, united her petitions with his, in order that by her faithful companionship She might move the eternal Father to so much the greater mercy. And the Father looked upon Them both, graciously accepting the prayers respectively of the Son and Mother for the salvation of men. Besides prayer, her divine Son left the performance of yet another work in her charge. In order to understand what this was, it must be remembered (as I mentioned in the preceding chapter) that

Lucifer was present at the washing of the Apostles' feet, and that, being forced to remain and witness the doings of Christ in the Cenacle, he astutely conjectured some great blessings to be intended for the Apostles. Although the dragon felt his forces much diminished and altogether unavailing against the Redeemer, he nevertheless sought with implacable fury and pride to spy out these mysteries for the concoction of future malicious plans. The great Lady perceived these intentions of Lucifer and knew that the foiling of them was to be left in her hands. Therefore, inflamed by zeal and love for the Most High, She, as sovereign Queen, commanded the dragon and all his squadrons to leave the hall and descend to the depths of hell.

479. To accomplish this the arm of the Almighty gave new power to the Blessed Virgin, so that neither the rebellious Lucifer nor all his hosts could resist. They were hurled into the infernal abysses, there to remain until they should again be permitted to issue as witnesses to the passion and death of the Savior in order to be finally convinced of his being the Messias and Redeemer, true God and man. Let it then be understood, that Lucifer and his demons were present at the legal supper and washing of the feet, and also afterwards at the entire passion of Christ! but that they were not present at this institution of the holy Eucharist, nor at the Communion of the disciples. Then the great Queen was raised to a most sublime state of contemplation of the mysteries about to be enacted, and the holy angels, as to another valorous Judith, sang to Her of this glorious triumph over the dragon. At the same time Christ our Lord offered up to the eternal Father exalted thanksgiving and praise for the blessings conceded to the human race in consequence of his petition.

480. Thereupon Christ our Lord took into his venerable hands the bread, which lay upon the plate, and interiorly asked the permission and co-operation of the eternal Father, that now and ever afterwards in virtue of the words about to be uttered by Him, and later to be repeated in his holy Church, He should really and truly become present in the host, Himself to yield obedience to these sacred words. While making this petition He raised his eyes toward heaven with an expression of such sublime majesty, that He inspired the Apostles, the angels and his Virgin Mother with new and deepest reverence. Then He pronounced the words of consecration over the bread, changing its substance into the substance of his true body and immediately thereupon He uttered the words of consecration also over the wine, changing it into his true blood. As an answer to these words of consecration was heard the voice of the eternal Father, saying: "This is my beloved Son, in whom I delight, and shall take my delight to the end of the world; and He shall be with men during all the time of their banishment." In like manner was this confirmed by the Holy Ghost. The most sacred humanity of Christ, in the Person of the Word, gave tokens of profoundest veneration to the Divinity contained in the Sacrament of his body and blood. The Virgin Mother, in her retreat, prostrated Herself on the ground and adored her Son in the blessed Sacrament with incomparable reverence. Then also the angels of her guard, all the angels of heaven, and among them likewise the souls of Enoch and Elias, in their own name and in the name of the holy Patriarchs and Prophets of the old law, fell down in adoration of their Lord in the holy Sacrament.

481. All the Apostles and disciples, who, with the exception of the traitor, believed in this holy Sacrament,

adored it with great humility and reverence according to each one's disposition. The great high priest Christ raised up his own consecrated body and blood in order that all who were present at this first Mass might adore it in a special manner, as they also did. During this elevation his most pure Mother, saint John, Enoch and Elias, were favored with an especial insight into the mystery of his presence in the sacred species. They understood more profoundly, how, in the species of the bread, was contained his body and in those of the wine, his blood; how in both, on account of the inseparable union of his soul with his body and blood, was present the living and true Christ; how with the Person of the Word, was also therein united the Person of the Father and of the Holy Ghost; and how therefore, on account of the inseparable existence and union of the Father, Son and Holy Ghost, the holy Eucharist contained the perfect humanity of the Lord with the three divine Persons of the Godhead. All this was understood most profoundly by the heavenly Lady and by the others according to their degree. They understood also the efficacy of the words of the consecration, now endowed with such divine virtue, that as soon as they are pronounced with the intention of doing what Christ did at that time, by any priest since that time over the proper material, they would change the bread into his body and the wine into his blood, leaving the accidents to subsist in a new way and without their proper subject. They saw, that this change would take place so certainly and infallibly, that heaven and earth would sooner fall to pieces, than that the effect of these words of consecration, when pronounced in the proper manner by the sacerdotal minister of Christ, should ever fail.

482. The heavenly Queen understood also by a special

vision how the most sacred body of Christ is hidden beneath the accidents of bread and wine without change in them or alteration of the sacred humanity; for neither can the Body be the subject of the accidents, nor can the accidents be the form of the body. The accidents retain the same extension and qualities as before, and each of their parts retain the same position after the host has been consecrated; and the sacred body is present in an invisible form, also retaining the same size without intermingling of parts. It remains in the whole host, and all of it in every particle of the host, without being strained by the host, or the host by the body. For neither is the extension of his body correlative with the accidental species, nor do they depend upon the sacred body for their existence. They therefore have a totally different mode of existence and the body interpenetrates the accidents without hindrance. Although naturally the head would demand a different place than the hands, or these a different one from the breast or any other part of the body; yet by the divine power the consecrated body places itself unimpaired in its extent in one and the same place, because it bears no relation to the space which it would naturally occupy, having thrown aside all these relations though still remaining a quantitative body. Moreover it need not necessarily remain in one determined place only, or in only one host, but at the same time it can be present in many innumerable consecrated hosts.

483. She understood likewise, that the sacred body, although not naturally depending upon the accidents as above declared, yet does not continue to exist sacramentally in these accidents after the corruption of the species of the bread and wine; and this for no other reason than because it was so willed by Christ the Author of these

wonders. The co-existence of the sacred body and blood of our Lord with the incorrupted species of bread and wine therefore rests upon the arbitrary and voluntary disposition of the Creator of this Sacrament. As soon as they deteriorate and disappear on account of the natural process destructive of these species (for instance, as happens in holy Communion with the sacramental host, which is changed and corrupted by the heat of the stomach, or when this is effected by other causes) then God, in the last instant, when the species are ready for their last transformation, again creates another substance. This new substance, being now devoid of the Divinity, nourishes the human body and finally coalesces with the human form of existence, which is the soul. This wonderful creation of a new substance for the assumption of the changed and corrupted species is consequent upon the will of the Lord, who wishes not to continue the existence of his body in the corrupted accidents, and this process is demanded also by the laws of nature; for the substance of man cannot grow except by some other substance, which, being newly added, prevents the accidents from continuing to exist.

484. All these and other wonders the right hand of the Almighty perpetuated in this most august sacrament of the holy Eucharist. All of them the Mistress of heaven and earth understood and comprehended profoundly. In like manner saint John, the Fathers of the ancient Law, and the Apostles who were present, perceived these mysteries each in their degree. Aware of the great blessing contained therein for all men, Mary foresaw also the ingratitude of mortals in regard to this ineffable Sacrament, established for their benefit, and She resolved to atone, with all the powers of her being, for our shameless and ungrateful behavior. She took

upon Herself the duty of rendering thanks to the eternal Father and to his divine Son for this extraordinary and wonderful benefit to the human race. This earnest desire dwelled in her soul during her whole life and many times did She shed tears of blood welling forth from her purest heart in order to satisfy for our shameful and torpid forgetfulness.

485. Still greater was my admiration when Jesus our God, having raised the most holy Sacrament, as I said before, for their adoration, divided it by his own sacred hands, first partook of it Himself as being the First and Chief of all the priests. Recognizing Himself, as man, inferior to the Divinity, which He was now to receive in this his own consecrated body and blood. He humiliated and, as it were, with a trembling of the inferior part of his being, shrank within Himself before that Divinity, thereby not only teaching us the reverence with which holy Communion is to be received; but also showing us what was his sorrow at the temerity and presumption of many men during the reception and handling of this exalted and sublime Sacrament. The effects of holy Communion in the body of Christ were altogether miraculous and divine; for during a short space of time the gifts of glory flowed over in his body just as on mount Tabor, though the effects of this transfiguration were manifest only to his blessed Mother, and partly also to saint John, Enoch and Elias. This was the last consolation He permitted his humanity to enjoy as to its inferior part during his earthly life, and from that moment until his Death He rejected all such alleviation. The Virgin Mother, by a special vision, also understood how Christ her divine Son received Himself in the blessed Sacrament and what was the manner of its presence in his divine Heart. All this caused inestimable affection in our Queen and Lady.

486. While receiving his own body and blood Christ our Lord composed a canticle of praise to the eternal Father and offered Himself in the blessed Sacrament as a sacrifice for the salvation of man. He took another particle of the consecrated bread and handed it to the archangel Gabriel who brought and communicated it to the most holy Mary. By having such a privilege conferred on one of their number, the holy angels considered themselves sufficiently recompensed for being excluded from the sacerdotal dignity and for yielding it to man. The privilege of merely having even one of their number hold the sacramental body of their Lord and true God filled them with a new and immense joy. In abundant tears of consolation the great Queen awaited holy Communion. When saint Gabriel with innumerable other angels approached, She received it, the first after her Son, imitating his self-abasement, reverence and holy fear. The most blessed Sacrament was deposited in the breast and above the heart of the most holy Virgin Mother, as in the most legitimate shrine and tabernacle of the Most High. There the ineffable sacrament of the holy Eucharist remained deposited from that hour until after the Resurrection, when saint Peter said the first Mass and consecrated anew, as I shall relate in its place. The Almighty wished to have it so for the consolation of the great Queen and in order to fulfill his promise, that He would remain with the children of men until the consummation of the ages (Matth. 28, 20); for after his death his most holy humanity could not remain in his Church any other way than by his consecrated body and blood. This true manna was then deposited in the most pure Mary as in the living ark together with the whole evangelical law, just as formerly its prophetic figures were deposited in the ark of Moses (Heb. 9, 4).

The sacramental species were not consumed or altered in the heart of the Lady and Queen of heaven until the next consecration. Having received holy Communion, the blessed Mother gave thanks to the eternal Father and to her divine Son in new canticles similar to the ones the incarnate Word had rendered to his Father.

487. After having thus favored the heavenly Princess, our Savior distributed the sacramental bread to the Apostles (Luke 22, 17), commanding them to divide it among themselves and partake of it. By this commandment He conferred upon them the sacerdotal dignity and they began to exercise it by giving Communion each to Himself. This they did with the greatest reverence, shedding copious tears and adoring the body and blood of our Lord, whom they were receiving. They were established in the power of the priesthood, as being founders of the holy Church and enjoying the distinction of priority over all others (Ephes. 2, 20). Then saint Peter, at the command of Christ the Lord, administered two of the particles of holy Communion to the two patriarchs, Enoch and Elias. This holy Communion so rejoiced these two holy men, that they were encouraged anew in their hope of the beatific vision, which for them was to be deferred for so many ages, and they were strengthened to live on in this hope until the end of the world. Having given most fervent and humble thanks to the Almighty for this blessing, they were brought back to their abiding-place by the hands of the holy angels. The Lord desired to work this miracle in order to pledge Himself to include the ancient natural and written laws in the benefits of the Incarnation, Redemption and general resurrection; since all these mysteries were contained in the most holy Eucharist. By thus communicating Himself to the two holy men, Enoch and Elias, who were still in their mortal

flesh, these blessings were extended over the human race such as it existed under the natural and the written laws, while all the succeeding generations were to be included in the new law of grace, the Apostles at the head. This was all well understood by Enoch and Elias, and, returning to the midst of their contemporaries, they gave thanks to their and our Redeemer for this mysterious blessing.

488. Another very wonderful miracle happened at the Communion of the Apostles. The perfidious and treacherous Judas, hearing the command of his Master to partake of holy Communion, resolved in his unbelief not to comply, but if he could do so without being observed, determined to secrete the sacred body and bring it to the priests and pharisees in order to afford them a chance of incriminating Jesus by showing them what He had called his own body; or if he should not succeed therein, to consummate some other vile act of malice with the divine Sacrament. The Mistress and Queen of heaven, who by a clear vision was observing all that passed and knew the interior and exterior effects and affections in the Apostles at holy Communion, saw also the accursed intentions of the obstinate Judas. All the zeal for the glory of her Lord, existing in Her as his Mother, Spouse and Daughter, was aroused in her purest heart. Knowing that it was the divine will, that She should make use of her power as Mother and Queen, She commanded the holy angels to extract from the mouth of Judas the consecrated particles as well of the bread as of the wine and replace them from whence they had been taken. It well befitted Her on this occasion to defend the honor of her divine Son and prevent Judas from heaping such an ignominious injury upon Christ the Lord. The holy angels obeyed their Queen, and when it was the turn of Judas to communicate, they withdrew the consecrated

species one after the other, and, purifying them from
their contact with Judas, the most wicked of living men,
they restored them to their place, altogether unobserved
by the disciples. Thus the Lord shielded the honor of
his malicious and obstinate Apostle to the end. This was
attended to by the angels in the shortest space of time
and the others then received holy Communion, for Judas
was neither the first nor the last to communicate. Then
our Savior offered thanks to the eternal Father and there-
with ended both the legal and the sacramental Supper
in order to begin the mysteries of his Passion, which I
will relate in the subsequent chapters. The Queen of
heaven attended to all full of wonder and joyful praise,
magnifying the Most High.

INSTRUCTION GIVEN TO ME BY THE QUEEN OF HEAVEN.

489. O my daughter! Would that the believers in the
holy Catholic faith opened their hardened and stony
hearts in order to attain to a true understanding of the
sacred and mysterious blessing of the holy Eucharist!
If they would only detach themselves, root out and reject
their earthly inclinations, and, restraining their passions,
apply themselves with living faith to study by the divine
light their great happiness in thus possessing their eternal
God in the holy Sacrament and in being able, by its
reception and constant intercourse, to participate in the
full effects of this heavenly manna! If they would only
worthily esteem this precious gift, begin to taste its
sweetness, and share in the hidden power of their omnipotent God! Then nothing would ever be wanting to them
in their exile. In this, the happy age of the law of grace,
mortals have no reason to complain of their weakness
and their passions; since in this bread of heaven they

have at hand strength and health. It matters not that they are tempted and persecuted by the demon; for by receiving this Sacrament frequently they are enabled to overcome him gloriously. The faithful are themselves to blame for all their poverty and labors, since they pay no attention to this divine mystery, nor avail themselves of the divine powers, thus placed at their disposal by my most holy Son. I tell thee truly, my dearest, that Lucifer and his demons have such a fear of the most holy Eucharist, that to approach it, causes them more torments than to remain in hell itself. Although they do enter churches in order to tempt souls, they enter them with aversion, forcing themselves to endure cruel pains in the hope of destroying a soul and drawing it into sin, especially in the holy places and in the presence of the holy Eucharist. Their wrath against the Lord and against the souls alone could induce them to expose themselves to the torment of his real sacramental presence.

490. Whenever He is carried through the streets they usually fly and disperse in all haste; and they would not dare to approach those that accompany Him, if by their long experience they did not know, that they will induce some to forget the reverence due to their Lord. Therefore they make special efforts to tempt the faithful in the churches; for they know what great injury they can thereby do to the Lord himself, who in his sacramental love is there waiting to sanctify men and to receive the return of his sweetest and untiring love. Hence thou canst also understand the strength of those who prepare themselves to partake of this bread of the angels and how the demons fear the souls, who receive the Lord worthily and devoutly and who strive to preserve themselves in this purity until the next Communion. But there are very few who live with this intention, and the enemy is

ceaselessly alert in striving to throw them back into their
forgetfulness, distraction and indifference, so that he
may not be obliged to encounter such powerful weapons
in the hands of men.   Write this admonition in thy
heart; and since without thy merit the Almighty has
ordained, that thou receive holy Communion daily, seek
by all possible means to preserve thyself in the good dispositions from one Communion to the other.   It is the
will of the Lord and my own, that with this sword thou
fight the battles of the Almighty in the name of the holy
Church against the invisible enemies.   For in our days
they are heaping affliction and sorrow upon the mistress
of nations, while there is none to console her or to take
it to heart (Thren. 1, 1).   Do thou thyself weep for
the same reason and let thy heart be torn in sorrow.
But while the omnipotent and just Judge who is so
greatly incensed against the Catholics for having outraged his justice by their unmeasurable and continual
transgressions even under the aegis of their grand faith,
none are found to consider and weigh the fearful damage,
nor to approach the easy remedy of receiving the holy
Eucharist with a contrite and humble heart; nor does any
one ask for my intercession.

491. Though all the children of the Church largely
incur this fault, yet more to be blamed are the unworthy and wicked priests; for by the irreverence with
which they treat the blessed Sacrament the other Catholics have been drawn to undervalue it.   If the people see
that their priests approach the divine mysteries with holy
fear and trembling, they learn to treat and receive their
God in like manner.   Those that so honor Him shall shine
in heaven like the sun among the stars; for the glory of
my divine Son's humanity will redound in a special
measure in those who have behaved well toward Him

in the blessed Sacrament and have received Him with all reverence; whereas this will not happen to those who have not frequented this holy table with devotion. Moreover the devout will bear on their breast, where they have so often harbored the holy Eucharist, most beautiful and resplendent inscriptions, showing that they were most worthy tabernacles of the holy Sacrament. This will be a great accidental reward for them and a source of jubilation and admiration for the holy angels and all the rest of the blessed. They will also enjoy the special favor of being able to penetrate deeper into the mystery of the presence of the Lord in the sacrament and to understand all the rest of the wonders hidden therein. This will be such a privilege, that it alone would suffice for their eternal happiness, even if there were no other enjoyment in heaven. Moreover the essential glory of those, who have worthily and devoutly received the holy Eucharist, will in several respects exceed the glory of many martyrs who have not received the body and blood of the Lord.

492. I wish thee also to hear, my dearest daughter, from my own mouth, what were my sentiments when in mortal life I was about to receive holy Communion. In order that thou mayest better understand what I say, reflect on all I have commanded thee to write about my gifts, merits and labors in life. I was preserved from original sin and, at the instant of my Conception, I received the knowledge and vision of the Divinity, as thou hast often recorded. I knew more than all the saints; I surpassed the highest seraphim in love; I never committed any fault; I constantly practiced all the virtues in a heroic degree and in the least of them I was greater than all the saints in their highest perfection; the intention and object of my actions were most exalted

and my habits and gifts were noble without measure;
I imitated my most holy Son most closely; I labored
most faithfully; I suffered with eagerness and co-operated with the doings of the Lord exactly as was becoming
to me; I ceased not to exercise my love and gain new
and supereminent merits of grace.   Yet I thought myself to have been fully repaid by being allowed to receive
Him even once in the holy Eucharist; yea, I did not consider myself worthy of this one favor.   Reflect then
what should be thy sentiments, and those of the rest of
the children of Adam, on being admitted to the reception
of this admirable Sacrament.   And if for the greatest
of saints one holy Communion is a superabundant reward, what must the priests and the faithful think, when
they are allowed to receive it so frequently?   Open thy
eyes in the deep darkness and blindness which overwhelm men around thee, and raise them up to the divine
brightness in order to understand these mysteries.   Look
upon all thy works as insufficient, all thy sufferings as
most insignificant, all thy thanksgiving as falling far
short of what thou owest for such an exquisite blessing
as that of possessing in the holy Church, Christ my
divine Son, present in the holy Sacrament in order to
enrich all the faithful.   If thou hast not wherewith to
show thy thanks for this and the other blessings which
thou receivest, at least humiliate thyself to the dust and
remain prostrate upon it; confess thyself unworthy in
all the sincerity of thy heart.   Magnify the Most High,
bless and praise Him, preserving thyself at all times
worthy to receive Him and to suffer many martyrdoms
in return for such a favor.

CHAPTER III

THE PRAYER OF OUR LORD IN THE GARDEN AND ITS
MYSTERIES. WHAT HIS MOST BLESSED MOTHER KNEW
OF IT.

493. By the wonderful mysteries, which our Savior
Jesus had celebrated in the Cenacle, the reign which,
according to his inscrutable decree, his eternal Father had
consigned to Him, was well established; and the Thursday night of his last Supper having already advanced
some hours, He chose to go forth to that dreadful battle
of his suffering and death by which the Redemption was
to be accomplished. The Lord then rose to depart from
the hall of the miraculous feast and also most holy
Mary left her retreat in order to meet Him on the way.
At this face to face meeting of the Prince of eternity
and of the Queen, a sword of sorrow pierced the heart
of Son and Mother, inflicting a pang of grief beyond
all human and angelic thought. The sorrowful Mother
threw Herself at the feet of Jesus, adoring Him as her
true God and Redeemer. The Lord, looking upon Her
with a majesty divine and at the same time with the
overflowing love of a Son, spoke to Her only these
words: "My Mother, I shall be with thee in tribulation;
let Us accomplish the will of the eternal Father and the
salvation of men." The great Queen offered Herself
as a sacrifice with her whole heart and asked his blessing. Having received this She returned to her retire-
ment, where, by a special favor of the Lord, She was
enabled to see all that passed in connection with her

divine Son. Thus She was enabled to accompany Him and co-operate with Him in his activity as far as devolved upon Her. The owner of the house, who was present at this meeting, moved by a divine impulse, offered his house and all that it contained to the Mistress of heaven, asking Her to make use of all that was his during her stay in Jerusalem; and the Queen accepted his offer with humble thanks. The thousand angels of her guard, in forms visible to Her, together with some of the pious women of her company, remained with the Lady.

494. Our Redeemer and Master left the house of the Cenacle with all the men, who had been present at the celebration of the mysterious Supper; and soon many of them dispersed in the different streets in order to attend to their own affairs. Followed by his twelve Apostles, the Lord directed his steps toward mount Olivet outside and close to the eastern walls of Jerusalem. Judas, alert in his treacherous solicitude for the betrayal of his divine Master, conjectured that Jesus intended to pass the night in prayer as was his custom. This appeared to him a most opportune occasion for delivering his Master into the hands of his confederates, the scribes and the pharisees. Having taken this dire resolve, he lagged behind and permitted the Master and his Apostles to proceed. Unnoticed by the latter he lost them from view and departed in all haste to his own ruin and destruction. Within him was the turmoil of sudden fear and anxiety, interior witnesses of the wicked deed he was about to commit. Driven on in the stormy hurricane of thoughts raised by his bad conscience, he arrived breathless at the house of the high priests. On the way it happened, that Lucifer, perceiving the haste of Judas in procuring the death of Jesus Christ, and (as I have related in chapter the tenth), fearing that after all Jesus

might be the true Messias, came toward him in the shape
of a very wicked man, a friend of Judas acquainted with
the intended betrayal. In this shape Lucifer could speak
to Judas without being recognized. He tried to persuade
him that this project of selling his Master did at first
seem advisable on account of the wicked deeds attributed
to Jesus; but that, having more maturely considered the
matter, he did not now deem it advisable to deliver Him
over to the priests and pharisees; for Jesus was not so
bad as Judas might imagine; nor did He deserve death;
and besides He might free Himself by some miracles and
involve his betrayer into great difficulties.

495. Thus Lucifer, seized by new fear, sought to
counteract the suggestions with which he had previously
filled the heart of the perfidious disciple against his
Author. He hoped to confuse his victim; but his new
villainy was in vain. For Judas, having voluntarily lost
his faith and not being troubled by any such strong suspicions as Lucifer, preferred to take his Master's life
rather than to encounter the wrath of the pharisees for
permitting Him to live unmolested. Filled with this fear
and his abominable avarice, he took no account of the
counsel of Lucifer, although he had no suspicion of his
not being the friend, whose shape the devil had assumed.
Being stripped of grace he neither desired, nor could be
persuaded by any one, to turn back in his malice. The
priests, having heard that the Author of life was in
Jerusalem, had gathered to consult about the promised
betrayal. Judas entered and told them that he had left
his Master with the other disciples on their way to
mount Olivet; that this seemed to be the most favorable
occasion for his arrest, since on this night they had already made sufficient preparation and taken enough precaution to prevent his escaping their hands by his arti-

fices and cunning tricks. The sacrilegious priests were much rejoiced and began to busy themselves to procure an armed force for the arrest of the most innocent Lamb.

496. In the meanwhile our divine Lord with the eleven Apostles was engaged in the work of our salvation and the salvation of those who were scheming his death. Unheard of and wonderful contest between the deepest malice of man and the unmeasurable goodness and charity of God! If this stupendous struggle between good and evil began with the first man, it certainly reached its highest point in the death of the Repairer; for then good and evil stood face to face and exerted their highest powers: human malice in taking away the life and honor of the Creator and Redeemer, and his immense charity freely sacrificing both for men. According to our way of reasoning, it was as it were necessary that the most holy soul of Christ, yea that even his Divinity, should revert to his blessed Mother, in order that He might find some object in creation, in which his love should be recompensed and some excuse for disregarding the dictates of his justice. For in this Creature alone could He expect to see his Passion and Death bring forth full fruit; in her immeasurable holiness did his justice find some compensation for human malice; and in the humility and constant charity of this great Lady could be deposited the treasures of his merits, so that afterwards, as the new Phœnix from the rekindled ashes, his Church might arise from his sacrifice. The consolation which the humanity of Christ drew from the certainty of his blessed Mother's holiness gave Him strength and, as it were, new courage to conquer the malice of mortals; and He counted Himself well recompensed for suffering such atrocious pains by the fact that to mankind belonged also his most beloved Mother.

497. All that happened the great Lady observed from her retreat. She perceived the sinister thoughts of the obstinate Judas, how he separated himself from the rest of the Apostles, how Lucifer spoke to him in the shape of his acquaintance, and all the rest that passed when he reached the priests and helped them to arrange with so much haste the capture of the Lord. The sorrow which then penetrated the chaste heart of the Virgin Mother, the acts of virtue which She elicited at the sight of such wickedness, and what else She then did, cannot be properly explained by us; we can only say that in all She acted with the plenitude of wisdom and holiness, and with the approbation of the most holy Trinity. She pitied Judas and wept over the loss of that perfidious disciple. She sought to make recompense for his malice by adoring, confessing, praising and loving the Lord, whom he delivered by such fiendish and insulting treachery. She offered Herself with eagerness to die in her Son's stead, if necessary. She prayed for those who were plotting the capture and death of her divine Lamb, for She regarded them as prizes to be estimated according to the infinite value of his precious life-blood for which this most prudent Lady foresaw they would be bought.

498. Our Savior pursued his way across the torrent of Cedron (John 18, 1) to mount Olivet and entered the garden of Gethsemane. Then He said to all the Apostles: "Wait for Me, and seat yourselves here while I go a short distance from here to pray (Matth. 26, 36); do you also pray, in order that you may not enter into temptation" (Luke 22, 40). The divine Master gave them this advice, in order that they might be firm in the temptations, of which He had spoken to them at the Supper: that all of them should be scandalized on account of what

they should see Him suffer that night, that Satan would assail them to sift and stir them up by his false suggestions; for the Pastor (as prophesied) was to be illtreated and wounded and the sheep were to be dispersed (Zach. 13, 7). Then the Master of life, leaving the band of eight Apostles at that place and taking with Him saint Peter, saint John, and saint James, retired to another place, where they could neither be seen nor heard by the rest (Mark 14, 33). Being with the three Apostles He raised his eyes up to the eternal Father confessing and praising Him as was his custom; while interiorly He prayed in fulfillment of the prophecy of Zacharias, permitting death to approach the most innocent of men and commanding the sword of divine justice to be unsheathed over the Shepherd and descend upon the Godman with all its deathly force. In this prayer Christ our Lord offered Himself anew to the eternal Father in satisfaction of his justice for the rescue of the human race; and He gave consent, that all the torments of his Passion and Death be let loose over that part of his human being, which was capable of suffering. From that moment He suspended and restrained whatever consolation or relief would otherwise overflow from the impassible to the passible part of his being, so that in this dereliction his passion and sufferings might reach the highest degree possible. The eternal Father granted these petitions and approved this total sacrifice of the sacred humanity.

499. This prayer was as it were the floodgate through which the rivers of his suffering were to find entrance like the resistless onslaught of the ocean, as was foretold by David (Ps. 68, 2). And immediately He began to be sorrowful and feel the anguish of his soul and therefore said to the Apostles: "My soul is sorrowful unto

death" (Mark 14, 34).   As these words and the sorrow
of Christ our Lord contain such great mysteries for our
instruction, I will say something of what has been shown
me and as far as I can understand concerning them.   The
Lord permitted this sorrow to reach the highest degree
both naturally and miraculously possible in his sacred
humanity.   This sorrow penetrated not only all the
lower faculties of his human life in so far as his natural
appetites were concerned; but also all the highest faculties of his body and soul, by which He perceived the inscrutable judgments and decrees of the divine justice,
and the reprobation of so many, for whom He was to
die.   This was indeed by far the greater source of his
sorrow, as we shall see farther on.   He did not say that
He was sorrowful on account of his death, but unto
death; for the sorrow naturally arising from the repugnance to the death He was about to undergo, was a
minor fear.   The sacrifice of his natural life, besides
being necessary for our Redemption, was also demanded
as a return for the joy of having in his human body experienced the glory of the Transfiguration.   On account of
the glory then communicated to his sacred body He held
Himself bound to subject it to suffering, deeming that a
recompense of what He had received.   This we see verified also in the three Apostles, who were witnesses as
well of the glorious as of the sorrowful mystery.   This
they themselves now understood, being informed thereof
by an especial enlightenment.

500. Moreover the immense love of our Savior for us
demanded that full sway be given to this mysterious sorrow.   For if He had caused it to stop short of the highest which that sorrow was capable of, his love would
not have rested satisfied, nor would it have been so evident that his love was not to be extinguished by the mul-

titude of tribulations (Cant. 8, 7). At the same time He showed thereby his charity toward the Apostles, who were with Him and were now much disturbed by perceiving, that his hour of suffering and death, which He had so often and in so many ways foretold them, was now at hand. This interior disturbance and fear confounded and confused them without their daring to speak of it. Therefore the most loving Savior sought to put them more at rest by manifesting to them his own sorrow unto death. By the sight of his own affliction and anxiety they were to take heart at the fears and anxieties of their own souls. There was still another mystery contained in this sorrow of the Lord, which referred especially to the three Apostles, saint Peter, John and James. For, more than all the rest, they were imbued with an exalted conception of the greatness and Divinity of their Master as far as the excellence of his doctrine, the holiness of his works, and the power of his miracles were concerned. They realized more completely and wondered more deeply at his dominion over all creation. In order that they might be confirmed in their belief of his being a man capable of suffering, it was befitting that they should know as eye-witnesses his truly human sorrow and affliction. By the testimony of these three Apostles who were distinguished by such favors, the holy Church was afterwards to be well fortified against the errors, which the devil would try to spread against the belief in the humanity of Christ our Savior. Thus would the rest of the faithful have the consolation of this firmly established belief in their own affliction and sorrow.

501. Interiorly enlightened in this truth, the three Apostles were exhorted by the Author of life by the words: "Wait for Me, watch and pray with Me." He

wished to inculcate the practice of all that He had taught
them and to make them constant in their belief. He
thereby reminded them of the danger of backsliding
and of the duty of watchfulness and prayer in order to
recognize and resist the enemy, remaining always firm
in the hope of seeing his name exalted after the ignominy
of his Passion. With this exhortation the Lord separated
Himself a short distance from the 'three Apostles. He
threw himself with his divine face upon the ground and
prayed to the eternal Father: "Father, if it is possible,
let this chalice pass from Me" (Matth. 26, 38). This
prayer Christ our Lord uttered, though He had come
down from heaven with the express purpose of really
suffering and dying for men; though He had counted
as naught the shame of his Passion, had willingly em-
braced it and rejected all human consolation; though
He was hastening with most ardent love into the jaws
of death, to affronts, sorrows and afflictions; though He
had set such a high price upon men, that He determined
to redeem them at the shedding of his life-blood. Since
by virtue of his divine and human wisdom and his inextinguishable love He had shown Himself so superior
to the natural fear of death, that it seems this petition
did not arise from any motive solely coming from Himself. That this was so in fact, was made known to me
in the light which was vouchsafed me concerning the
mysteries contained in this prayer of the Savior.

502. In order to explain what I mean, I must state,
that on this occasion Jesus treated with the eternal
Father about an affair, which was by far the most
important of all, namely, in how far the Redemption
gained by his Passion and Death should affect the hidden
predestination of the saints. In this prayer Christ
offered, on his part, to the eternal Father his torments,

his precious blood and his Death for all men as an abundant price for all the mortals and for each one of the human born till that time and yet to be born to the end of the world; and, on the part of mankind, He presented the infidelity, ingratitude and contempt with which sinful man was to respond to his frightful Passion and Death; He presented also the loss which He was to sustain from those who would not profit by his clemency and condemn themselves to eternal woe. Though to die for his friends and for the predestined was pleasing to Him and longingly desired by our Savior; yet to die for the reprobate was indeed bitter and painful; for with regard to them the impelling motive for accepting the pains of death was wanting. This sorrow was what the Lord called a chalice, for the Hebrews were accustomed to use this word for signifying anything that implied great labor and pain. The Savior himself had already used this word on another occasion, when in speaking to the sons of Zebedee He asked them: whether they could drink the chalice, which the Son of man was to drink (Matth 20, 22). This chalice then was so bitter for Christ our Lord, because He knew that his drinking it would not only be without fruit for the reprobate, but would be a scandal to them and redound to their greater chastisement and pain on account of their despising it (I Cor. 1, 23).

503. I understood therefore that in this prayer Christ besought his Father to let this chalice of dying for the reprobate pass from Him. Since now his Death was not to be evaded, He asked that none, if possible, should be lost; He pleaded, that as his Redemption would be superabundant for all, that therefore it should be applied to all in such a way as to make all, if possible, profit by it in an efficacious manner; and if this was not

possible, He would resign Himself to the will of his
eternal Father.   Our Savior repeated this prayer three
times at different intervals (Matth. 26, 44), pleading
the longer in his agony in view of the importance and
immensity of the object in question (Luke 22, 43).
According to our way of understanding, there was a contention or altercation between the most sacred humanity
and the Divinity of Christ.   For this humanity, in its
intense love for men who were of his own nature, desired that all should attain eternal salvation through his
Passion; while his Divinity, in its secret and high judgments, had fixed the number of the predestined and in
its divine equity could not concede its blessings to those
who so much despised them, and who, of their own free
will, made themselves unworthy of eternal life by repel-
ling the kind intentions of Him who procured and offered
it to them.   From this conflict arose the agony of Christ,
in which He prayed so long and in which He appealed
so earnestly to the power and majesty of his omnipotent
and eternal Father.

504. This agony of Christ our Savior grew in proportion to the greatness of his charity and the certainty of
his knowledge, that men would persist in neglecting to
profit by his Passion and Death (Luke 22, 44).   His
agony increased to such an extent, that great drops of
bloody sweat were pressed from Him, which flowed to
the very earth.   Although this prayer was uttered subject to a condition and failed in regard to the reprobate
who fell under this condition; yet He gained thereby a
greater abundance and secured a greater frequency of
favors for mortals.   Through it the blessings were multiplied for those who placed no obstacles, the fruits of
the Redemption were applied to the saints and to the
just more abundantly, and many gifts and graces, of

which the reprobates made themselves unworthy, were diverted to the elect. The human will of Christ, conforming itself to that of the Divinity, then accepted suffering for each respectively: for the reprobate, as sufficient to procure them the necessary help, if they would make use of its merits, and for the predestined, as an efficacious means, of which they would avail themselves to secure their salvation by co-operating with grace. Thus was set in order, and as it were realized, the salvation of the mystical body of his holy Church, of which Christ the Lord was the Creator and Head.

505. As a ratification of this divine decree, while yet our Master was in his agony, the eternal Father for the third time sent the archangel Michael to the earth in order to comfort Him by a sensible message and confirmation of what He already knew by the infused science of his most holy soul; for the angel could not tell our Lord anything He did not know, nor could he produce any additional effect on his interior consciousness for this purpose. But, as I related above (No. 498), Christ had suspended the consolation, which He could have derived from his human nature from this knowledge and love, leaving it to its full capacity for suffering, as He afterwards also expressed Himself on the Cross (No. 684). In lieu of this alleviation and comfort, which He had denied Himself, He was recompensed to a certain extent, as far as his human senses were concerned, by this embassy of the archangel. He received an experimental knowledge of what He had before known by interior consciousness; for the actual experience is something superadded and new and is calculated to move the sensible and bodily faculties. Saint Michael, in the name of the eternal Father, intimated and represented to Him in audible words, what He al-

ready knew, that it was not possible for those to be
saved who were unwilling; that the complaisance of the
eternal Father in the number of the just, although
smaller than the number of the reprobate was great;
that among the former was his most holy Mother, a
worthy fruit of his Redemption; that his Redemption
would also bear its fruits in the Patriarchs, Prophets,
Apostles, Martyrs, Virgins and Confessors, who should
signalize themselves in his love and perform admirable
works for the exaltation of the name of the Most High.
Among these the angel moreover mentioned some of the
founders of religious orders and the deeds of each one.
Many other great and hidden sacraments were touched
upon by the archangel, which it is not necessary to
mention here, nor have I any command to do so; and
therefore what I have already said, will suffice for continuing the thread of this history.

506. During the intervals of Christ's prayer, the
Evangelists say, He returned to visit the Apostles and
exhort them to watch and pray lest they enter into temptation (Matth. 14, 41; Mark 14, 38; Luke 22, 42). This
the most vigilant Pastor did in order to show the dignitaries of his Church what care and supervision they were
to exercise over their flocks. For if Christ, on account
of his solicitude for them interrupted his prayer, which
was so important, it was in order to teach them, how
they must postpone other enterprises and interests to
the salvation of their subjects. In order to understand
the need of the Apostles, I must mention, that the infernal dragon, after having been routed from the Cenacle and forced into the infernal caverns, was permitted by the Savior again to come forth, in order that
he might, by his malicious attempts, help to fulfill the
decrees of the Lord. At one fell swoop many of these

demons rushed to meet Judas and, in the manner already
described, to hinder him, if possible, from consummating
the treacherous bargain. As they could not dissuade
him, they turned their attention to the other Apostles,
suspecting that they had received some great favor at
the hands of the Lord in the Cenacle. What this favor
was Lucifer sought to find out, in order to counteract
it. Our Savior saw this cruelty and wrath of the prince
of darkness and his ministers; therefore as a most loving
Father and vigilant Superior He hastened to the assistance of his little children and newly acquired subjects,
his Apostles. He roused them and exhorted them to
watch and pray against their enemies, in order that they
might not enter unawares and unprovided into the threatening temptation.

507. He returned therefore to the three Apostles,
who, having been more favored, also had more reasons
for watchfulness in imitation of their Master. But He
found them asleep; for they had allowed themselves to
be overcome by insidious disgust and sorrow and in it
had been seized by such a remissness and lukewarmness,
that they fell asleep. Before speaking to them or waking
them, the Lord looked at them for a moment and wept
over them. For He saw them oppressed and buried in
this deathly shade by their own sloth and negligence.
He spoke to Peter and said to him: "Simon, sleepest
thou? couldst not thou watch one hour?" And immediately He gave him and the others the answer: "Watch
ye, and pray that you enter not into temptation (Mark
14, 37); for my enemies and your enemies sleep not as
you do." That He reprehended Peter especially was
not only because he was placed as head of the rest, and
not only because he had most loudly protested that he
would not deny Him and was ready to die for Him,

though all the others should be scandalized in Him and leave Him; but also because Peter, having from his whole heart made freely these protests, deserved to be corrected and admonished before all the rest. For no doubt the Lord chastises those whom He loves and is always pleased by our good resolutions, even when we afterwards fall short in their execution, as happened with the most fervent of all the Apostles, saint Peter. When the Lord came the third time and woke up all the twelve, Judas was already approaching in order to deliver Him into the hands of his enemies, as I shall relate in the next chapter.

508. Let us now return to the Cenacle, where the Queen of heaven had retired with the holy women of her company. From her retreat, by divine enlightenment, She saw most clearly all the mysteries and doings of her most holy Son in the garden. At the moment when the Savior separated Himself with the three Apostles Peter, John and James, the heavenly Queen separated Herself from the other women and went into another room. Upon leaving them She exhorted them to pray and watch lest they enter into temptation, but She took with Her the three Marys, treating Mary Magdalen as the superior of the rest. Secluding Herself with these three as her more intimate companions, She begged the eternal Father to suspend in Her all human alleviation and comfort, both in the sensitive and in the spiritual part of her being, so that nothing might hinder Her from suffering to the highest degree in union with her divine Son. She prayed that She might be permitted to feel and participate in her virginal body all the pains of the wounds and tortures about to be undergone by Jesus. This petition was granted by the blessed Trinity and the Mother in consequence suffered all the torments

of her most holy Son in exact duplication, as I shall relate later. Although they were such, that, if the right hand of the Almighty had not preserved Her, they would have caused her death many times over; yet, on the other hand, these sufferings, inflicted by God himself, were like a pledge and a new lease of life. For in her most ardent love She would have considered it incomparably more painful to see her divine Son suffer and die without being allowed to share in his torments.

509. The three Marys were instructed by the Queen to accompany and assist Her in her affliction, and for this purpose they were endowed with greater light and grace than the other women. In retiring with them the most pure Mother began to feel unwonted sorrow and anguish and She said to them: "My soul is sorrowful, because my beloved Son is about to suffer and die, and it is not permitted me to suffer and die of his torments. Pray, my friends, in order that you may not be overcome by temptation." Having said this She went apart a short distance from them, and following the Lord in his supplications. She, as far as was possible to Her and as far as She knew it to be conformable to the human will of her Son, continued her prayers and petitions, feeling the same agony as that of the Savior in the garden. She also returned at the same intervals to her companions to exhort them, because She knew of the wrath of the demon against them. She wept at the perdition of the foreknown; for She was highly enlightened in the mysteries of eternal predestination and reprobation. In order to imitate and co-operate in all things with the Redeemer of the world, the great Lady also suffered a bloody sweat, similar to that of Jesus in the garden, and by divine intervention She was visited by the archangel saint Gabriel, as Christ her Son was vis-

ited by the archangel Michael. The holy prince expounded to Her the will of the Most High in the same
manner as saint Michael had expounded it to Christ
the Lord. In both of Them the prayer offered and the
cause of sorrow was the same; and therefore They were
also proportionally alike to one another in their actions
and in their knowledge. I was made to understand that
the most prudent Lady was provided with some cloths
for what was to happen in the Passion of her most beloved Son; and on this occasion She sent some of her
angels with a towel to the garden in which her Son was
then perspiring blood, in order to wipe off and dry his
venerable countenance. The Lord, for love of his
Mother and for her greater merit, permitted these ministers of the Most High to fulfill her pious and tender
wishes. When the moment for the capture of our
Savior had arrived, it was announced to the three Marys
by the sorrowful Mother. All three bewailed this in-
dignity with most bitter tears, especially Mary Magdalen, who signalized herself in tenderest love and piety
for her Master.

INSTRUCTION WHICH MARY, THE QUEEN OF
HEAVEN, GAVE ME.

510. My daughter, all that thou hast understood and
written in this chapter will serve as a most potent incen-
tive to thee and to all the mortals who will consider it
carefully. Estimate then, and weigh within thy soul,
how important is the eternal predestination or reprobation of the souls, since my most holy Son looked upon
it with such great anxiety, that the difficulty or impossibility of saving all men added such immense bitterness to
the Death, which He was about to suffer for all. By
this conflict He manifests to us the importance and grav-

ity of the matter under consideration, He prolonged his supplications and prayers to his eternal Father and his love for men caused his most precious blood to ooze forth from his body on perceiving, that the malice of men would make them unworthy of participation in the benefits of his Death. The Lord my Son has indeed justified his cause in thus having lavished his love and his merits without measure for the purchase of man's salvation; and likewise the eternal Father has justified Himself in presenting to the world such a remedy and in having made it possible for each one freely to reach out for such widely different lots, as death and life, fire and water (Eccli. 15, 71).

511. But what pretense or excuse will men advance for having forgotten their own eternal salvation, when my divine Son and I have desired and sought to procure it for them with such sacrifices and untiring watchfulness? None of the mortals will have any excuse for their foolish negligence, and much less will the children of the holy Church have an excuse, since they have received the faith of these admirable sacraments and yet show in their lives little difference from that of infidels and pagans. Do not think, my daughter, that it is written in vain: "Many are called, but few are chosen" (Matth. 20, 16): fear this sentence and renew in thy heart the care and zeal for thy salvation, conformable to the sense of obligation arising from the knowledge of such high mysteries. Even if it were not a question of eternal salvation for thee, thou shouldst correspond to the loving kindness with which I manifest to thee such great and divine secrets. That I call thee my daughter and a spouse of my Lord, should cause thee to pay no attention to any visible thing and embrace only love and suffering for his sake. This I have shown thee by

my example, since I applied all my faculties continually
to these two things with the highest perfection. In order
that thou mayest attain this, I wish that thy prayer be
without intermission and that thou watch one hour with
me, that is during the whole of thy life; for, compared
with eternity, life is less than one hour, yea less than
one moment. With such sentiments I wish that thou
follow up the mysteries of the Passion, writing them,
feeling them and imprinting them upon thy heart.

CHAPTER IV

512. While our Savior occupied Himself in praying to his Father for the spiritual salvation of the human race, the perfidious disciple Judas sought to hasten the delivery of Christ into the hands of the priests and pharisees. At the same time Lucifer and his demons, not being able to divert the perverse will of Judas and of the other enemies of Christ from their designs on the life of Christ their Creator and Master, changed the tactics of their satanic malice and began to incite the Jews to greater cruelty and effrontery in their dealings with the Savior. As I have already said several times, the devil was filled with great suspicions lest this most extraordinary Man be the Messias and the true God. He now resolved to ascertain whether his misgivings were well founded or not by instigating the Jews and their ministers to the most atrocious injuries against the Savior. He imparted to them his own dreadful envy and pride, and thus literally fulfilled the prophecy of Solomon (Wis. 2, 7). For it seemed to the demon, that if Christ was not God and only a man, He certainly must weaken and be conquered in these persecutions and torments. If on the other hand He was God, He would manifest it by freeing Himself and performing new miracles.

513. Similar motives urged on the priests and phari-

sees. At the instigation of Judas they hastily gathered
together a large band of people, composed of pagan soldiers, a tribune, and many Jews. Having consigned to
them Judas as a hostage, they sent this band on its way
to apprehend the most innocent Lamb, who was awaiting
them and who was aware of all the thoughts and schemes
of the sacrilegious priests, as foretold expressly by Jeremias (Jer. 11, 19). All these servants of malice, bearing
arms and provided with ropes and chains, in the glaring
torch and lantern-light, issued from the city in the direction of mount Olivet. The prime mover of the treachery, Judas, had insisted upon so much precaution; for,
in his perfidy and treachery, he feared that the meekest
Master, whom he believed to be a magician and sorcerer,
would perform some miracle for his escape. As if arms
and human precautions could ever have availed if Jesus
should have decided to make use of his divine power!
As if He could not have brought this power into play in
the same way as He had done on other occasions, should
He now choose not to deliver Himself to suffering and
to the ignominies of the Cross!

514. While they were approaching, the Lord returned
the third time to his Apostles and finding them asleep
spoke to them: "Sleep ye now, and take your rest. It
is enough: the hour is come; behold the Son of man
shall be betrayed into the hands of sinners. Rise up,
let us go. Behold he that will betray Me is at hand"
(Mark 14, 41). Such were the words of the Master of
holiness to the three most privileged Apostles; He was
unwilling to reprehend them more severely than in this
most meek and loving manner. Being oppressed, they
did not know what to answer their Lord, as Scripture
says (Mark 14, 40). They arose and Jesus went with
them to join the other eight disciples. He found them

likewise overcome and oppressed by their great sorrow and fallen asleep. The Master then gave orders, that all of them together, mystically forming one body with Him their Head, should advance toward the enemies, thereby teaching them the power of mutual and perfect unity for overcoming the demons and their followers and for avoiding defeat by them. For a triple cord is hard to tear, as says Ecclesiastes (4, 12), and he that is mighty against one, may be overcome by two, that being the effect of union. The Lord again exhorted all the Apostles and forewarned them of what was to happen. Already the confused noise of the advancing band of soldiers and their helpmates began to be heard. Our Savior then proceeded to meet them on the way, and, with incomparable love, magnanimous courage and tender piety prayed interiorly: "O sufferings longingly desired from my inmost soul, ye pains, wounds, affronts, labors, afflictions and ignominious death, come, come, come quickly, for the fire of love, which burns for the salvation of men, is anxious to see you meet the Innocent one of all creatures. Well do I know your value, I have sought, desired, and solicited you and I meet you joyously of my own free will; I have purchased you by my anxiety in searching for you and I esteem you for your merits. I desire to remedy and enhance your value and raise you to highest dignity. Let death come, in order that by my accepting it without having deserved it I may triumph over it and gain life for those who have been punished by death for their sins (Osee 13, 14). I give permission to my friends to forsake Me; for I alone desire and am able to enter into this battle and gain for them triumph and victory" (Is. 53, 3).

515. During these words and prayers of the Author of life, Judas advanced in order to give the signal upon

which he had agreed with his companions (Matth. 26, 48), namely the customary, but now feigned kiss of peace, by which they were to distinguish Jesus as the One whom they should single out from the rest and immediately seize. These precautions the unhappy disciple had taken, not only out of avarice for the money and hatred against his Master, but also, on account of the fear with which he was filled. For he dreaded the inevitable necessity of meeting Him and encountering Him in the future, if Christ was not put to death on this occasion. Such a confusion he feared more than the death of his soul, or the death of his divine Master, and, in order to forestall it, he hastened to complete his treachery and desired to see the Author of life die at the hands of his enemies. The traitor then ran up to the meekest Lord, and, as a consummate hypocrite, hiding his hatred, he imprinted on his countenance the kiss of peace, saying: "God save Thee, Master." By this so treacherous act the perdition of Judas was matured and God was justified in withholding his grace and help. On the part of the unfaithful disciple, malice and temerity reached their highest degree; for, interiorly denying or disbelieving the uncreated and created wisdom by which Christ must know of his treason, and ignoring his power to destroy him, he sought to hide his malice under the cloak of the friendship of a true disciple; and all this for the purpose of delivering over to such a frightful and cruel death his Creator and Master, to whom he was bound by so many obligations. In this one act of treason he committed so many and such formidable sins, that it is impossible to fathom their immensity; for he was treacherous, murderous, sacrilegious, ungrateful, inhuman, disobedient, false, lying, impious and unequalled in hypocrisy; and all this was included in one and the same crime perpetrated against the person of God made man.

516. On the part of the Lord shone forth his ineffable mercy and equity, since those words of David were fulfilled in an eminent manner: "With them that hated peace I was peaceable; when I spoke to them they fought against Me without cause" (Ps. 119, 7). So completely did the Lord fulfill this prophecy, that when, in answer to the kiss of Judas, He said: "Friend, whereto art thou come?" He sent into the heart of the traitorous disciple a new and most clear light, by which Judas saw the atrocious malice of his treason, the punishment to follow, if he should not make it good by true penitence, and the merciful pardon still to be obtained from the divine clemency. What Judas clearly read in those few words of Christ was: "Friend, take heed lest thou cause thy perdition and abuse my meekness by this treason. If thou seek my friendship, I will not refuse it to thee on account of this deed, as soon as thou art sorry for thy sin. Consider well thy temerity in delivering Me by false friendship and under cover of a false peace and a kiss of reverence and love. Remember the benefits thou hast received of my charity, and that I am the Son of the Virgin, by whom thou hast been so often favored and rejoiced with motherly advice and counsel during thy apostolate. Even if it were only for her sake, thou shouldst not commit such a treason as to sell and deliver her Son. In no wise does her loving meekness deserve such an outrageous wrong, for She has never been unkind to thee. But although thou hast now committed this wrong, do not despise her intercession, for She alone will be powerful with Me and for her sake I offer thee pardon and life, since She has many times besought Me to do so. I assure thee, that We love thee; for thou art yet in life, where there is hope and where we will not

deny thee our friendship, if thou seek it. But if thou
refuse it, thou wilt merit our abhorrence and eternal
chastisement and pain." The seed of the divine words
took no root in the heart of that unhappy reprobate. It
was harder than adamant and more inhuman than that
of a wild beast. Resisting the divine clemency he finally
fell into despair, as I shall relate in the next chapter.

517. The signal of the kiss having been given by
Judas, the Lord with his disciples and the soldiers, who
had come to capture Him, came face to face, forming
two squadrons the most opposed and hostile that ever
the world saw. For on the one side was Christ our
Lord, true God and man, as the Captain of all the just,
supported by his eleven Apostles the chieftains and cham-
pions of his Church with innumerable hosts of angelic
spirits full of adoring wonder at this spectacle. On the
other side were Judas, the originator of the treason, filled
with hypocrisy and hatred, and many Jews and gentiles,
bent on venting their malice with the greatest cruelty.
Surrounding these were Lucifer and a multitude of
demons, inciting and assisting Judas and his helpers
boldly to lay their sacrilegious hands upon their Creator.
With unfathomable love for suffering and great force
and authority the Lord then spoke to the soldiers, saying: "Whom seek ye?" (John 18, 4-5). They answered:
"Jesus of Nazareth." Jesus said to them: "I am He."
By these inestimably precious and blessed words Christ
declared Himself as our Redeemer and Savior; for only
by his offering Himself freely to redeem us by his Passion and Death, could our hope of eternal life ever rest
on firm foundation.

518. His enemies could not understand or fathom the
true meaning of these words: I am He. But his most
blessed Mother and the angels understood them, as did

also, to a great extent, the Apostles. It was as if He had said: "I am who am" (Exod. 3, 14), as I have said to my prophet Moses; for I am of Myself, and all creatures have their being and existence from Me: I am eternal, immense, infinite, one in substance and attributes; and I have made Myself man hiding my glory, in order that, by means of my Passion and Death, to which you wish to condemn Me, I might save the world. As the Lord spoke with divine power, his enemies could not resist and when his words struck their ears, they all fell backwards to the ground (John 18, 6). This happened not only to the soldiers, but to the dogs, which they had brought with them, and to the horses on which some of them rode: all of them fell to the ground and remained motionless like stones. Lucifer and his demons were hurled down with them, deprived of motion and suffering new confusion and torture. Thus they remained for some seven or eight minutes, showing no more signs of life than if they had died. O word of a God, so mysterious in meaning and more than invincible in power! Let not the wise glory before Thee in their wisdom and astuteness; nor the powerful in their valor (Jer. 9, 23); let the vanity and arrogance of the children of Babylon be humbled, since one word from the mouth of the Lord, spoken with so much meekness and humility, confounds, destroys and annihilates all the pride and power of man and hell. Let us children of the Church also learn, that the victories of Christ are gained by confessing the truth, by giving place unto wrath (Rom. 12, 19), by showing meekness and humility of heart (Matth. 11, 29), by overcoming and being overcome with dove-like simplicity, by the peacefulness and resignment of sheep free from resistance of furious and ravenous wolves.

519. Sadly our divine Lord contemplated the picture of eternal damnation exhibited in them and listened to the prayer of his most holy Mother to let them rise, for upon her intercession his divine will had made that dependent. When it was time for them to come to themselves, He prayed to the eternal Father, saying: "My Father and eternal God, in my hands Thou hast placed all things (John 13, 3), and hast consigned to Me the Redemption required by thy justice. I wish to satisfy it and give Myself over to death with all my heart, in order to merit for my brethren participation in thy treasures and the eternal happiness held out to them." By this expression of his efficacious will the Lord gave permission to that whole miserable band of men, demons and animals to arise and be restored to the same condition as before their falling down. A second time the Savior said to them: "Whom seek ye?" and they again answered: "Jesus of Nazareth." The Lord answered most meekly: "I have already told you, that I am He. If therefore you seek Me, let these go their way" (John 18, 8). With these words He gave permission to the servants and the soldiers to take Him prisoner and execute their designs, which, without their understanding it, meant nothing else than to draw upon his divine Person all our sorrows and infirmities (Is. 53, 4).

520. The first one who hastened to approach in order to lay hands upon the Master of life, was a servant of the highpriests named Malchus. In spite of the fear and consternation of all the Apostles, saint Peter, more than all the rest, was roused with zeal for the defense of the honor and life of the divine Master. Drawing a cutlass which he had with him, he made a pass at Malchus and cut off one of his ears, severing it entirely from the head (John 18, 10). The stroke would have resulted in a

much more serious wound, if the divine providence of the Master of patience and meekness had not diverted it. The Lord would not permit that any other death than his own should occur at his capture; his wounds, his blood and suffering alone should rescue to eternal life the human race, as many of it as are willing. Nor was it his will, or according to his teaching, that his Person be defended by tne use of arms, and He did not wish to leave such an example in his Church as one to be principally imitated for her defense. In order to confirm this doctrine, which He had always inculcated, He picked up the severed ear and restored it to its place, perfectly healing the wound and making Malchus more sound and whole than he was before. But He first turned to saint Peter and reprehended him, saying: "Put up thy sword into the scabbard, for all that shall take it to kill with it, shall perish. Dost thou not wish that I drink the chalice, which my Father hath given Me? Thinkst thou that I cannot ask my Father, and He will give me presently many legions of angels for my defense? But how then shall the Scriptures and the Prophets be fulfilled?" (John 18, 11; Matth. 26, 53).

521. Thus saint Peter, the head of the Church, by this loving exhortation had been taught and enlightened, that his arms for the establishment and defense of the Church were to be spiritual and that the law of the Gospel does not inculcate battles and conquests with material weapons, but conquests of humility, patience, meekness and perfect charity, which overcome the demon, the world, and the flesh; that divine virtue would triumph over its enemies and over the power and intrigues of this world; that arms for attack and defense were not for the followers of Christ our Savior, but for the princes of the earth to safeguard their earthly possessions; while the sword of

the Church was to be spiritual, reaching rather the soul
than the body.   Then Christ our Lord, turning toward
his enemies and the servants of the Jews, spoke to them
with great majesty and grandeur: "You are come as it
were to a robber with swords and clubs to apprehend
Me.   I sat daily with you, teaching in the temple, and
you laid not hands on Me.   But this is your hour and
the power of darkness" (Matth. 26, 55; Luke 22, 53).
All the words of our Savior contained the profoundest
mysteries, and it is impossible to comprehend them all
or explain them, especially those which He spoke at his
Passion and Death.

522. Well might those ministers have been softened
and made ashamed of their wickedness by this reprehen-
sion of the divine Master; but they were far from it,
because they were of the cursed and sterile earth, drained
of the dew of virtue and human kindness.   Nevertheless
the Author of life wished to admonish them of the truth
to that extent.   Thereby their malice would be so much
the more inexcusable and this sin and all the others, committed in the very presence of the highest holiness and
justice, would have its due correction and they themselves
a powerful help for conversion, if they should desire it;
moreover it would thereby become evident that He knew
all that was to happen, that He delivered Himself into
their hands and over to this Death of his own free will.
For these, and for many other sublime reasons, the Lord
spoke the above words, penetrating their inmost mind.
For He knew and fully understood the cause of their
malice, hatred and envy: namely, because He had publicly reprehended the vices of the priests and pharisees;
because He had taught the truth and the way of life
to the people; because He had, by his example and his
miracles, captured the good will of the humble and the

pious and brought many sinners to his friendship and grace. He reminded them, that one who had power to bring about all these results in public, and who could not be apprehended in the temple or in the city in which He taught, could certainly not be captured in the open field without his consent. He clearly made them sensible, that the reason of their failing to do so before, was because He himself had not given his permission to men or demons until the hour chosen by Himself. In order to signify to them, that the hour of his being captured, illtreated and afflicted had come He said: "This is your hour and the power of darkness." As if He had said to them: Until now it was necessary for Me to be with you as your Master for your instruction, therefore I did not permit you to take my life. But I desire to consummate by my death the work of the Redemption consigned to Me by my eternal Father; and therefore I now permit you to take Me prisoner and to execute your will upon my Person. Thereupon they fell upon the most meek Lamb like fierce tigers, binding Him securely with ropes and chains in order thus to lead Him to the house of the highpriest, as I shall presently relate.

523. The most pure Mother of Christ our Lord was most attentive to all that passed in his capture, and by means of her clear visions saw it more clearly than if She had been present in person; for by means of her supernatural visions She penetrated into all the mysteries of his words and actions. When She beheld the band of soldiers and servants issuing from the house of the high priest, the prudent Lady foresaw the irreverence and insults with which they would treat their Creator and Redeemer; and in order to do what was within her power, She invited the holy angels and many

others in union with Her to render adoration and praise
to the Lord of creation as an offset to the injuries and
affronts He would sustain at the hands of those ministers of darkness. The same request She made to the
holy women who were praying with Her. She told
them, that her most holy Son had now given permission
to his enemies to take him prisoner and illtreat him,
and that they were about to make use of this permission in a most impious and cruel manner. Assisted by
the holy angels and the pious women the faithful Queen
engaged in interior and exterior acts of devoted faith
and love, confessing, adoring, praising and magnifying
the infinite Deity and the most holy humanity of her
Creator and Lord. The holy women imitated Her in
the genuflections and prostrations, and the angelic
princes responded to the canticles with which She magnified, celebrated and glorified the Divinity and humanity
of Christ. In the measure in which the children of
malice increased their irreverence and injuries, She
sought to compensate them by her praise and veneration.
Thus She continued to placate the divine justice, lest it
should be roused against his persecutors and destroy
them; for only most holy Mary was capable of staying
the punishment of such great offenses.

524. And the great Lady not only placated the just
Judge, but even obtained favors and blessings from the
divine clemency for the very persons who irritated Him
and thus secured a return of good for those who were
heaping wrongs upon Christ the Lord for his doctrine
and benefits. This mercy attained its highest point in
the disloyal and obstinate Judas; for the tender Mother,
seeing him deliver Jesus by the kiss of feigned friendship, and considering how shortly before his mouth had
contained the sacramental body of the Lord, with whose

sacred countenance so soon after those same foul lips were permitted to come in contact, was transfixed with sorrow and entranced by charity. She asked the Lord to grant new graces, whereby this man, who had enjoyed the privilege of touching the face whereon angels desire to look, might, if he chose to use them, save himself from perdition. In response to this prayer of most holy Mary, her Son and Lord granted Judas powerful graces in the very consummation of his treacherous delivery. If the unfortunate man had given heed and had commenced to respond to them, the Mother of mercy would have obtained for him many others and at last also pardon for his sin. She has done so with many other great sinners, who were willing to give that glory to Her, and thus obtain eternal glory for themselves. But Judas failed to realize this and thus lost all chance of salvation, as I shall relate in the next chapter.

525. Likewise, when the great Lady saw all the servants and soldiers who had come to take Him, fall to the ground at his divine word, She, in company with the angels, broke out in a song of praise of his infinite power and of the virtue of his humanity, which thereby renewed the victory of the Most High over Pharao and his troops in the Red sea (Exod. 15, 4). She exalted the Lord of hosts, because He was about to deliver Himself in an admirable manner to suffering and death in order to save the human race from the captivity of Lucifer. Then She besought the Lord to permit all these dumbfounded and vanquished enemies to regain their senses and to arise. She was moved to the petition by her most generous kindness and deep compassion for these men created by the Lord according to his own image and likeness; on the other hand, She wanted to fulfill in an eminent degree the law of loving our enemies

and doing good to those who persecute us, inculcated and
practiced by her own Son and Master (Matth. 5, 44),
and finally because She knew that the prophecies of holy
Scripture were to be fulfilled in the Redemption of man.
Although all these were infallible, this did not hinder
the most holy Mary from giving voice to her prayer
and thereby moving the Most High to grant these
favors; for in the infinite wisdom and in the decrees of
his eternal will all these means were foreseen as producing these effects in the manner most conformable to the
foreknowledge and foresight of the Lord. But it is not
necessary to enter into further explanation of such mysteries at present. When the servants of the high priest
laid hands on and bound the Savior, the most blessed
Mother felt on her own hands the pains caused by the
ropes and chains, as if She Herself was being bound and
fettered; in the same manner She felt in her body the
blows and torments further inflicted upon the Lord,
for, I have already said, this favor was granted to his
Mother, as we shall see in the course of the Passion.
Thus her sensible participation in his sufferings was some
kind of relief of the pain, which She would have suffered in her loving soul at the thought of not being with
Him in his torments.

INSTRUCTION WHICH THE QUEEN OF HEAVEN, MOST HOLY MARY, GAVE ME.

526. My daughter, in all that thou art made to understand and write concerning these mysteries, thou drawest
upon thyself (and upon mortals) a severe judgment, if
thou dost not overcome thy pusillanimity, ingratitude
and baseness by meditating day and night on the Passion
and Death of Jesus crucified. This is the great science
of the saints, so little heeded by the worldly; it is the

bread of life and the spiritual food of the little ones, which gives wisdom to them and the want of which starves the lovers of this proud world (Wis. 15, 3). In this science I wish thee to be studious and wise, for with it thou canst buy thyself all good things (Wis. 7, 11). My Son and Lord taught us this science when He said: "I am the way, the truth and the life: no one cometh to my Father except through Me" (John 14, 6). Tell me then, my daughter: if my Lord and Master has made Himself the life and the way for men through his Passion and Death, is it not evident that in order to go that way and live up to this truth, they must follow Christ crucified, afflicted, scourged and affronted? Consider the ignorance of men who wish to come to the Father without following Christ, since they expect to reign with God without suffering or imitating his Passion, yea without even a thought of accepting any part of his suffering and Death, or of thanking Him for it. They want it to procure for them the pleasures of this life as well as of eternal life, while Christ their Creator has suffered the most bitter pains and torments in order to enter heaven and to show them by his example how they are to find the way of light.

527. Eternal rest is incompatible with the shame of not having duly labored for its attainment. He is not a true son of his father, who does not imitate him, nor he a good disciple, who does not follow his Master, nor he a good servant, who does not accompany his lord; nor do I count him a devoted child, who does not suffer with me and my divine Son. But our love for the eternal salvation of men obliges us, who see them forgetful of this truth and so adverse to suffering, to send them labors and punishments, so that if they do not freely welcome them, they may at least be forced to

undergo them and so be enabled to enter upon the way of salvation. And yet even all this is insufficient, since their inclinations and their blind love of visible things detains them and makes them hard and heavy of heart; they rob them of remembrance and affection toward these higher things, which might raise them above themselves and above created things. Hence it comes, that men do not find joy in their tribulations, nor rest in their labors, nor consolation in their sorrows, nor any peace in adversities. For, altogether different from the saints who glory in tribulation as the fulfillment of their most earnest desires, they desire none of it and abhor all that is painful. In many of the faithful this ignorance goes still farther; for some of them expect to be distinguished by God's most intimate love, others, to be pardoned without penance, others, to be highly favored. Nothing of all this will they attain, because they do not ask in the name of Christ the Lord and because they do not wish to imitate Him and follow Him in his Passion.

528. Therefore, my daughter, embrace the Cross and do not admit any consolation outside of it in this mortal life. By contemplating and feeling within thyself the sacred Passion thou wilt attain the summit of perfection and attain the love of a spouse. Bless and magnify my most holy Son for the love with which He delivered Himself up for the salvation of mankind. Little do mortals heed this mystery; but I, as an Eyewitness, assure thee, next to ascending to the right hand of his eternal Father, nothing was so highly estimated and so earnestly desired by Him, as to offer Himself for suffering and death and to deliver Himself up entirely to his enemies. I wish also that thou lament with great sorrow the fact that Judas, in his malice and treachery, has

many more followers than Christ. Many are the infidels, many the bad Catholics, many the hypocrites, who under the name of a Christian, sell and deliver Him and wish to crucify Him anew. Bewail all these evils, which thou understandest and knowest, in order that thou mayest imitate and follow me in this matter.

CHAPTER V

THE FLIGHT AND DISPERSION OF THE APOSTLES AFTER THE CAPTURE OF THEIR MASTER; HOW HIS MOST BLESSED MOTHER WAS AWARE OF ALL THAT HAPPENED AND HOW SHE ACTED IN CONSEQUENCE; THE PERDITION OF JUDAS AND THE WORRY OF THE DEMONS OVER WHAT THEY WERE OBLIGED TO EXPERIENCE.

529. After the seizure of our Savior Jesus, his prophecy at the Supper, that all of the Apostles would be greatly scandalized in his Person (Matth. 26, 31) and that satan would attack them in order to sift them like wheat, was fulfilled. For when they saw their divine Master taken prisoner and when they perceived, that neither his meekness, nor his words so full of sweetness and power, nor his miracles, nor his doctrine exemplified by such an unblamable life, could appease the envy of the priests and pharisees, they fell into great trouble and affliction. Naturally the fear of personal danger diminished their courage and confidence in the counsels of their Master, and beginning to wander in their faith, each one became possessed with anxious thoughts as to how he could escape the threatening persecutions foreshadowed by what had happened to their Captain and Master. The Apostles, availing themselves of the pre-occupation of the soldiers and servants in binding and fettering the meek Lamb of God, betook themselves to flight unnoticed. Certainly their enemies,

if they had been permitted by the Author of life, would
have captured all the Apostles, especially if they had
seen them fly like cowards or criminals (Matth. 26, 56).
But it was not proper that they should be taken and
made to suffer at that time. This was clearly indicated
as the will of the Lord, when He said: that if they
sought Him, they should let his companions go free;
these words had the force of a divine decree and were
verified in the event. For the hatred of the priests and
pharisees extended to the Apostles, and was deep enough
to make them desire the death of all of them. That is
the reason why the highpriest Annas asked the divine
Master about his disciples and his doctrine (John 18, 8).

530. At the flight of the Apostles, Lucifer, already
troubled and vaguely perplexed, betook himself off hesi-
tating between different projects of his redoubled malice.
He certainly wished to see the doctrine of the Savior
and all his disciples blotted out from the world, so that
not even the memory of them be left. Hence he would
have been well satisfied, if the Jews had imprisoned and
killed them all. But he had no hope of easily attaining
this wish, and therefore he busied himself in disquieting
the Apostles by various suggestions and inciting them to
flight, in order that they might not witness the patience
and virtues of their Master in his sufferings. The astute
dragon feared, that by this new proof of his doctrine
in his living example the Apostles might be confirmed
and fortified in their faith and thus resist the temptations
which he planned for them; therefore it seemed to him,
that if he could weaken them now, he could more easily
cause them to fall away entirely by subsequent persecutions easily to be raised against them among the only
too ready enemies of their Master. Thus the demon
deceived himself by his own malicious calculations.

When therefore he saw the Apostles filled with cowardly
fear and much disturbed by the sorrow of their hearts,
he rejoiced in their evil plight and considered it the
best time to begin his temptations. He assailed them
with rabid fury, filling them with strong doubts and
suspicions against the Master of life and urging them
to give Him up and betake themselves to flight. They
easily yielded to his suggestions of flight; but they resisted many of the doubts against faith, although some
failed more, some less, not all of the Apostles being
equally disturbed or scandalized.

531. They separated from each other, scattering in
different directions; for it would have been difficult for
all of them to hide as they wished, if they remained
together. Only saint Peter and saint John kept each
other company to follow their God and Master and see
the end of his misfortune (Matth. 26, 58). But in the
soul of each one of the eleven Apostles raged a battle
of sorrow and grief, which wrung their hearts and left
them without consolation or the least rest. On the one
side battled reason, grace, faith, love and truth; on the
other temptation, suspicion, fear, cowardice and sorrow.
Reason and truth reproached them with their incon-
stancy and disloyalty in having forsaken their Master
by cowardly flying from danger, after having been
warned of it and after having offered themselves so
shortly before to die for Him if necessary. They remembered their disobedience in neglecting to pray and
strengthen themselves against temptations, as the Lord
had commanded them. Their love for his sweet conversation and company, for his teaching and miraculous
power, and their conviction that He was true God, urged
them to return and seek Him, and to offer themselves
to danger and death like faithful servants and disciples.

To all this was joined the memory of his most sweet Mother, the consideration of her intense sorrow, and the desire to seek Her and attend upon Her in her trouble. But on the other hand was their timidity, exaggerating their fears of the Jews, their dread of death, of shame and confusion. In regard to seeking the company of the sorrowful Mother, they feared lest She would oblige them to return to their Master, and lest they should be more easily found if they stayed with Her in the same house. Dreadful above all were the impious and horrible suggestions of the demons. For the dragon filled them with harassing doubts, whether it would not be suicide to thus deliver themselves to a certain death; that, if their Master could not free Himself, much less could He free them from the hands of the priests; that He would now certainly be put to death, and that therefore all ties between Him and them were dissolved, since they would not see Him any more; that, although his life seemed to be blameless, yet He had taught some very hard doctrines, some of them unheard of until that time, whence He had incurred the hatred of those learned in the law and of the priests, as well as the indignation of all the people. Moreover it was a serious matter to follow a Man, who was to be condemned to an infamous and frightful death.

532. Such was the interior contention and strife in the hearts of the Apostles. Satan under cover of this excitement, continually sought to instill into their minds doubts concerning the teachings of Christ and concerning the prophecies, that treated of the mysteries of his Passion. As in their sad interior conflict they failed to see the least assurance of seeing their Master escape the hands of the priests alive, their fears settled into a profound sorrow and melancholy, in which they decided to fly

from the danger and save their own lives. And they
were seized with such timidity and cowardice, that during
this night they felt nowhere safe, and every shadow or
noise made them tremble with fear. The consideration
of the treachery of Judas added still more to their fear;
for, as he had not been seen in the company of any of
the eleven after his treacherous delivery of the Lord,
they dreaded lest he should excite against them the
hatred of the priests. Saint Peter and saint John, being
more fervent in the love of their Master, made a greater
show of resistance to fear and to the demon; and the
two together resolved to follow their Master at a distance. In taking this resolve, they relied much upon the
acquaintance of saint John with the highpriest Annas,
who with Caiphas alternated in the office of highpriest.
In that year it was held by Caiphas, who in the meeting
had given the prophetic counsel, asking whether one man
had not better die in order that the whole world might
not perish (John 18, 15, 49). This acquaintance had
arisen from the fact, that saint John was esteemed as a
man, distinguished and of noble lineage, of affable and
courteous manners and amiable in person. Trusting to
these favorable circumstances the two Apostles followed
the Lord with less fear. The thought of their heavenly
Queen was deep in their hearts, and they reflected on her
bitter sorrow and desired to bring relief and console Her
if possible. In this pious and loving desire especially
saint John excelled all the others.

533. The heavenly Princess, from the Cenacle, clearly
understood and saw all: not only her most holy Son in
captivity and suffering, but all that happened inwardly
and outwardly to the Apostles. She observed their tribulation and temptations, their thoughts and resolves,
where each one was and what he did. But although all

was known to the most gentle Dove, She allowed Herself
no feeling of indignation against the Apostles, nor did
She ever in the least reproach them for their disloyalty;
on the contrary, She was the One, who was principally
instrumental in restoring them to a better mind, as I
shall show later on (746, 747). From that hour on
She commenced to pray for them. In sweetest charity
and with the compassion of a Mother, She interiorly
addressed them: "O ye simple sheep, chosen by the Lord,
do ye forsake your most loving Pastor, who cares for
you and feeds you on the pastures of eternal life? Why,
being disciples of such a truthful doctrine, do you leave
your Benefactor and Master? How can you forget the
sweet and loving intercourse, which so attracted your
hearts? Why do you listen to the master of lies and
follow the ravenous wolf, who seeks your ruin? O most
patient and sweetest Lord, how meek, and kind and merciful does the love of men make Thee! Extend thy gentle
love to this little flock, which is now troubled and dispersed by the fury of the serpent. Do not deliver over
to the beasts those souls, who have confessed thy name
(Ps. 73, 19). Great hopes hast thou set in those, whom
Thou hast chosen as thy servants and through whom
Thou hast already accomplished great things. Let not
such graces be in vain, nor reject those whom Thou hast
freely chosen for the foundations of thy Church. Let
not Lucifer glory in having, beneath thy very eyes, vanquished the best of thy family and household. My Son
and Lord, look upon thy beloved disciples John, Peter
and James, so much favored by thy love and good will.
Turn an eye of clemency also upon the rest, crush the
pride of the dragon, which now pursues them with implacable fury."

534. In all that most holy Mary did on this occasion

and in the pleasure She caused the Almighty by her
holiness, She exceeded in grandeur all that was ever
possible in men and angels. Over and above the sensible
and spiritual sorrows caused by the torments of her
divine Son and the affronts perpetrated against his divine
Person (for which the blessed Mother entertained the
highest veneration attainable by a creature), She was
overwhelmed with the sorrow caused by the fall of the
Apostles, the greatness of which She alone could properly estimate. She was obliged to witness their weakness
and forgetfulness in the face of his divine favors, his
doctrines and exhortations, and in so short a time after
the last Supper, when He had warned them so lovingly,
given them holy Communion and elevated them to such
a high dignity as the priesthood. She saw also the danger
of their falling into even greater sins on account of the
astute and furious attacks of Lucifer and his demons,
and on account of the heedlessness of the Apostles in
their greater or less confusion and fear. Yet notwith-
standing this great sea of sorrow She multiplied and
intensified her petitions in order to merit for them sufficient assistance and speedy pardon from her Son, so that
they might again return to their faith and to his friendship in grace. She alone was the powerful and efficacious
instrument of these results. During these hours the
great Lady united within Herself all the faith, all the
holiness, all the worship and divine cult of the Church;
for in Her was preserved and enclosed as in the living
and incorruptible ark and as in the temple and sanctuary,
the evangelical law and sacrifice. She by Herself alone
then constituted the entire Church, because She alone
preserved full faith, hope and love, complete worship and
adoration for the great object of our faith, not only supplying her full share for Herself, but for the Apostles

and for the whole human race. She it was who compensated, as far as was possible to a creature, for the
deficiencies and faults in the rest of the mystical members of the Church. She performed heroic acts of faith,
hope, love toward Her Son and true God, She venerated
and adored Him by her prostrations and genuflections,
She blessed Him with wonderful songs of praise, not
allowing her deep and bitter sorrow to interfere with the
beautiful and harmonious disposition and the full operation of all her faculties, as pre-ordained by the Almighty.
What Ecclesiasticus says of music: that it is inopportune
in time of sorrow (Eccli. 22, 6), does not apply to Her;
for only the blessed Mary was able and knew how to
augment the beautiful harmony of virtues in the midst
of sorrow.

535. Leaving the twelve Apostles in the sad state
above mentioned, I now proceed to relate the most
unhappy end of the traitor Judas, somewhat anticipating
the course of events, in order to have done with his
lamentable and unfortunate lot and continue the narra-
tive of the Passion. With the band that had taken the
Lord prisoner, the sacrilegious disciple arrived at the
house of the highpriest, that of Annas first, and then
at that of Caiphas, who, with the scribes and pharisees
were awaiting results. When the perfidious disciple saw
his divine Master overwhelmed with blasphemies and
injuries and how He suffered all with such admirable
silence, meekness and patience, he began to reflect upon
his own treachery and that it alone caused such cruel
injustice to be heaped upon an innocent Man and his
Benefactor. He recalled the miracles he had witnessed,
the doctrines he had heard, and the benefits enjoyed at his
hands, and he remembered the kindness and meekness
of the most holy Mary, the charity with which She had

solicited his conversion, and the malice with which he
had offended the Son and the Mother for such insignificant gain. All the sins he had committed piled themselves up before his interior gaze like a dark and chaotic,
impenetrable mountain.

536. As I have stated above, Judas was forsaken by
divine grace at the time when he consummated his treachery by his perfidious kiss and by his contact with Christ
our Savior. According to the hidden judgments of the
Most High, although he was now left to his own counsels, the divine justice and equity, ingrained in the natural
reason, permitted these reflections to arise and to be
supplemented by many suggestions of Lucifer who possessed him. But though Judas thus reasoned correctly
in these matters, it was the devil who awakened these
truths and added many other false and deceitful suggestions, in order to deduct from them not the salutary
hope of remedy, but to convince him of the impossibility
of repairing the damage and to lead him to the despair
to which he at last yielded. Lucifer roused in him a
keen sorrow for his misdeeds; not however for a good
purpose, nor founded upon having offended the divine
Truth, but upon his disgrace among men and upon the
fear of retribution from his Master, whom he knew to be
miraculously powerful and One whom he would be able
to escape nowhere in the whole world. Everywhere the
blood of the just One would forever cry for vengeance
against him. Filled with these thoughts and others
aroused by the demon, he was involved in confusion,
darkness and rabid rage against himself. Fleeing from
all human beings he essayed to throw himself from the
highest roof of the priests' house without being able to
execute his design. Gnawing like a wild beast at the
flesh of his arms and hands, striking fearful blows at his

head, tearing out his hair and raving in his talk, he rushed away and showered maledictions and execrations upon himself as the most unfortunate and miserable of men.

537. Seeing him thus beside himself Lucifer inspired him with the thought of hunting up the priests, returning to them the money and confessing his sin. This Judas hastened to do, and he loudly shouted at them those words: "I have sinned, betraying innocent blood!" (Matth. 27, 4). But they, not less hardened, answered that he should have seen to that before. The intention of the demon was to hinder the death of Christ if possible, for reasons already given and yet to be given (No. 419). This repulse of the priests, so full of impious cruelty, took away all hope from Judas and he persuaded himself that it was impossible to hinder the death of his Master. So thought also the demon, although later on he made more efforts to forestall it through Pilate. But as Judas could be of no more use to him for his purpose, he augmented his distress and despair, persuading him that in order to avoid severer punishments he must end his life. Judas yielded to this terrible deceit, and rushing forth from the city, hung himself on a dried-out figtree (Matth. 27, 5). Thus he that was the murderer of his Creator, became also his own murderer. This happened on Friday at twelve o'clock, three hours before our Savior died. It was not becoming that his death and the consummation of our Redemption should coincide too closely with the execrable end of the traitorous disciple, who hated him with fiercest malice.

538. The demons at once took possession of the soul of Judas and brought it down to hell. His entrails burst from the body hanging upon the tree (Acts 1, 18). All that saw this stupendous punishment of the perfidious

and malicious disciple for his treason, were filled with astonishment and dread. The body remained hanging by the neck for three days, exposed to the view of the public. During that time the Jews attempted to take it down from the tree and to bury it in secret, for it was a sight apt to cause great confusion to the pharisees and priests, who could not refute such a testimony of his wickedness. But no efforts of theirs sufficed to drag or separate the body from its position on the tree until three days had passed, when, according to the dispensation of divine justice, the demons themselves snatched the body from the tree and brought it to his soul, in order that both might suffer eternal punishment in the profoundest abyss of hell. Since what I have been made to know of the pains and chastisements of Judas, is worthy of fear-inspiring attention, I will according to command reveal what has been shown me concerning it. Among the obscure caverns of the infernal prisons was a very large one, arranged for more horrible chastisements than the others, and which was still unoccupied; for the demons had been unable to cast any soul into it, although their cruelty had induced them to attempt it many times from the time of Cain unto that day. All hell had remained astonished at the failure of these attempts, being entirely ignorant of the mystery, until the arrival of the soul of Judas, which they readily succeeded in hurling and burying in this prison never before occupied by any of the damned. The secret of it was, that this cavern of greater torments and fiercer fires of hell, from the creation of the world, had been destined for those, who, after having received Baptism, would damn themselves by the neglect of the Sacraments, the doctrines, the Passion and Death of the Savior, and the intercession of his most holy Mother. As Judas had been the first one who had so signally participated in these blessings, and as he had so fearfully misused them, he was also the first to suffer the torments of this place, prepared for him and his imitators and followers.

539. This mystery I was commanded to reveal more particularly for a dreadful warning to all Christians, and especially to the priests, prelates and religious, who are accustomed to treat with more familiarity the body and blood of Christ our Lord, and who, by their office and state are his closer friends. In order to avoid blame I would like to find words and expressions sufficiently strong to make an impression on our unfeeling obduracy, so that we all may take a salutary warning and be filled with the fear of the punishments awaiting all bad Christians according to the station each one of us occupies.   The demons torment Judas with inexpressible cruelty, because he persisted in the betrayal of his Master, by whose Passion and Death they were vanquished and despoiled of the possession of the world. The wrath which they had conceived against the Savior and his blessed Mother, they wreck, as far as is allowed them, on all those who imitate the traitorous disciple and who follow him in his contempt of the evangelical law, of the Sacraments and of the fruits of the Redemption. And in this the demons are but executing just punishment on those members of the mystical body of Christ, who have severed their connection with its head Christ, and who have voluntarily drifted away and delivered themselves over to the accursed hate and implacable fury of his enemies. As the instruments of divine justice they chastise the redeemed for their ingratitude toward their Redeemer. Let the children of the Church consider well this truth, for it cannot fail to move their hearts and induce them to evade such a lamentable fate.

540. During the whole course of the Passion Lucifer with his demons moved about, eagerly spying out all the circumstances of each event in order to ascertain whether Christ the Lord was really the Messias and Redeemer of the world. On the one hand the miracles seemed to argue the truth of his suspicions, on the other very often the doings and the sufferings, so much like those of weak human nature, argued the contrary. The strongest argument for the truth of his suspicions was Lucifer's personal experience of the power of the Redeemer, when He said "I am He," which caused him and all his associates to fall prostrate, annihilated in the presence of the Lord; and this had happened only a short time after he had been permitted to issue from hell, whither the demons had been hurled from the Cenacle. It was true, Mary had routed them from the hall of the last Supper; yet Lucifer with his ministers connected it with the power exercised by Jesus and they could not but admit, that this power of both Mother and Son was something altogether new and unexperienced by them. When he had received permission to rise from his fall in the garden, he conferred with the rest and expressed his opinion, that this could not be merely human power, but without doubt the power of One, who is God and at the same time man. "If He shall die, as we have planned, He will accomplish the Redemption of man and satisfy the justice of God; then our sway will cease and all our intentions will be frustrated. We have erred in seeking his death. If now we cannot prevent his death, let us see how far his endurance will go and excite his enemies to torture Him with most impious cruelty. Let us stir up their fury against Him; let us suggest to their minds new insults, affronts, ignominies and torments to be inflicted upon his Person; let us drive them to vent upon

Him all their wrath in order to exhaust his patience, and let us carefully study the results." These proposals the demons sought to realize, although, on account of the hidden mysteries alluded to above (and to be mentioned later, No. 579, 627, 631), they found that not all of their plans succeeded. Whenever they incited the executioners to inflict tortures unbecoming his royal and divine Person, the Lord would not permit such indignities farther than was becoming, while He gave free scope to their inhuman barbarities and savage fury in all the rest.

541. The great Lady of heaven, Mary, likewise interfered in order to curb the insolent malice of Lucifer; for She was well aware of all the designs of the infernal dragon. At times She would make use of her sovereign power as Queen to prevent some of the hellish suggestion to reach the ministers of the Passion; at others She prevented their execution by her prayers, or She enlisted the service of her holy angels to drive away and confuse the persecutors of her Son. Those sufferings, which by her great wisdom She knew, that her Son wished to undergo, She permitted, fulfilling in all things the divine will. She knew all about the unhappy death of Judas, his torments and place of imprisonment in hell; the bed of fire, which He was to occupy for all eternity, as the master of hypocrisy and the leader of all those who were to deny Christ our Redeemer, as well in thought as in their works, who, according to Jeremias (17, 3), leave the veins of living waters, that is Christ, and whose names are written and sealed upon the earth, far from heaven, where are written the names of the predestined. All this the Mother of mercy knew and She wept over his fate most bitterly, praying for the welfare of men and for

their salvation from such great blindness and ruinous destruction. Yet in all this She conformed Herself to the just and hidden decrees of divine Providence.

INSTRUCTION WHICH THE QUEEN OF HEAVEN, MARY, GAVE ME.

542. My daughter, thou art astonished, not without cause, at what thou hast learned and recorded of the unhappy fate of Judas and of the fall of the Apostles, who were all disciples in the school of Christ, nursed at his breast by his doctrine, by the example of his life, and by his miracles, enjoying his sweetest and gentlest intercourse, and many other benefits of my assistance and intercession. But I truly say to thee, if all the children of the Church would attentively consider this example, they would find a salutary exhortation and warning in this mortal state of life against the danger surrounding them even in the midst of the favors and blessings they continually receive at the hands of the Lord. All of them cannot be equal to seeing Him with bodily eyes and having intercourse with Him as the living image of all sanctity. The Apostles received from me personal exhortations and they were eye-witnesses of my blameless and holy conduct; they received great tokens of my kindness and my charity flowed directly from God through me upon them. If they, in the very act of receiving such favors and in the very presence of their God and Savior, forgot all of them and all of their obligation of corresponding to them: who then shall be so presumptuous in this mortal life as not to fear the danger of eternal ruin, no matter how many favors he has received from the Almighty? They were Apostles chosen by their divine Master, their true God; yet one of them fell lower than any other individual of the human race;

and the others failed in faith, the foundation of all virtue. Yet all this was conformable to the just judgments of the Most High. Why then should those who are not Apostles, be without fear, who have not so labored in the school of Christ and who have not so merited my intercession?

543. Concerning the perdition of Judas and of his most just punishment thou hast written enough in order to set forth to what extremes a man can be brought by yielding to vices and to the devil, and by refusing to hear and follow the pleading of grace. I moreover inform thee, that not only the torments of the traitorous disciple Judas, but also those of many other Christians, who condemn themselves and shall be sent to the same place of punishment, which was assigned to them and Judas from the beginning of the world, are greater than the torments of many demons. For my most holy Son did not die for the angels, but for men; nor were the fruits and results of the Redemption for the demon, but entirely at the disposal of the children of the Church in the holy Sacraments. The contempt for these incomparable benefits is not properly the sin of the devils, but of the Christians; and therefore they must expect a special and appropriate punishment for this contempt. The mistake of not having recognized Christ as the true God causes the deepest and most tormenting regret to Lucifer and his evil spirits for all eternity. Hence, on account of this error, they are filled with special wrath against those that were redeemed, particularly against the Christians, who derived the greatest benefits from the Redemption and the blood of the Lamb. That is why the devils are so eager to cause forgetfulness and misuse of these graces in them and why afterwards in hell, they are permitted to vent so much the greater fury

and wrath upon the wicked Christians. If it were not
for the equitable dispositions of divine justice by which
the pains are proportioned to the guilt, they would wreck
still fiercer vengeance upon them. But the goodness of
the Lord extends even to this place and restrains the
malice of the demons by his infinite power and wisdom.

544. In the fall of the other eleven Apostles, I wish,
my dearest, that thou learn the frailty of human nature,
since even in such great blessings and favors received
of the Lord, it easily falls into the habit of gross negligence and ingratitude, such as the Apostles manifested
in flying from their heavenly Master and leaving Him
in a spirit of doubt. Men incur this danger from their
earthly and sensuous inclinations, the result of past sins
and of the habits formed by a terrestrial, carnal and
sensuous life, void of spirituality. On account of it
they desire and love the divine favors and benefits only
in a carnal manner. As soon as they fail to find that
kind of enjoyment in them, they turn to other sensible
enjoyments, are moved by them and lose the true conception of a spiritual life; for they treat it and estimate
it according to the low standard of mere sensuality.
Hence the Apostles, though they were so greatly favored
by my most holy Son, fell into such gross heedlessness
and sins; for the miracles, the teachings and the examples
affected them only in a sensible manner; and as they, in
spite of their being raised to justice and perfection, permitted themselves to be affected by them only outwardly,
they were presently disturbed by temptation and yielded
to it. They acted like men who had done little to penetrate into the mysteries and into the spirit of what they
had seen and heard in the school of their Master. By
this example, my daughter, and by my teachings thou
oughtest to be well instructed, a spiritual disciple of

mine, and not a terrestrial, accustoming thyself to despise mere outwardness, even in favors bestowed upon thee by the Lord or myself. When thou receivest them, do not attach thyself merely to the material or sensible in them, but raise thy mind to the exalted and the spiritual contained therein; to that which is perceived by the interior and spiritual, and not by the animal senses (I Cor. 2, 14). If even the merely sensible can hinder the spiritual life, how much is this true of that which pertains altogether to earthly, animal and carnal life? Clearly I desire of thee to forget and blot out of thy faculties all images and remembrances of mere creatures in order that thou mayest be fit to receive my salutary teaching and be capable of imitating me.

CHAPTER VI

545. Fit were it to speak of the suffering, the affronts
and the Death of our Savior Jesus in such vivid and
efficacious words, that they enter into the soul like a
two-edged sword, piercing with deepest sorrow our
inmost hearts (Heb. 4, 13). Not of an ordinary kind
were the pains He suffered and there is no sorrow like
unto his sorrow (Thren. 1, 12). For his body was not
like the bodies of the rest of men, nor did the Lord
suffer for Himself, nor for his own sins, but for us and
for our sins (I Pet. 2, 21). Hence the words and
expressions, by which we describe his torments and sorrows, should not be of the common or ordinary kind.
But, woe is me, who cannot give sufficient force to my
words, and cannot find those my soul seeks in order
to manifest this mystery! I will speak according to my
capacity and as far as is given me, although my powers
constrain and limit the greatness of what I understand,
and my inadequate words cannot reach the secret concepts of the heart. Let then the vividness and force of
the faith, which we profess as children of the Church,
supply what is defective in my words. If our words
are but of the ordinary kind, let our compassion and
our sorrow be extraordinary; let our thoughts be of
the loftiest, our comprehension most real, our consideration of the deepest, our thankfulness heartfelt, and

our love most fervent; for all that we can do shall fall short of what the reality demands, of what we owe as servants, as friends, and as children adopted through his most sacred Passion and Death.

546. Having been taken prisoner and firmly bound, the most meek Lamb Jesus was dragged from the garden to the house of the highpriests, first to the house of Annas (John 18, 13). The turbulent band of soldiers and servants, having been advised by the traitorous disciple that his Master was a sorcerer and could easily escape their hands, if they did not carefully bind and chain Him securely before starting on their way, took all precautions inspired by such a mistrust (Mark 14, 44). Lucifer and his compeers of darkness secretly irritated and provoked them to increase their impious and sacrilegious illtreatment of the Lord beyond all bounds of humanity and decency. As they were willing accomplices of Lucifer's malice, they omitted no outrage against the person of their Creator within the limits set them by the Almighty. They bound Him with a heavy iron chain with such ingenuity, that it encircled as well the waist as the neck. The two ends of the chain, which remained free, were attached to large rings or handcuffs, with which they manacled the hands of the Lord, who created the heavens, the angels and the whole universe. The hands thus secured and bound, they fastened not in front, but behind. This chain they had brought from the house of Annas the highpriest, where it had served to raise the portcullis of a dungeon. They had wrenched it from its place and provided it with padlock handcuffs. But they were not satisfied with this unheard-of way of securing a prisoner; for in their distrust they added two pieces of strong rope: the one they wound around the throat of Jesus and, crossing it

at the breast, bound it in heavy knots all about the body, leaving two long ends free in front, in order that the servants and soldiers might jerk Him in different directions along the way. The second rope served to tie his arms, being bound likewise around his waist. The two ends of this rope were left hanging free to be used by two other executioners for jerking Him from behind.

547. In this manner the almighty and holy One permitted Himself to be bound and made helpless, as if He were the most criminal of men and the weakest of the woman-born; for He had taken upon Himself all the iniquities and weaknesses of our sins (Is. 53, 6). They bound Him in the garden, adding to the chains and ropes insulting blows and vilest language; for like venomous serpents they shot forth their sacrilegious poison in abuse and blasphemy against Him who is adored by angels and men, and who is magnified in heaven and on earth. They left the garden of Olives in great tumult and uproar, guarding the Savior in their midst. Some of them dragged Him along by the ropes in front and others retarded his steps by the ropes hanging from the handcuffs behind. In this manner, with a violence unheard of, they sometimes forced Him to run forward in haste, frequently causing Him to fall; at others they jerked Him backwards; and then again they pulled Him from one side to the other, according to their diabolical whims. Many times they violently threw Him to the ground and as his hands were tied behind He fell upon it with his divine countenance and was severely wounded and lacerated. In his falls they pounced upon Him, inflicting blows and kicks, trampling upon his body and upon his head and face. All these deviltries they accompanied with festive shouts and opprobrious insults, as was foretold by Jeremias (3, 30).

548. During all this time Lucifer, while inciting these ministers of evil, watched all the actions and movements of our Savior. His patience he thus put to the test in order to find out, whether Jesus was only a man; for this doubt and perplexity tormented his wicked pride above all others. As he was obliged to acknowledge the meekness, patience and sweetness of Christ, his serene majesty without change or disturbance amid all these injuries and sufferings, the infernal dragon was enraged only so much the more and at one time, like one crazed by fury, he attempted to seize the ropes in order that he and his fellow-demons might pull at them more violently than his human foes and thus perhaps overcome the meekness of the Savior. But he was withheld by the most holy Mary, who, from her retreat by a clear vision saw all that happened to her divine Son. When She noticed this attempt of Lucifer, She made use of her power as sovereign Queen and commanded him to desist. All strength immediately left Lucifer and he could not proceed in his presumptuous intent. It was not becoming that his malice should add to the sufferings and death of the Redeemer in such a manner. He was however given permission to excite all his fellow-demons against the Lord, and these again were left a free hand to incite his mortal enemies among the Jews; since the latter had liberty of will to consent or not. Lucifer used this freedom to its full extent, and therefore said to the other evil spirits: "What kind of a man is this, now born into the world, who by his patience and by his works so torments us and annihilates us? None ever maintained such equanimity and such long-suffering in tribulations since the time of Adam until now. Never have we found among mortals such humility and meekness. How can we rest, when we see in the world such a rare and

powerful example, drawing others after Him? If this is
the Messias, He will certainly open heaven and close
up the highway, by which we have so far led men into
our eternal torments; we shall be vanquished and all
our plans will be frustrated. Even if He is but a mere
man, I cannot permit such an example for the rest of
mankind. Haste then, ministers of my exalted power,
let us persecute Him through his human foes, who, obe-
dient to my sway, have conceived of me some of our
own furious envy."

549. The Author of our salvation, hiding his power
of annihilating his enemies in order that our Redemption
might be the more abundant, submitted to all the consequences of the impious fury which Lucifer and his
hellish squadron fomented in the Jews. They dragged
Him bound and chained under continued ill-treatment
to the house of Annas, before whom they presented Him
as a malefactor worthy of death. It was the custom of
the Jews to present thus bound those criminals who
merited capital punishment; and they now made use of
this custom in regard to Jesus, in order to intimate his
sentence even before the trial. The sacrilegious priest
Annas seated himself in proud and arrogant state on the
platform or tribunal of a great hall. Immediately Lucifer placed himself at his side with a multitude of evil
spirits. The servants and soldiers brought before Him
Jesus, bound and fettered, and said: "At last we bring
hither this wicked Man, who by his sorceries and evil
deeds has disturbed all Jerusalem and Judea. This time
his magic art has not availed Him to escape our hands
and power."

550. Our Savior Jesus was attended by innumerable
angels, who confessed and adored Him, full of admiration for the incomprehensible judgments of his wisdom

(Rom. 11, 33) by which the Lord consented to be held
as a sinner and a criminal. The iniquitous highpriest
pretended to be just and zealous for the honor of the
Lord, whose life he was seeking. The most meek Lamb
was silent and opened not his mouth, as Isaias prophesied
(53, 7). Imperiously and haughtily the highpriest asked
Him about his disciples (John 18, 19), and what doctrine He was preaching and teaching. This question was
put merely for the purpose of misinterpreting his answer, if Jesus should utter any word that afforded such
a chance. But the Master of holiness, who is the Guide
and the Corrector of the most wise (Wis. 7, 15), offered
to the eternal Father the humiliation of being presented
as a criminal before the highpriest and of being ques-
tioned by him as a prevaricator and author of a false
doctrine. Our Redeemer with an humble and cheerful
countenance answered the question as to his doctrines:
"I have spoken openly to the world: I have always taught
in the synagogue and in the temple, whither all the Jews
resort: and in secret I have spoken nothing. Why askest
thou Me? ask those, who have heard what I have spoken
unto them: behold they know what I have said." As
the doctrine of Christ our Lord came from his eternal
Father, He spoke for it and defended its honor. He
referred them to his hearers, both because those by whom
He was now surrounded, would not believe Him and
wished to distort all He should say, and because the
truth and force of his teachings recommended and forced
themselves upon the minds of his greatest enemies by
their own excellence.

551. Concerning the Apostles He said nothing, because it was not necessary on this occasion and because
they were not reflecting much credit upon their Master
by their present conduct. Though his answer was so

full of wisdom and so well suited to the question, yet
one of the servants of the highpriest rushed up with
raised hand and audaciously struck the venerable and
sacred face of Jesus, saying: "Answerest Thou the high
priest so?" The Lord accepted this boundless injury,
praying for the one who had inflicted it; and holding
Himself ready, if necessary, to turn and offer the other
cheek for a second stroke, according to the doctrine
He had himself inculcated (Matth. 5, 39). But in order
that the atrocious and daring offender might not shame-
lessly boast of his wickedness, the Lord replied with
great tranquillity and meekness: "If I have spoken evil,
give testimony of the evil; if well, why strikest thou
Me?" O sight most astounding to the supernal spirits!
Since this is He, at the mere sound of whose voice the
foundations of the heavens tremble and ought to tremble
and the whole firmament is shaken! This is the Lord
of whom Job says, He is wise of heart and mighty in
strength; who hath resisted Him and hath peace? Who
hath removed mountains, and they, whom He overthrew
in his wrath, knew it not; He who moveth the earth
out of its place; who commandeth the sun, and it riseth
not; and shutteth up the stars as it were under a seal;
who doth things great and incomprehensible, whose
wrath no man can resist, and under whom they stoop,
that bear up the world (Job 9, 4, etc.); this is the One,
who for the love of men patiently suffers a servant to
strike and wound Him in the face by a buffet!

552. By the humble and appropriate reply of the Lord,
the wickedness of the sacrilegious servant stood repri-
manded. Yet neither the shame of this reprimand, nor
the shameful negligence of the highpriest, which permitted such a criminal unfairness in his very presence,
moved either him or the other Jews to moderate their

conduct toward the Author of life. While this ill-
treatment of the Lord was going on, saint Peter and
the other disciple, who was none other than saint John,
arrived at the house of Annas. Saint John, as being well
known there, readily obtained entrance, while saint
Peter remained outside. Afterwards the servant maid,
who was an acquaintance of saint John, allowed also him
to enter and see what would happen to the Lord (John
18, 16). The two disciples remained in the portico
adjoining the court-hall of the priest, and saint Peter
approached the fire, which the soldiers, on account of
the coldness of the night, had built in the enclosure near
the portico. The servant maid, on closer inspection,
noticed the depressed bearing of saint Peter. Coming
up to him she recognized him as a disciple of Jesus, and
said: "Art thou not perhaps one of the disciples of this
Man?" This question was asked by the maid with an
air of contempt and reproach. Peter in his great weakness and hesitancy yielded to a sense of shame. Overcome also by his fear he answered: "I am not his disciple." Having given this answer, he slipped away to
avoid further conversation, and left the premises. But
he soon afterwards followed his Master to the house
of Caiphas, where he denied Him again at two different
times, as I shall relate farther on.

553. The denial of Peter caused greater pain to the
Lord than the buffet which He had received; for this
sin was directly opposed and abhorrent to his immense
charity, while pains and sufferings were sweet and welcome to Him, since He could thereby atone for our sins.
After this first denial of Peter, Christ prayed for him
to his eternal Father and ordained that through the
intercession of the blessed Mary he should obtain pardon
even after the third denial. The great Lady witnessed

all that passed from her oratory, as I have said. As
She contained in her own breast the propitiatory and
sacrifice of her Son and Lord in sacramental form, She
directed her petitions and loving aspirations to Him,
eliciting most heroic acts of compassion, thanksgiving,
adoration and worship. She bitterly wept over the denial
of saint Peter, and ceased not, until She perceived that
the Lord would not refuse him the necessary helps for
effectually rising from his fall. The purest Mother also
felt all the wounds and torments of her Son in the same
portions of her virginal body as the Savior. When the
Lord was bound with the chains and ropes, She felt on
her wrists such pains, that the blood oozed from her
fingernails, as if they had been really bound and crushed:
in the same manner also the other wounds affected her
body. As to these tortures were added the sorrows of
her heart in seeing Christ our Lord suffer, She shed miraculous tears of blood. She felt also the buffet in the
same way, as if that sacrilegious hand had struck at the
same time her Son and Herself. At this wicked affront
and at the blasphemous insult offered to the Lord, She
called out to her holy angels to join Her in magnifying
and adoring their Creator in compensation for the injuries offered Him by sinners, and in many most sorrowful lamentations She conferred with the angels concerning the cause of her affliction and mourning.

INSTRUCTION WHICH THE GREAT QUEEN AND LADY GAVE ME.

554. My daughter, to great deeds art thou called and
invited on account of the divine enlightenment thou receivest concerning the mysteries of the sufferings of my
most holy Son and of myself for the human race, and on
account of the knowledge which thou hast obtained con-

cerning the small return made by heartless and ungrateful men for all our pains. Thou livest yet in mortal flesh and art thyself subject to this ignorance and weakness; but by the force of truth thou art now roused to great wonder, sorrow and compassion at the want of attention displayed by mortals toward these great sacraments and at the losses sustained by them through their lukewarmness and negligence. What then are the thoughts of the angels and saints, and what are my thoughts in beholding this world and all the faithful in such a dangerous and dreadful state of carelessness, when they have the Passion and Death of my divine Son before their eyes, and when they have me, for their Mother and Intercessor and his most pure life and mine for an example? I tell thee truly, my dearest, only my intercession and the merits of his Son, which I offer to the eternal Father, can delay the punishment and placate his wrath, can retard the destruction of the world and the severe chastisement of the children of the Church, who know his will and fail to fulfill it (John 15, 15). But I am much incensed to find so few who condole with me and try to console my Son in his sorrows, as David says (Ps. 68, 21). This hardness of heart will cause great confusion to them on the day of judgment; since they will then see with irreparable sorrow, not only that they were ungrateful, but inhuman and cruel toward my divine Son, toward me and toward themselves.

555. Consider then thy duty, my dearest, and raise thyself above all earthly things and above thyself; for I am calling thee and choose thee to imitate and follow me into the solitude, in which I am left by creatures, whom my Son and I have pursued with so many blessings and favors. Weigh in thy heart, how much it cost my Lord to reconcile mankind to the eternal Father

(Colos. 1, 22) and regain for them his friendship. Weep
and afflict thyself that so many should live in such forgetfulness and that so many should labor with all
their might at destroying and losing what was bought
by the blood of God itself and all that I from the first
moment of my Conception have sought to procure and
am procuring for their salvation. Awaken in thy heart
the deepest grief, that in his holy Church there should
be many followers of the hypocritical and sacrilegious
priests who, under cover of a false piety, still condemn
Christ; that pride and sumptuousness with other grave
vices should be raised to authority and exalted, while
humility, truth, justice and all virtues be so oppressed
and debased and avarice and vanity should prevail. Few
know the poverty of Christ, and fewer embrace it. Holy
faith is hindered and is not spread among the nations
on account of the boundless ambition of the mighty
of this earth; in many Catholics it is inactive and dead;
and whatever should be living, is near to death and to
eternal perdition. The counsels of the Gospel are forgotten, its precepts trodden under foot, charity almost
extinct. My son and true God offers his cheeks in patience and meekness to be buffeted and wounded (Thren.
3, 30). Who pardons an insult for the sake of imitating
Him? Just the contrary is set up as law in this world,
not only by the infidels, but by the very children of the
faith and of light.

556. In recognizing these sins I desire that thou imitate me in what I did during the Passion and during my
whole life, namely practice the virtues opposed to these
vices. As a recompense for their blasphemies, I blessed
God; for their oaths, I praised Him; for their unbelief,
I excited acts of faith, and so for all the rest of the sins
committed. This is what I desire thee to do while living

in this world. Fly also the dangerous intercourse with creatures, taught by the example of Peter, for thou art not stronger than he, the Apostle of Christ; and if thou fall in thy weakness, weep over thy fault and immediately seek my intercession. Make up for thy ordinary faults and weaknesses by thy patience in adversities, accept them with a joyous mien and without disturbance, no matter what they may be, whether they be sickness or the molestations coming from creatures, or whether they arise from the opposition of the flesh to the spirit, or from the conflicts with visible or invisible enemies. In all these things canst thou suffer and must thou bear up in faith, hope and magnanimous sentiment. I remind thee, that there is no exercise more profitable and useful for the soul than to suffer: for suffering gives light, undeceives, detaches the heart from visible things and raises it up to the Lord. He will come to meet those in suffering, because He is with the afflicted and sends to them his protection and help (Ps. 40, 15).

CHAPTER VII

CHRIST IS DRAGGED TO THE HOUSE OF THE PRIEST
CAIPHAS, WHERE HE IS FALSELY ACCUSED AND ASKED
WHETHER HE IS THE SON OF GOD; SAINT PETER
DENIES HIM FOR THE SECOND AND THIRD TIME;
WHAT MOST HOLY MARY DID ON THIS OCCASION, AND
OTHER MYSTERIES.

557. After Jesus had been thus insulted and struck in
the house of Annas, He was sent, bound and fettered as
He was, to the priest Caiphas, the son-in-law of
Annas, who in that year officiated as the prince and high
priest; with him were gathered the scribes and distinguished men of the Jews in order to urge the condemnation of the most innocent Lamb (Matth. 26, 57). The
invincible patience and meekness of the Lord of all virtues (Ps. 23, 10) astounded the demons, and they were
filled with a confusion and fury so great as no words
can describe. Since they could not penetrate into the
interior of the sanctuary of his humanity, and since they
noticed in the meekest Lord no inordinate movement, nor
any sign of complaint, nor any sighing, nor the least
attempt at human relief, by which they are wont to search
the hearts of other men, the dragon was in the utmost
torments and surprised as at something altogether new
and unheard of among weak and imperfect mortals. In
his fury he redoubled his efforts to irritate the scribes
and servants of the priests against Him and excite them
to shower their abominable insults and affronts upon his

devoted head. In all that the demon suggested to them they showed themselves most eager and they executed it as far as the divine will allowed.

558. The whole rabble of infernal spirits and merciless foes of Christ left the house of Annas and dragged our Lord Savior through the streets to the house of Caiphas, exercising upon Him all the cruelty of their ignominious fury. The highpriests and his attendants broke out in loud derision and laughter, when they saw Jesus brought amid tumultuous noise into their presence and beheld Him now subject to their power and jurisdiction without hope of escape. O mystery of the most exalted wisdom of heaven! O foolishness and ignorance of hell, and blind stupidity of mortals! What a distance immeasurable do I see between the doings of the Most High and yours! At the very time when the King of glory, as the Lord of all virtues and mighty in battles, (Ps. 23, 8), is vanquishing vice, and death, and all sin by the virtues of patience, humility and charity, the world boasts of having overcome and subjected Him to its arrogance and proud presumption! How different were the thoughts of Christ our Lord from those of the ministers of wickedness! The Author of life offered up to the eternal Father the triumph, which his meekness and humility won over sin; He prayed for the priests, the scribes and servants, presenting his patience and sufferings as a compensation for their persecutions and excusing them on account of their ignorance. The same prayer and petition was sent up at the same time by his blessed Mother, for her enemies and the enemies of her divine Son, thus following and imitating the Lord in all his doings; for, as I have many times said, She saw all as if personally present. Between the actions of the Son

and the Mother there was a most sweet and wonderful
harmony and a correspondence, most pleasing to the
eyes of the eternal Father.

559. The highpriest Caiphas, filled with a deadly envy
and hatred against the Master of life, was seated in his
chair of state or throne. With him were Lucifer and
all his demons, who had come from the house of Annas.
The scribes and pharisees, like bloodthirsty wolves, surrounded the gentle Lamb; all of them were full of the
exultation of the envious, who see the object of their
envy confounded and brought down. By common consent they sought for witnesses, whom they could bribe
to bring false testimonies against Jesus our Savior
(Matth. 26, 59). Those that had been procured, advanced to proffer their accusations and testimony; but
their accusations neither agreed with each other, nor
could any of their slander be made to apply to Him, who
of his very nature was innocence and holiness (Mark
25, 56; Heb. 7, 26). In order not to be foiled, they
brought two other false witnesses, who deposed, that
they had heard Jesus say, He could destroy the temple
of God made by the hands of men, and build up another
one in three days, not made by them (Mark 16, 58).
This testimony did not seem to be of much value, although they founded upon it the accusation, that He
arrogated to Himself divine power. Even if this testimony had not been false in itself, the saying, if uttered
by the Lord Almighty, would have been infallibly true
and could not have been presumptuous or false. But
the testimony was false; since the Lord had not uttered
these words in reference to the material temple of God,
as the witnesses wished to inculcate. At the time when
He expelled the buyers and sellers from the temple and
when asked by what power He did it, He answered:

"Destroy this temple" that is: destroy this sacred humanity, and on the third day I shall restore it, which He certainly did at his Resurrection in testimony of his divine power.

560. Our Savior Jesus answered not a word to all the calumnies and lies brought forward against his innocence. Caiphas, provoked by the patient silence of the Lord, rose up in his seat and said to Him: "Why dost Thou not answer to what so many witnesses testify against Thee?" But even to this the Lord made no response. For Caiphas and the rest were not only indisposed to believe Him; but they treacherously wished to make use of his answer in order to calumniate Him and satisfy the people in their proceedings against the Galileean, so that they might not be thought to have condemned Him to death without cause. This humble silence, which should have appeased the wicked priest, only infuriated him so much the more because it frustrated his evil purpose. Lucifer, who incited the high priest and all the rest, intently watched the conduct of the Savior. But the intention of the dragon was different from that of the high priest. He merely wanted to irritate the Lord, or to hear some word, by which he could ascertain whether he was true God.

561. With this purpose satan stirred up Caiphas to the highest pitch of rage and to ask in great wrath and haughtiness: "I adjure Thee by the living God, that Thou tell us, if Thou be the Christ, the Son of God." This question of the highpriest certainly convicted him at once of the deepest folly and of dreadful blasphemy; for if it was sincere, he had permitted Christ to be brought before his tribunal in doubt whether He was the true God or not, which would make him guilty of the most formidable and audacious crime. The doubt

in such a matter should have been solved in quite another way, conformable to the demands of right reason and justice. Christ our Savior, hearing Himself conjured by the living God, inwardly adored and reverenced the Divinity, though appealed to by such sacrilegious lips. Out of reverence for the name of God He therefore answered: "Thou hast said: I am He. Nevertheless I say to you, hereafter you shall see the Son of man (who I am) sitting on the right hand of the power of God, and coming in the clouds of heaven" (Matth. 26, 64). At this divine answer the demons and the men were affected in different ways. Lucifer and his devils could not bear it; but immediately felt a superior force, which hurled them down into the abyss and oppressed them by the truth it contained. And they would not have dared to come again into the presence of Christ our Savior, if the divine Providence had not allowed them to fall again into doubts, whether this Man Christ had really spoken the truth or had merely sought this means of freeing Himself from the hands of the Jews. This uncertainty gave them new courage and they came forth once more to the battlefield. The ultimate triumph over the demons was reserved to the Cross itself, on which the Savior was to vanquish both them and death, as Zachary had prophesied and as will appear later.

562. But the highpriest, furious at the answer of the Lord, instead of looking upon it as a solution of his doubt, rose once more in his seat, and rending his garments as an outward manifestation of his zeal for the honor of God, loudly cried out: "He hath blasphemed; what further need have we of witnesses? Behold, now you have heard the blasphemy: what think you?" (Matth. 26, 65.) The real blasphemy however consisted rather in these words of Caiphas, since he

denied the certain fact that Christ was the Son of
God by his very nature, and since he attributed to
the divine Personality sinfulness, which was directly
repugnant to his very nature. Such was the folly of the
wicked priest, who by his office should have recognized
and proclaimed the universal truth. He made of himself
an execrable blasphemer in maintaining that He, who
is holiness itself, had blasphemed. Having previously,
with satanical instinct, abused his high office in prophe-
sying that the death of one man is better than the ruin
of all the people, he now was hindered by his sins from
understanding his own prophecy. As the example and
the opinions of princes and prelates powerfully stirs up
the flattery and subserviency of inferiors, that whole gathering of wickedness was incensed at the Savior Jesus:
all exclaimed in a loud voice: "He is guilty of death
(Matth. 26, 66), let Him die, let Him die!" Roused
by satanic fury they all fell upon their most meek Master
and discharged upon Him their wrath. Some of them
struck Him in the face, others kicked Him, others tore
out his hair, others spat upon his venerable countenance,
others slapped or struck Him in the neck, which was a
treatment reserved among the Jews only for the most
abject and vile of criminals.

563. Never among men were such outrageous and
frightful insults heaped upon any one as were then
heaped upon the Redeemer. Saint Luke and saint Mark
say that they covered his face and then struck Him
with their hands and fists saying: Prophesy, prophesy to
us, Thou Prophet, who was it that struck Thee? The
reason for their doing this was mysterious: namely, the
joy with which our Savior suffered all these injuries and
blasphemies (as I will soon relate) made his face shine
forth in extraordinary beauty, and on this account those

ministers of wickedness were seized with unbearable consternation and shame.   They sought to attribute it to
sorcery and magic and, by a resolution befitting also
well their unworthiness, they covered the face of the
Lord with an unclean cloth, so that they might not be
hindered and tormented by its divine light in venting
their diabolical wrath.   All these affronts, reproaches
and insults were seen and felt by the most holy Mary,
causing in Her the same pains and wounds in the same
parts of her body and at the same time as inflicted upon
the Lord.   The only difference was, that in our Lord
the blows and torments were inflicted by the Jews themselves, while in his most pure Mother they were caused
by the Almighty in a miraculous manner and upon request of the Lady.   According to natural laws, the
vehemence of her interior sorrow and anxiety would
have put an end to her life; but She was strengthened
by divine power, so as to be able to continue to suffer
with her beloved Son and Lord.

564. The interior acts performed by the Savior under
these barbarous and unheard of persecutions, cannot be
fathomed by human reason or faculties.   Mary alone
understood them fully, so as to be able to imitate them
with the highest perfection.   But as the divine Master
now experienced in his own Person, how necessary his
sympathy would be for those who were to follow him
and practice his doctrine, He exerted Himself so much
the more in procuring for them grace and blessings on
this occasion, in which He was teaching them by his
own example the narrow way of perfection.   In the
midst of these injuries and torments, and those which
followed thereafter, the Lord established for his perfect
and chosen souls the beatitudes, which He had promised
and proposed to them some time before. He looked upon

the poor in spirit, who were to imitate Him in this virtue and said: "Blessed are you in being stripped of the earthly goods; for by my Passion and Death I am to entail upon you the heavenly kingdom as a secure and certain possession of voluntary poverty. Blessed are those who meekly suffer and bear adversities and tribulations; for, besides the joy of having imitated Me, they shall possess the land of the hearts and the good will of men through the peacefulness of their intercourse and the sweetness of their virtues. Blessed are they that weep while they sow in tears; for in them, they shall receive the bread of understanding and life, and they shall afterwards harvest the fruits of everlasting joy and bliss."

565. "Blessed are also those who hunger and thirst for justice and truth; for I shall earn for them satiation far beyond all their desires, as well in the reign of grace as in the reign of glory. Blessed are they, who, imitating Me in my offers of pardon and friendship, mercifully pity those that offend and persecute them; for I promise them the fulness of mercy from my Father. Blessed be the pure of heart, who imitate Me in crucifying their flesh in order to preserve the purity of their souls. I promise them the vision of peace and of my Divinity, by becoming like unto Me and by partaking of Me. Blessed are the peaceful, who, yielding their rights, do not resist the evil-minded and deal with them with a sincere and tranquil heart without vengeance; they shall be called my children, because they imitate my eternal Father and I shall write them in my memory and in my mind as my adopted sons. Those that suffer persecution for justice's sake, shall be the blessed heirs of my celestial kingdom, since they suffer with Me; and where I am, there also they shall be in eternity. Rejoice,

ye poor; be consoled all ye that are and shall be afflicted; glory in your lot, ye little ones and despised ones of this world, you who suffer in humility and longanimity, suffer with an interior rejoicing; since all of you are following Me in the path of truth. Renounce vanity, despise the pomp and haughtiness of the false and deceitful Babylon; pass ye through the fires and the waters of tribulation until you reach Me, who am the light, the truth and your guide to the eternal rest and refreshment."

566. In such divine acts and in other aspirations for the good of sinners, our Savior Jesus occupied Himself, while He was surrounded by his malignant enemies as by ravenous dogs (Ps. 21, 17), who pursued Him and satiated Him with insults, affronts, blasphemies and wounds. The Virgin Mary, who was most attentive to all that passed, accompanied Him in all his acts and petitions; for She made the same petitions for his enemies. She took charge of the blessings lavished by her Son upon the just and the predestined, and constituted Herself as their Mother, their Helper and Protectress. In the name of all of them She composed hymns of praise and thanksgiving, because the Lord had assigned such an exalted position in the reign of grace to the despised and poor of this earth. On this account also, and on account of what She afterwards witnessed in the interior of Christ, She chose anew labor and contempt, tribulations and pains as her share during the Passion and during the rest of her most holy life.

567. Saint Peter had followed the Lord Jesus from the house of Annas to that of Caiphas, although he took care to walk at some distance behind the crowd of enemies for fear that the Jews might seize him. He partly repressed this fear on account of the love of his

Master and by the natural courage of his heart. Among
the great multitude which crowded in and out of the
house of Caiphas and in the darkness, it was not difficult for the Apostle to find entrance into the house of
Caiphas. In the gates of the courtyard a servant-maid,
who was a portress as in the house of Annas, likewise
noticed saint Peter; she immediately went up to the
soldiers, who stood at the fire with him and said: "This
man is one of those who were wont to accompany Jesus
of Nazareth." One of the bystanders said: "Thou art
surely a Galileean and one of them." Saint Peter denied
it and added an oath, that he was not a disciple of Jesus,
immediately leaving the company at the fire. Yet, in his
eagerness to see the end, although he left the courtyard,
he did not leave the neighborhood. His natural love
and compassion for the Lord still caused him to linger
in the place, where he saw Him suffer so much. So the
Apostle moved about, sometimes nearer, sometimes
farther from the hall of justice for nearly an hour. Then
a relative of that Malchus, whose ear he had severed,
recognized him and said: "Thou art a Galileean and a
disciple of Jesus; I saw thee with Him in the garden."
Then Peter deeming himself discovered, was seized with
still greater fear, and he began to assert with oaths and
imprecations, that he knew not the Man (Matth. 26, 72).
Immediately thereupon the cock crowed the second time,
and the prediction of his divine Master, that he should
deny Him thrice before the cock crowed twice, was fulfilled to the letter.

568. The infernal dragon was very anxious to destroy
saint Peter. It was Lucifer that incited the two maids,
whom he could more easily influence, and afterwards,
the soldiers, to molest the Apostle by their attention and
inquiries. At the same time as soon as he saw him in

his dangerous hesitation and change of mind he tried
to disturb saint Peter by vivid imaginations of impending cruelty. Thus tempted, Peter simply denied the
Lord at first, added an oath to the second denial, and
curses and imprecations against himself at the third.
Hence, from one sin he fell into another greater one,
yielding to the cruel persecutions of the enemies. But
saint Peter, now hearing the crowing of the cock, remembered the warning of his divine Master (Luke 22,
61) ; for, the great Queen in her gentle love having interceded for him, the Lord now cast upon him a look of
boundless mercy. From her oratory in the Cenacle She
had witnessed the denials together with all the circumstances and the causes which had brought the Apostle
to fall so deeply. She had seen him beset with natural
fear and much more by the merciless assaults of Lucifer.
She threw Herself upon the ground and tearfully interceded for him, alleging his frailty and appealing to the
merits of her divine Son. The Lord himself moved
the heart of Peter, and by means of the light sent to
him, gently reproached him, exhorting him to acknowledge his fault and deplore his sin. Immediately the
Apostle left the house of the highpriest, bursting with
inmost sorrow into bitter tears over his fall. In order
to weep in the bitterness of his heart he betook himself
to a cave, even now called that of the Crowing Cock;
there he poured forth his sorrow and confusion in a
flood of tears. At the end of three hours he had obtained
pardon for his crimes; and the holy impulses and inspirations had continued during that whole time until he
was again restored to grace. The most pure Mother
and Queen sent to him one of her angels, who secretly
consoled him and excited in him the hope of forgiveness,
so that he might not delay his full pardon by want of

trust in the goodness of God. The angel was ordered not to manifest himself, because the Apostle had so recently committed his sin. Hence the angel fulfilled his commission without being seen by the Apostle. Saint Peter was consoled and strengthened in his great sorrow by these inspirations and thus obtained full pardon through the intercession of most holy Mary.

INSTRUCTION WHICH THE GREAT QUEEN AND LADY GAVE ME.

569. My daughter, the mysterious sacrament of the patience of my Son, by which He bore all the affronts and insults, is a sealed book, which can be opened and understood only by the divine light. Thou hast come to the knowledge of it, as it has been partly laid open for thee, although on account of thy limited powers, thou writest much less than thou hast seen. But as this mystery is being made clear and intelligible to thee in the secret of thy heart, I wish that it be also written there and that thou study by this living example that divine science, which neither flesh nor blood can teach thee. For the world does not know, nor does it merit to know, this science. This philosophy consists in recognizing and loving the happy lot of the poor, the humble, the afflicted, the despised, and those unknown among the children of vanity. This school my most holy and loving Son established in his Church, when He proclaimed and set up the eight beatitudes (Matth. 5, 2-10). Afterwards, when He himself assumed all the sufferings of his Passion, He became for us a Teacher, who practices what He teaches, as thou hast seen. Nevertheless, although this is set before the eyes of the Catholics, and can be plainly read by them in this book of life during their whole earthly pilgrimage, there are but few and scattered souls

who enter into this school and study this book, while countless are the wayward and foolish, who ignore this science in their unwillingness to be taught.

570. All abhor poverty and thirst after riches, none of them being willing to recognize their emptiness. Infinite is the number of those who are carried away by their anger and vengeance, despising meekness. Few deplore their real miseries and struggle merely for terrestrial consolations; scarcely any love justice, or loyally pursue it in their dealings with the neighbors. Mercy is almost extinct, purity of heart is sullied and infringed upon, peace is constrained. None grant pardon, none wish to suffer for justice's sake, yea not even the least of the many torments and pains, which they have so justly merited. Thus, my dearest, there are few who attain the blessings promised by my divine Son and by me. Many times the just indignation and anger of the Almighty is roused against the professors of the true faith; since in the very sight of the living example of their Master, they live almost like infidels; many of them being even more abominable in their lives; for they are properly those who despise the fruits of the Redemption, which they have come to know and confess. In the land of saints they impiously perform the works of wickedness (Is. 26, 10), and make themselves unworthy of the remedies, which are put at their disposal in more merciful abundance.

571. Of thee I desire, my daughter, that thou labor valiantly for this blessedness, by seeking to imitate me perfectly according to thy grace of so deeply understanding this doctrine, which is hidden from the prudent and wise of this world (Mark 11, 25). Day for day I manifest to thee new secrets of my wisdom, in order that it may be established in thy heart and thou mayest extend

thy hands to valiant deeds (Prov. 31, 19). And now I will tell thee of an exercise which I practiced and which thou canst imitate to a certain degree. Thou knowest already, that from the very first instant of my Conception I was full of grace, without the least stain or participation of the least effect of original sin. On account of this singular privilege I was blessed in all the virtues, without feeling any repugnance or opposition in the exercise of them, and without being conscious of owing satisfaction for any sins of my own. Nevertheless the divine enlightenment taught me, that I was a Daughter of Adam by nature, which in him had sinned, and therefore I felt bound to humiliate myself to the very dust, even though I shared none of the guilt of that sin. And since I also possessed senses of the same kind as those, through which sin and its effects were contracted and which then and afterwards are operative in present human conditions, I thought myself obliged to mortify them, humiliate them and deprive them of the enjoyment proper to their nature, simply on account of this my parentage from Adam. I acted like a most faithful daughter of a family, who assumes the debt of her father and of her brothers as her own, though she had no share in contracting it, and who strives to pay and satisfy for it the more earnestly, the more she loves her family and the more they are unable to satisfy and free themselves from it, not giving herself any rest until she succeeds. This have I done with all the human race, whose miseries and transgressions I bewailed. Because I was a Daughter of Adam I mortified in me the senses and faculties with which he sinned, and I humiliated myself as one that had fallen and one guilty of his sin and disobedience, though I was entirely free from them. All this I did not only for Adam, but for all who by nature are my brethren.

Thou canst not imitate me under like conditions, since thou art a partaker in his sin and guilt. But I herewith impose upon thee to labor without ceasing for thyself and for thy neighbor, and to humiliate thyself to the very dust; since a contrite and humble heart draws down mercy from the divine goodness.

CHAPTER VIII

THE SUFFERINGS OF OUR SAVIOR JESUS CHRIST AFTER
THE DENIAL OF SAINT PETER UNTIL MORNING; AND
THE GREAT SORROW OF HIS MOST HOLY MOTHER.

572. The holy Evangelists pass over in silence what
and where the Savior suffered after the ill-treatment in
the house of Caiphas and the denial of saint Peter. But
they all take up again the thread of events, when they
speak of the council held by them in the morning in
order to deliver Him over to Pilate, as will be related in
the next chapter. I had some doubts as to the propriety
of speaking of this intervening time and of manifesting
that which was made known to me concerning it: for it
was intimated to me, that all cannot be known in this
life, nor is it proper that all should be made known to
all men. On the day of judgment these and many other
sacraments of the life and the Passion of our Lord shall
be published to the whole world. I cannot find words
for describing that which I might otherwise manifest:
I do not find adequate expressions for my concepts, and
much less for the reality itself; all is ineffable and above
my capacity. But in order to obey the orders given me,
I will say what I am able, so as not to incur the blame
of concealing the truth, which directly reproaches and
confuses our vanity and forgetfulness. In the presence
of heaven I confess my own hardness of heart, in not
dying of sorrow and shame for having committed such
great sins at such a cost to my God, the Originator of
my life and being. We cannot ignore the wickedness and

124

gravity of sin, which caused such ravages in the Author of grace and glory. I would be the most ungrateful of all the woman-born, if I would not now abhor sin more than death and as much as even the demon, and I cannot but intimate and assert, that this is the duty likewise of all the children of the holy Catholic church.

573. By the ill-treatment, which the Lord received in the presence of Caiphas, the wrath of this highpriest and of all his supporters and ministers was much gratified, though not at all satiated. But as it was already past midnight, the whole council of these wicked men resolved to take good care, that the Savior be securely watched and confined until the morning, lest He should escape while they were asleep. For this purpose they ordered Him to be locked, bound as He was, in one of the subterranean dungeons, a prison cell set apart for the most audacious robbers and criminals of the state. Scarcely any light penetrated into this prison to dispel its darkness. It was filled with such uncleanness and stench, that it would have infected the whole house, if it had not been so remote and so well enclosed; for it had not been cleaned for many years, both because it was so deep down and because of the degradation of the criminals that were confined in it; for none thought it worth while making it more habitable than for mere wild beasts, unworthy of all human kindness.

574. The order of the council of wickedness was executed; the servants dragged the Creator of heaven and earth to that polluted and subterranean dungeon there to imprison Him. As the Lord was still bound with the fetters laid upon Him in the garden, these malicious men freely exercised all the wrathful cruelty with which they were inspired by the prince of darkness; for they dragged Him forward by the ropes, inhumanly causing

Him to stumble, and loading Him with kicks and cuffs amid blasphemous imprecations. From the floor in one corner of the subterranean cavern protruded part of a rock or block, which on account of its hardness had not been cut out. To this block, which had the appearance of a piece of column, they now bound and fettered the Lord Jesus with the ends of the ropes, but in a most merciless manner. For they forced Him to approach it and tied Him to it in a stooping position, so that He could neither seat Himself nor stand upright for relief, forcing Him to remain in a most painful and torturing posture. Thus they left Him bound to the rock, closing the prison-door with a key and giving it in charge of one of the most malicious of their number.

575. But the infernal dragon rested not in his ancient pride. In the desire of finding out who this Christ was and of overcoming his imperturbable patience, he invented another scheme, to the execution of which he incited the jailer and some others of the servants. He inspired the one who held the key of the divine Treasure Trove, the greatest in heaven and earth, with the idea of inviting some of his equally evil-minded companions to descend to the dungeon and entertain themselves for awhile with the Master of life by forcing Him to speak of prophecy, or do some other strange or unheard of thing; for they believed Him to be a diviner or magician. Moved by this diabolical suggestion, he invited some of the soldiers and servants, who readily consented. While they were discussing this matter, a multitude of angels, who assisted the Redeemer in his Passion, when they saw Him so painfully bound in such an improper and polluted place, prostrated themselves before Him, adoring Him as their true God and Master, and showing Him so much the more reverence and worship the more they admired the

love which moved Him to subject Himself to such abuse for the sake of mankind. They sang to Him some of the hymns and canticles which his own Mother had composed in his praise, as I have mentioned above. The whole multitude of angelic spirits begged Him, in the name of the same Lady, that, since He would not permit his own almighty power to alleviate the sufferings of his humanity, He give them permission to unfetter and relieve Him of this torturing position and to defend Him from that horde of servants now instigated by the demons to heap upon Him new insults.

576. The Lord would not permit the angels to render this service and He said to them: "Ministering spirits of my eternal Father, I do not wish to accept any alleviation in my sufferings at present and I desire to undergo these torments and affronts in order to satiate my burning love for men and leave to my chosen friends this example for their imitation and consolation in their sufferings; and in order that all may properly estimate the treasures of grace, which I am gaining for them in great abundance through my pains. At the same time I wish to justify my cause, so that, on the day of my wrath, all may know how justly the reprobate shall be condemned for despising the most bitter sufferings by which I sought to save them. Tell my Mother to console Herself in this tribulation, since the day of rest and gladness shall come. Let Her accompany Me now in my works and sufferings for men; for her affectionate compassion and all her doings, afford Me much pleasure and enjoyment." Thereupon the holy angels betook themselves to their great Queen and Lady and consoled Her with this message, although She already knew in another way the will of her divine Son and all that happened in the house of Caiphas. When She perceived the new cruelty with

which they had left Christ the Lord bound in a posture so painful and hard, She felt in her purest body the same pains; just as She had felt that of the blows and cuffs and other insults inflicted upon the Author of life. All the sufferings of the Lord miraculously reacted upon the virginal body of this sincerest Dove; the same pains beset the Son and Mother, and the same sword pierced both their hearts; with only this difference, that Christ suffered as Godman and sole Redeemer of mankind, while Mary suffered as a creature and as a faithful helper of her most holy Son.

577. When the blessed Queen perceived that this band of vile miscreants, incited by the devil, would be permitted to enter the dungeon, She wept bitterly at what was to happen. Foreseeing the malicious intentions of Lucifer, She held Herself ready to make use of her sovereign power to prevent the executions of any designs upon the person of Christ that would imply indecency, such as the dragon sought to induce those unhappy men to carry out. For although all they did was most unbecoming and irreverent in his regard, yet there were insults, which would have been still more indecent, and by which the demon, not having succeeded hitherto, desired now to try the meek forbearance of the Lord. So exquisite and rare, wonderful and heroic, were the doings of the Lady at this time and during the whole Passion, that they could not worthily be mentioned or becomingly extolled, even if many books were written for this sole object; and as they are indescribable in this life, we must leave their full revelation to the beatific vision.

578. The ministers of wickedness therefore broke into the dungeon, blasphemously gloating over the expected feast of insult and ridicule, which they were now to hold with the Lord of all creation. Going up to Him

they began to defile Him with their loathsome spittle
and rain blows and cuffs upon Him with unmentionable
and insulting mockery. The Lord opened not his mouth
or made any answer; He raised not his divine eyes and
lost not the humble serenity of his countenance. The
sacrilegious buffoons wished to drive Him to some ridiculous or extraordinary saying or action, so that they
might make a laughing-stock of Him as a sorcerer; and
when they were compelled to witness his unchanging
meekness, they allowed themselves to be incited still more
by the demons. They untied the divine Master from
the stone block and placed Him in the middle of the
dungeon, at the same time blindfolding Him with a
cloth; there they began to come up one after the other
and strike Him with their fists, or slap or kick Him,
each one trying to outdo the other in vehemence of their
blasphemous cruelty and asking Him to prophesy who
had struck Him. This kind of sacrilegious treatment
these servants repeated even more often and continued
longer than before the tribunal of Annas, to which saint
Matthew (26, 67), saint Mark (14, 65), and saint Luke
(22, 64) refer, tacitly including all that followed.

579. The most meek Lamb silently bore this flood of
insults and blasphemies. Lucifer, tormented by his anxious desire of seeing some sign of impatience in Him,
was lashed into fury at the equanimity with which the
Savior bore it all. Therefore he inspired those slaves
and friends of his with the project of despoiling the Lord
of all his clothes and pursuing their ill-treatment according to suggestions which could only originate in the execrable demon. They readily yielded to this new inspira-
tion and set about its execution. But the most prudent
Lady was moved to most tearful prayers and aspirations
at this abominable attempt and interfered with her

power as the Queen. She asked the eternal Father to
withdraw his co-operation with the secondary or created
causes toward such a beginning and She commanded the
faculties of these servants not to perform their natural
functions. Thus it happened that none of the ruffians
could execute the indecencies, which the demon or their
own malice suggested to them. Some of these suggestions
they forgot immediately and others they could not follow
up, because their limbs became as it were frozen or paralyzed until they again changed their intent. As soon
as they desisted the use of their limbs would again be
restored, for this was not intended as a punishment, but
merely in order to prevent their practicing any indecencies. They were left entirely free to practice those cruel-
ties or indulge in other irreverence, which were not so
indecent, or were permitted by the Lord.

580. The powerful Queen also commanded the demons
to be silent and forbade them to follow out the indecent
intentions of Lucifer, their leader. By this command of
the powerful Lady the dragon completely lost his power
in those matters which Mary wished to include in her
prohibition. Neither could he further irritate the foolish
anger of those depraved men, nor could they go any
further in their indecency than She permitted. But while
experiencing within themselves the wonderful and extraordinary effects of her commands, they did not merit
to be undeceived or recognize the divine power, although
they thus saw themselves alternately paralyzed and suddenly restored to the full use of their powers. They
attributed it merely to the sorcery and magic of the
Master of truth. In their diabolical infatuation they continued to practice their insulting mockery and tortures
upon the person of Christ, until they noticed that the
night had already far advanced; then they again tied

Him to the column and leaving Him thus bound, they departed with all the demons. It was ordained by the divine Wisdom, that the power of the blessed Mother safeguard propriety and decency due to the person of her most pure Son against the improper intentions of Lucifer and his ministers.

581. Again the Savior was alone in the dungeon, surrounded by the angelic spirits, who were full of admiration at the doings and the secret judgments of the Lord in what He wished to suffer. They adored Him with deepest reverence and magnified his holy name in exalted praise. The Redeemer of the world addressed a long prayer to his eternal Father for the children of the evangelical Church, for the spreading of the holy faith, and for the Apostles, especially for saint Peter, who during that time was beweeping his sin. He prayed also for those who had injured and tormented Him; above all He included in his prayer his most holy Mother and all those who in imitation of Him were to be afflicted and despised in this world. At the same time He offered up his Passion and his coming Death for these ends. His grief-stricken Mother followed Him in these prayers, offering up the same petitions for the children of the Church and for its enemies without any movements of anger, indignation or dislike toward them. Only against the demon was She incensed, because he was entirely incapable of grace on account of his irreparable obstinacy. In sorrowful complaints She addressed the Lord, saying:

582. "Divine Love of my soul, my Son and Lord, Thou art worthy to be reverenced, honored and praised by all creatures, since Thou art the image of the eternal Father and the figure of his substance (Heb. 1, 3), infinite in thy being and in thy perfections. Thou art the beginning of all holiness (Apoc. 1, 8). But if the creatures

are to serve Thee in entire subjection, why do they now, my Lord and God, despise, vilify, insult and torture thy Person, which is worthy of the highest worship and adoration? Why has the malice of men risen to such a pitch? Why has pride dared to raise itself even above heaven? How can envy become so powerful? Thou art the only and unclouded Sun of justice, which enlightens and dispels the darkness of sin (John 1, 9). Thou art the fountain of grace, withholding its waters from no one. Thou art the One, who in his liberal love givest being and life to all that live upon this earth, and all things depend upon Thee, while Thou hast need of none (Acts 17, 28). What then have they seen in thy doings, what have they found in thy Passion, that they should treat Thee in so vile a manner? O most atrocious wickedness of sin, which has so disfigured the heavenly beauty and obscured the light of thy countenance! O cruel sin, which so inhumanly pursues the Repairer of all thy evil consequences! But I understand, my Son and Master, I understand that Thou art the Builder of true love, the Author of human salvation, the Master and Lord of virtues (Ps. 23, 10): Thou wishest to put in practice Thyself what Thou teachest the humble disciples of thy school: Thou wishest to humble pride, confound haughtiness and become the example of eternal salvation to all. And if Thou desirest that all imitate thy ineffable patience and charity, then that is my duty before all others, since I have administered to Thee the material and clothed Thee in this body now subjected to suffering, and wounded, spit upon and buffeted. O would that I alone should suffer these pains, and that Thou, my most innocent Son, be spared! And since this is not possible, let Me suffer with Thee unto death. You, O heavenly spirits, who full of wonder at the long-suffering

of my Son recognize his immutable Deity and the innocence and excellence of his humanity, seek ye to compensate for these injuries and blasphemies heaped upon
Him by men. Give Him glory and magnificence, wisdom
honor, virtue and power (Apoc. 5, 12). Invite the
heavens, the planets and the stars and the elements to acknowledge and confess Him; and see whether there is
another sorrow equal to mine!" (Thren. 1, 12). Such
and many more were the sorrowful aspirations of the
most pure Lady, in giving vent to the bitterness of her
grief and pain.

583. Peerless was the patience of the heavenly Princess in the Death and Passion of her beloved Son and
Lord; so that what She suffered never seemed to Her
much, nor her afflictions equal to those demanded by her
affection, which was measured only by the love and the
dignity of her Son and the greatness of his sufferings.
Nor did She in any of the injuries and affronts against
the Lord take any account of their being committed
against Herself. She reflected not on the share which
She herself had in them, although She was made to
suffer so much by all of them: She deplored them only
in so far as they outraged the divine Personality and
caused damage to the aggressors. She prayed for them
all, that the Most High might pardon them and grant
them salvation from the evils of sin and enlightenment
for gaining the fruits of Redemption.

INSTRUCTION GIVEN BY THE QUEEN OF HEAVEN,
MOST HOLY MARY.

584. My daughter, it is written in the holy Gospels
(John 5, 57) that the eternal Father has given to his
only Son and mine the power to judge and condemn
the reprobate on the last day, the day of universal judg-

ment. This was eminently proper, not only in order that all the sinners may see their Judge, who will sentence them according to the most just will of God; but also in order that they may behold and recognize his humanity, by which they were redeemed, and be confronted in it with the torments and injuries it suffered in order to rescue them from eternal damnation. The same Judge and Lord, who shall judge them, shall also advance the charge. As they cannot answer or satisfy for the crimes with which He charges them, their confusion will be only the beginning of the eternal torments, which they merit by their obstinate ingratitude; for then shall become evident to all the world the greatness of his most merciful and kind Redemption and the justice of their damnation. Great was the sorrow, most bitter the grief, of my most holy Son, that not all should make use of the fruits of his Redemption. This same thought also pierced my heart and immensely added to the sorrow of seeing Him spit upon, buffeted, and blasphemed more cruelly than can ever be understood by living man. But I understood all these sufferings clearly and as they should be understood; therefore my sorrow was great in proportion to this knowledge, just as it was also the measure of my reverence and love of the person of Christ, my Son and Lord. But next to this sorrow, my greatest one was to know, that after all these death-dealing sufferings of the Lord, so many men should still damn themselves even within sight of all the infinite treasures of grace.

585. I wish that thou imitate and follow me in this sorrow and that thou lament this fearful misfortune; for among all the losses sustained by men, there is none which deserves to be so deplored, nor which can ever be compared to it. My Son and I look with especial

love upon those who imitate this sorrow and afflict themselves on account of the perdition of so many souls. Seek thou, my dearest, to distinguish thyself in this exercise and continue to pray: for thou canst scarcely imagine how acceptable are such prayers to the Almighty. But remember his promise, that those who pray shall receive (Luke 11, 9), and that to those who knock the gates of his infinite treasures shall be opened. In order that thou mayest have something to offer in return, write into thy heart, what my most holy Son and thy Spouse suffered at the hands of those vile and depraved men, and the invincible patience, meekness and silence with which He submitted to their wicked whims. With this example, labor from now on, that no anger, nor any other passion of a daughter of Adam have any sway over thee. Let an interior and ever active horror of pride, and a dread of injuring thy neighbor, be engendered in thy bosom. Solicitously ask the Lord for patience, meekness, and peacefulness and for a love of sufferings and Christ's Cross. Embrace this Cross with a pious affection and follow Christ thy Spouse, in order that thou mayest at last possess Him (Matth. 16, 14).

CHAPTER IX

586. At the dawn of Friday morning, say the Evangelists (Matth. 27, 1; Mark 15, 1; Luke 22, 66; John 11, 47), the ancients, the chief priests and scribes, who according to the law were looked upon with greatest respect by the people, gathered together in order to come to a common decision concerning the death of Christ. This they all desired; however they were anxious to preserve the semblance of justice before the people. This council was held in the house of Caiphas, where the Lord was imprisoned. Once more they commanded Him to be brought from the dungeon to the hall of the council in order to be examined. The satellites of justice rushed below to drag Him forth bound and fettered as He was; and while they untied Him from the column of rock, they mocked Him with great contempt saying: "Well now, Jesus of Nazareth, how little have thy miracles helped to defend Thee. The power which Thou didst vaunt, of being able to rebuild the temple in three days, has failed altogether in securing thy escape. But Thou shalt now pay for thy presumption and thy proud aspirations shall be brought low. Come now to the chief priests and to the scribes. They are awaiting Thee to put an end to thy imposition and deliver Thee over to Pilate, who will quickly finish Thee." Having freed the

Lord from the rock they dragged Him up to the council.
The Lord did not open his lips; but the tortures, the
blows and the spittle, with which they had covered Him
and which He could not wipe off on account of his bonds,
had so disfigured Him, that He now filled the members
of the council with a sort of dreadful surprise, but not
with compassion. Too great was their envious wrath
conceived against the Lord.

587. They again asked Him to tell them, whether He
was the Christ (Luke 22, 1), that is, the Anointed. Just
as all their previous questions, so this was put with the
malicious determination not to listen or to admit the
truth, but to calumniate and fabricate a charge against
Him. But the Lord, being perfectly willing to die for
the truth, denied it not; at the same time He did not
wish to confess it in such a manner that they could
despise it, or borrow out of it some color for their cal-
umny; for this was not becoming his innocence and wisdom. Therefore He veiled his answer in such a way,
that if the pharisees chose to yield to even the least
kindly feeling, they would be able to trace up the mystery
hidden in his words; but if they had no such feeling,
then should it become clear through their answer, that
the evil which they imputed to Him was the result of
their wicked intentions and lay not in his answer. He
therefore said to them: "If I tell you that I am He of
whom you ask, you will not believe what I say; and if
I shall ask you, you will not answer, nor release Me.
But I tell you, that the Son of man, after this, shall
seat Himself at the right hand of the power of God"
(Luke 22, 67). The priests answered: "Then thou art
the Son of God?" and the Lord replied: "You say that
I am." This was as if He had said: You have made
a very correct inference, that I am the Son of God; for

my works, my doctrines, and your own Scripture, as
well as what you are now doing with Me, testify to the
fact, that I am the Christ, the One promised in the law.

588. But this council of the wicked was not disposed
to assent to divine truth, although they themselves
inferred it very correctly from the antecedents and could
easily have believed it.   They would neither give assent
nor belief, but preferred to call it a blasphemy deserving
death.   Since the Lord had now reaffirmed what He
had said before, they all cried out: "What need have we
of further witnesses, since He himself asserts it by his
own lips?"   And they immediately came to the unani-
mous conclusion that He should, as one worthy of death,
be brought before Pontius Pilate, who governed Judea
in the name of the Roman emperor and was the temporal Lord of Palestine.   According to the laws of the
Roman empire capital punishment was reserved to the
senate or the emperor and his representatives in the
remote provinces.   Cases of such importance as involved
the taking away of life were looked upon as worthy of
greater attention and as not to be decided without giving
the accused a hearing and an opportunity of defense and
justification.   In these affairs of justice the Roman people yielded to the requirements of natural reason more
faithfully than other nations.   In regard to this trial
of Christ the priests and scribes were pleased with the
prospect of having sentence of death passed upon Christ
our Lord by the heathen Pilate, because they could then
tell the people, that He was condemned by the Roman
governor and that this certainly would not have happened if He were not guilty of death.   To this extent
had they been blinded by their sins and their hypocrisy,
that they failed to see how much more guilty and sacrilegious they would even then be than the gentile judge.

But the Lord arranged it thus, in order that by their own behavior before Pilate they might reveal all their wickedness more plainly, as we shall see immediately.

589. The executioners therefore brought our Savior Jesus Christ to the house of Pilate, in order to present Him, still bound with the same chains and ropes in which they had taken Him from the garden, before his tribunal. The city of Jerusalem was full of strangers, who had come from all Palestine to celebrate the great Pasch of the Lamb and of the unleavened bread. As the rumor of this arrest was already spread among the people, and as the Master of life was known to all of them, a countless multitude gathered in the streets to see Him brought in chains through the streets. They were divided in their opinion concerning the Messiah; some of them shouted out: Let Him die, let Him die, this wicked impostor, who deceives the whole world. Others answered: His doctrines do not appear to be so bad, nor his works; for He has done good to many. Still others, who had believed in Him, were much afflicted and wept; while the whole city was in confusion and uproar concerning the Nazarene. Lucifer and all his demons were very attentive to what was passing; for, seeing himself secretly overcome by the invincible patience and meekness of Christ the Lord, he was stirred to uncontrollable fury by his own pride and haughtiness at the haunting suspicion, that such virtues could not be those of a mere human being. On the other hand, he could not understand how his allowing Himself to be despised and illtreated and his succumbing to so much bodily weakness and, as it were, total annihilation, could ever harmonize with his being true God; for, if He were God, said the dragon to himself, his Divinity would never consent to such annihilation, and the power inherent in his

divine nature and communicated to the humanity, would certainly prevent such weakness. Lucifer argued like one who knew nothing of the suspension of the overflow of the divine upon the human nature; which the Lord had secretly ordained for the purpose of securing the highest degree of suffering possible, as I have mentioned above (No. 498). By these misgivings, the pride of satan was lashed to still more furious efforts in the persecution of the Lord so as to ascertain who this One was that knew how to suffer torments in such a manner.

590. The sun had already arisen while these things happened and the most holy Mother, who saw it all from afar, now resolved to leave her retreat and follow her divine Son to the house of Pilate and to his death on the Cross. When the great Queen and Lady was about to set forth from the Cenacle, saint John arrived, in order to give an account of all that was happening; for the beloved disciple at that time did not know of the visions, by which all the doings and sufferings of her most holy Son were manifest to the blessed Mother. After the denial of saint Peter, saint John had retired and had observed, more from afar what was going on. Recognizing also the wickedness of his flight in the garden, he confessed it to the Mother of God and asked her pardon as soon as he came into her presence; and then he gave an account of all that passed in his heart and of what he had done and what he had seen in following his Master. Saint John thought it well to prepare the afflicted Mother for her meeting with her most holy Son, in order that She might not be overcome by the fearful spectacle of his present condition. Therefore He sought to impress Her beforehand with some image of his sufferings by saying: "O my Lady, in what a state of suf-

fering is our divine Master! The sight of Him cannot
but break one's heart; for by the buffets and the blows
and by the spittle, his most beautiful countenance is so
disfigured and defiled, that Thou wilt scarcely recognize
Him with thy own eyes." The most prudent Lady listened to his description, as if She knew nothing of the
events; but She broke out in bitterest tears of heart-
rending sorrow. The holy women, who had came forth
with the Lady, also listened to saint John, and all of
them were filled with grief and terror at his words. The
Queen of heaven asked the Apostle to accompany Her
and the devout women, and, exhorting them all, She
said: "Let us hasten our steps, in order that my eyes
may see the Son of the eternal Father, who took human
form in my womb; and you shall see, my dearest friends,
to what the love of mankind has driven Him, my Lord
and God, and what it costs Him to redeem men from sin
and death, and to open for them the gates of heaven."

591. The Queen of heaven set forth through the
streets of Jerusalem accompanied by saint John and by
some holy women. Of these not all, but only the three
Marys and other very pious women, followed Her to
the end. With Her were also the angels of her guard,
whom She asked to open a way for Her to her divine
Son. The holy angels obeyed and acted as her guard.
On the streets She heard the people expressing their
various opinions and sentiments concerning the sorrowful events now transpiring in reference to Jesus of Nazareth. The more kindly hearted lamented over his fate,
and they were fewest in number. Others spake about
the intention of his enemies to crucify Him; others related where He now was and how He was conducted
through the streets, bound as a criminal; others spoke of
the illtreatment He was undergoing; others asked, what

evil He had done, that He should be so misused; others again in their astonishment and in their doubts, exclaimed: To this then have his miracles brought Him! Without a doubt they were all impostures, since He cannot defend or free Himself! All the streets and squares were full of people and excited talk. But in the midst of this excitement the invincible Queen, though filled with the bitterest sorrow, preserved her constancy and composure, praying for the unbelievers and the evil-doers, as if She had no other care than to implore grace and pardon for their sins. She loved them as sincerely as if She were receiving favors and blessings at their hands. She permitted no indignation or anger to arise in her heart against the sacrilegious ministers of the Passion and Death of her beloved Son, nor any sign of such feelings in her exterior conduct. All of them She looked upon with charity and the desire of doing them good.

592. Some of them that met Her on the streets, recognized Her as the Mother of Jesus of Nazareth and moved by their natural compassion, said: "O sorrowful Mother! What a misfortune has overtaken Thee! How must thy heart be wounded and lacerated with grief!" Others again impiously said: "Why didst Thou permit Him to introduce such novelties among the people? It would have been better to restrain and dissuade Him; but it will be a warning for other mothers, and they will learn from thy misfortunes, how to instruct their children." These and other more horrible sentiments were expressed in the hearing of this sincerest Dove; but all of them She met with burning charity, accepting the pity of the kind-hearted, and suffering the malice of the unbelievers. She was not surprised at the ingratitude of the unresponsive and the ignorant; but implored the eternal Father to impart suitable blessings to all.

593. Through the swarming and confused crowds the angels conducted the Empress of heaven to a sharp turn of the street, where She met her most holy Son. With the profoundest reverence She prostrated Herself before his sovereign Person and adored it more fervently and with a reverence more deep and more ardent than ever was given or ever shall be given to it by all the creatures. She arose and then the Mother and Son looked upon each other with ineffable tenderness, interiorly conversing with each other in transports of an unspeakable sorrow. The most prudent Lady stepped aside and then followed Christ our Lord, continuing at a distance her interior communication with Him and with the eternal Father. The words of her soul are not for the mortal and corruptible tongue: but among other prayers the afflicted Mother said: "Most high God and my Son, I am aware of thy burning love for men, which leads Thee to hide the infinite power of thy Divinity beneath a form of passible flesh (Phil. 2, 7) formed in my womb. I confess thy incomprehensible wisdom in accepting such affronts and torments, and in sacrificing Thyself, who art the Lord of all creation, for the rescue of man, who is but a servant, dust and ashes (Gen. 3, 19). Thy goodness is to be praised, blessed, confessed and magnified by all creatures; but how shall I, thy Mother, ever cease to desire that all these injuries be heaped upon me and not upon thy divine Person, who art the beauty of the angels and the glory of the eternal Father? How shall I cease to desire the end of these pains? With what sorrow is my heart filled to behold Thee so afflicted, thy most beautiful countenance so defiled, and when I see, that to the Creator and Redeemer alone is denied pity and compassion in such bitter suffering? But if it is not possible, that I relieve Thee as Mother, do Thou

accept my sorrowful sacrifice in not being able to bring
Thee the relief which is due to the true and holy Son
of God."

594. The image of her divine Son, thus wounded, defiled and bound, remained so firmly fixed and imprinted
in the soul of our Queen, that during her life it was
never effaced, and remained in her mind as distinctly,
as if She were continually beholding Him with her own
eyes. Christ our God arrived at the house of Pilate,
followed by many of the council and a countless multitude of the people. The Jews, wishing to preserve themselves as clean before the law as possible for the celebration of the Pasch and the unleavened bread, excused
themselves before Pilate for their refusing to enter the
pretorium or court of Pilate in presenting Jesus. As
most absurd hypocrites they paid no attention to the sacrilegious uncleanness, with which their souls were affected
in becoming the murderers of the innocent Godman.
Pilate, although a heathen, yielded to their ceremonious
scruples, and seeing that they hesitated to enter his pretorium, he went out to meet them. According to the
formality customary among the Romans, he asked them
(John 18, 28) : "What accusation have you against this
Man?" They answered: "If He were not a criminal,
we would not have brought Him to thee thus bound and
fettered." This was as much as to say: We have convinced ourselves of his misdeeds and we are so attached
to justice and to our obligations, that we would not have
begun any proceedings against Him, if He were not a
great malefactor. But Pilate pressed his inquiry and
said: "What then are the misdeeds, of which He
has made Himself guilty?" They answered: "He is
convicted of disturbing the commonwealth, He wishes to
make Himself our king and forbids paying tribute to

Cæsar (Luke 23, 2) ; He claims to be the son of God, and has preached a new doctrine, commencing in Galilee, through all Judea and Jerusalem." "Take Him then yourselves," said Pilate, "and judge Him according to your laws; I do not find a just cause for proceeding against Him." But the Jews replied: "It is not permitted us to sentence any one to death, nor to execute such a sentence."

595. The most holy Mary, with saint John and the women who followed Her, was present at this interview; for the holy angels made room for them where they could hear and see all that was passing. Shielded by her mantle She wept tears of blood, pressed forth by the sorrow which pierced her virginal heart. In her interior acts of virtue She faithfully reproduced those practiced by her most holy Son, while in her pains and endurance She copied those of his body. She asked the eternal Father to grant Her the favor of not losing sight of her divine Son, as far as was naturally possible, until his Death; and this was conceded to Her, excepting during the time in which He was in prison. Considering it but just, that amid all the false accusations of the Jews the innocence of the Savior and the injustice of the sentence should become known, the most prudent Lady fervently prayed, that the judge be not deceived and that he obtain clearest insight into Christ's being delivered over to him by the envy of the priests and scribes. In virtue of this prayer, Pilate clearly saw the truth, was convinced of the innocence of Christ and of his being a victim of their envy (Matth. 28, 18). On her account also the Lord declared Himself more openly to Pilate, although the latter did not co-operate with the truth made known to him. It profited not him, but us; and it served to convict the priests and pharisees of their treachery.

596. In their wrath the Jews were anxious to dispose Pilate favorably toward their project and they wished him to pronounce the sentence of death against Jesus without the least delay. When they perceived his hesitation, they ferociously raised their voices, accusing Jesus over and over again of revolting against the government of Judea, deceiving and stirring up the people (Luke 23, 5), calling Himself Christ, that is an anointed King. This malicious accusation they pressed particularly, hoping to stir Pilate to fear for the temporal welfare of his government, with which he was charged by the Romans. Among the Jews the kings were anointed; therefore they insisted, that Jesus in having called Himself Christ, intended to constitute Himself as King, and, as Pilate was a heathen and knew nothing of the anointing of kings, they wished to persuade him, that calling oneself Christ among the Jews was identical with calling oneself king of the Jews. Pilate asked the Lord: "What dost Thou answer to the accusations which they bring against Thee?" But the Savior answered not one word in the presence of his accusers, causing much wonder in Pilate at such silence and patience. But, desiring to inquire more closely, whether Jesus was truly a King, he withdrew from the clamoring Jews and brought Jesus into the pretorium. There he asked Him face to face: "Tell me, can it be that Thou art a King of the Jews?" Pilate could not bring himself to think that He was a King in fact; since he knew that Christ was not reigning. Therefore he wished to find out, whether Jesus claimed or really possessed any right to the title of King. Our Savior answered him: "Sayst thou this thing of thyself, or have others told it thee of Me?" (John 18, 34). Pilate replied: "Am I a Jew? Thy own nation and the chief priests have delivered Thee up to

me. What hast Thou done?" Jesus answered: "My
kingdom is not of this world. If my kingdom were of
this world, my servants would certainly strive that I be
not delivered to the Jews: but now my kingdom is not
from hence." The judge partly believed this assertion
of Jesus and therefore answered: "Art Thou a king
then?" Jesus answered: "Thou sayest that I am a king.
For this I was born and for this I came into the world.
Every one that is of the Truth, heareth my voice."
Pilate wondered at this answer and asked: "What is
truth?" But without waiting for an answer, he left Him
in the pretorium, and said to the Jews: "I find no cause
in Him. But you have a custom, that I should release
one unto you at the Pasch: will you, therefore, that I
release unto you the King of the Jews, or Barabbas?"
This Barabbas was a thief and murderer, who had killed
some one in a quarrel. All the people raised their voice
and said: "We desire that you release Barabbas, and
crucify Jesus." In this demand they persisted until it
was granted.

597. Pilate was much disturbed by the answers of
Jesus and the obstinacy of the Jews. For on the one
hand, seeing that they were so determined on the death
of Jesus, he well knew, that it would be difficult to satisfy
them without consenting to their demands; and on the
other hand, he clearly saw that they persecuted Him out
of mortal envy and that their accusations about his disturbing the people, were false and ridiculous (Matth.
17, 18). In regard to the imputation, that He had made
Himself King, he was likewise satisfied of the contrary
by the answers of Christ and by his humility, poverty
and patient forbearance toward their calumnies. By the
light and grace which Pilate received, he became fully
convinced that Jesus was truly innocent, although he

never pierced the mystery of his Divinity and the greatness of this innocence.   The living words of Christ
created an exalted idea of Him in his mind and made
him think that some great mystery was connected with
Him; therefore he desired to free Him and finally determined to send Him to Herod.   But all these shifts failed,
because Pilate made himself unworthy by his sin and
paid attention only to his worldly prospects, allowing
himself to be governed by them and not by the dictates
of justice, but more by the suggestions of Lucifer,
as I have related above (No. 423), than by the truth,
which he so clearly knew.   Fully understanding the true
circumstances, he acted the part of a wicked judge in
continuing to treat the cause of an innocent Man with
those who were his declared enemies and false accusers.
Thus he committed the still greater crime of condemning
Jesus to such an inhuman scourging and then to death,
without having any other cause than to satisfy the Jews.

598. But though Pilate for these and other reasons
was a most wicked and unjust judge in thus condemning
Christ, whom he held to be a mere man, though good
and innocent; yet his crime was much smaller than that
of the priests and pharisees.   And this not only because
they were moved by envy, cruelty and other vices, but
also because they sinned in not acknowledging Christ as
their true Messias and Redeemer, God and Man, such
as He had been promised in the Law, which they believed
and professed.   For their own condemnation the Lord
permitted, that in their very accusations they called Him
Christ and anointed King, thus confessing with their
lips what they denied and discredited in their proceedings.   They were bound to believe this truth, which they
confessed in their words, and thus come to the understanding of the true anointment of the Savior, which

was an unction prefigured in the kings and priests of
the olden times and consisted in the anointment mentioned
by David (Ps. 44, 8) and different from theirs; namely,
the unction of the Divinity resulting from its union with
the humanity and by which Christ's soul was anointed
with the gifts of grace and glory corresponding to the
hypostatic union. All these mysteries of truth were
providentially hidden beneath the accusations of the
Jews, although they in their perfidy would not believe
them, and in their envy interpreted them falsely. For
they imputed to the Savior the desire of making Himself king, without his being one, while just the contrary
was really the truth: He was in every respect the
supreme Lord, but did not wish to show or make use
of the power of a temporal king. He had not come
into this world to command men, but to obey (Matth.
20, 28). Still greater was the blindness of the Jews
in hoping for a temporal king as their Messias and at
the same time calumniously asserting that Jesus made of
Himself a king. It seems that they sought for their
Messias a King so powerful, that they would not be
able to resist Him; although they then would have to
receive a king by compulsion and not with the free will
benevolently desired by the Lord.

599. Our great Lady profoundly understood these
hidden sacraments and the wisdom of her chaste heart
made use of them to excite heroic acts of all the virtues.
Other children of Adam, conceived in original sin and
defiled by their own, are wont to be disturbed and oppressed in proportion to the increase of sorrow and tribulation, and excited to impatience and other inordinate
passions; but most holy Mary, who was actuated not
by sin or its effects, or by mere nature, was impelled
by exalted grace to just the contrary course of action.

For the great persecutions and the vast waters of affliction and sorrow extinguished not in her bosom the fire
of divine love (Cant. 8, 7); but they were new incen-
tives to the fires of divine love in her soul, breaking forth
in petitions for the sinners so much the more ardently,
as the malice of men reached greater excesses. O
Queen of virtues, Mistress of creatures and sweetest
Mother of mercy! How hard of heart am I, how slow
and insensible, that my soul is not annihilated by sorrow
at what I understand of thy sufferings and those of
thy divine Son! That I still live, knowing all I do
know, should cause in me a sorrow unto death. It is a
crime against love and piety to beg favors from the innocent, whom we see suffering torments. With what truth
can we then say as creatures, that we love God, our
Redeemer, and Thee, my Queen, who art his Mother, if
Thou and He alone drink out the chalice of such torments and pains, while we are draining the chalice of
the pleasures of Babylon? O that I might understand
this truth! O that it might penetrate into my deepest
heart and that it might pierce my very soul at the sight
of such inhuman torments of my Savior and his afflicted
Mother! How can I conceive, that any one can do me
an injustice in persecuting me, that they offend me by
despising me, that they insult me by abhorring me?
How can I complain of suffering, even if I am blamed,
neglected and contemned by the world? O great Chief-
tainess of the martyrs, Queen of the courageous, Mistress of all the imitators of thy Son, if I am thy daughter
and disciple, as Thou condescendest to call me, and as
my Lord wishes me to merit, do not reject my longing
desire to follow thy footsteps on the way of the cross.
If in my weakness I have fallen, do Thou, my Lady
and Mother, obtain for me the courage of a contrite

heart, justly humiliated on account of its vile ingratitude. Gain for me through thy prayers the love of the eternal Father, which is so precious, that only thy powerful intercession can obtain it and only my Lord and Redeemer can merit it for me.

INSTRUCTION WHICH THE GREAT QUEEN OF HEAVEN GAVE ME.

600. My daughter, great is the neglect and the inattention of men in failing to consider the works of my most holy Son and to penetrate with humble reverence the mysteries which He has concealed within them for the salvation of all. But many do not know, and others are astonished, that the Lord should have consented to be presented as a criminal before iniquitous judges and be examined by them as a wicked malefactor; that they should have been allowed to treat Him as an ignorant fool; and that He should not have made use of his divine wisdom to defend his innocence, convict the Jews and all his enemies of their malice, since He could so easily have done it. But these sentiments of wonder should be especially united to a deep veneration for the judgments of the Lord, who disposed all things connected with the Redemption according to his equity, goodness and rectitude and in a manner befitting all his attributes, denying none of his enemies sufficient help to follow the good, if only they wished to use their freedom for that purpose. He wished all of them to be saved (I Tim. 2, 4), and if not all of them attained this salvation, no one can justly complain of his superabundant kindness.

601. But besides this, I wish, my dearest, that thou understand the instructive lessons contained in these works; for in each one of them my Son acted as Re-

deemer and Teacher of men. In the silence and the meekness, which He maintained during his Passion, permitting Himself to be reputed as a wicked and foolish man, He left to mankind a lesson just as important as it is unnoticed and unpracticed by the children of Adam. Because they do not heed the contagion of Lucifer through sin, which is perpetuated in the world, they do not seek in the Physician the medicine of suffering, which the Lord in his immense charity has left to the world in word and deed. Let men then consider themselves conceived in sin (Ps. 50, 7), and let them realize how strong has grown in them the hellish seed of pride, of presumption, vanity, self-esteem, avarice, hypocrisy, deceitfulness, and all other vices. Each one ordinarily seeks to advance his honor and vainglory, struggling to be applauded and renowned. The learned and those who think themselves wise, wish to be applauded and looked up to, bragging about their knowledge. The unlearned try to appear wise. The rich glory in their riches and wish to be respected on their account. The poor strive to be and appear rich, anxious to gain the approbation of the wealthy. The powerful seek to be feared, worshipped and obeyed. All of them are pursuing the same deceit of seeking to appear what they are not in fact, and fail in reality to come up to what they appear to be. They palliate their faults, extol their virtues and abilities, they attribute to themselves the goods and the blessings as if they had not received them from God. They receive them as if they were their due and not owing to his liberal kindness; instead of being thankful for them they abuse them as weapons against God and against their own selves. Commonly all are swollen up by the mortal poison of the serpent and so much the more anxious to drink it, the more deeply they are already wounded and weakened by his lamentable assaults. The way of the cross and imitation of Christ in humble Christian sincerity is deserted, because they are so few that walk upon it.

602. In order to crush the head of Lucifer and overcome pride and arrogance, my Son observed this patient silence in his Passion, permitting Himself to be treated as an ignorant and foolish criminal. As the Teacher of this philosophy and as the Physician of the sickness of sin, He would not deny the charges nor defend or justify Himself, nor refute those who accused Him, showing us by his own living example, how to oppose and counteract the intentions of the serpent. In the Lord was that teaching of the wise man put into practice: More precious is a little foolishness in its time than wisdom and glory (Eccles. 10, 1) ; for it is better that human frailty be at times considered ignorant and wicked, than that it make a vain show of virtue and wisdom. Infinite is the number of those who are entangled in this dangerous error, who, desiring to appear wise, speak much and multiply words like the foolish (Eccles. 1, 14). They only lose what they strive so much to attain, since they become known as foolish. All these vices arise from the pride rooted in human nature. But do thou, my daughter, preserve the doctrine of my divine Son and that which comes from me. Abhor human ostentation, suffer in silence and let the world consider thee ignorant; for it does not know where true wisdom dwells.

CHAPTER X

603. One of the accusations of the Jews and the priests
before Pilate was, that Jesus our Savior had begun to
stir up the people by his preaching in the province of
Galilee (Luke 23, 6). This caused Pilate to inquire,
whether He was a Galileean; and as they told him, that
Jesus was born and raised in that country, he thought
this circumstance useful for the solution of his difficulties
in regard to Jesus and for escaping the molestations of
the Jews, who so urgently demanded his death. Herod
was at that time in Jerusalem, celebrating the Pasch of
the Jews. He was the son of the first Herod, who had
murdered the Innocents to procure the death of Jesus
soon after his birth (Matth 2, 16). This murderer had
become a proselyte of the Jews at the time of his mar-
riage with a Jewish woman. On this account his son
Herod likewise observed the law of Moses, and he had
come to Jerusalem from Galilee, of which he was governor. Pilate was at enmity with Herod, for the two
governed the two principal provinces of Palestine,
namely, Judea and Galilee, and a short time before it had
happened that Pilate, in his zeal for the supremacy of
the Roman empire, had murdered some Galileeans during a public function in the temple, mixing the blood

of the insurgents with that of the holy sacrifices. Herod was highly incensed at this sacrilege, and Pilate, in order to afford him some satisfaction without much trouble to himself, resolved to send to him Christ the Lord to be examined and judged as one of the subjects of Herod's sway. Pilate also expected that Herod would set Jesus free as being innocent and a Victim of the malice and envy of the priests and scribes.

604. Christ our Lord therefore went forth from the house of Pilate to the palace of Herod, being still bound and chained as before and accompanied by the scribes and priests as his accusers. There were also a large number of soldiers and servants, who dragged Him along by the ropes and cleared the streets, which had been filled with multitudes of the people to see the spectacle. The military broke their way through the crowds; and as the servants and priests were thirsting so eagerly for the blood of the Savior and wished to shed it on this very day, they hastened with the Lord through the streets nearly on a run and with great tumult. Mary also set forth from the house of Pilate with her company in order to follow her sweetest Son Jesus and accompany Him on the ways, which He was still to go until his death on the Cross. It would not have been possible for the Lady to follow her Beloved closely enough to be in his sight, if She had not ordered her holy angels to open a way for Her. They made it possible for Her to be constantly near her Son, so that She could enjoy his presence, though that also brought with it only a fuller participation in all torments and sorrows. She obtained the fulfillment of all her wishes; for walking along through the streets near the Savior She saw and heard the insults of the servants, the blows they dealt Him, the reproaches of the people, expressed either as their own or repeated from hearsay.

605. When Herod was informed that Pilate would send Jesus of Nazareth to him, he was highly pleased. He knew that Jesus was a great friend of John the Baptist, whom he had ordered to be put to death (Mark 6, 27), and had heard many reports of his preaching. In vain and foolish curiosity he harbored the desire of seeing Jesus do something new and extraordinary for his entertainment and wonder (Luke 23, 8). The Author of life therefore came into the presence of the murderer Herod, against whom the blood of the Baptist was calling more loudly to this same Lord for vengeance, than in its time the blood of Abel (Gen. 4, 10). But the unhappy adulterer, ignorant of the terrible judgment of the Almighty, received Him with loud laughter as an enchanter and conjurer. In this dreadful misconception he commenced to examine and question Him, persuaded that he could thereby induce Him to work some miracle to satisfy his curiosity. But the Master of wisdom and prudence, standing with an humble reserve before his most unworthy judge, answered him not a word. For on account of his evil-doing he well merited the punishment of not hearing the words of life, which he would certainly have heard if he had been disposed to listen to them with reverence.

606. The princes and priests of the Jews stood around, continually rehearsing the same accusations and charges which they had advanced in the presence of Pilate. But the Lord maintained silence also in regard to these calumnies, much to the disappointment of Herod. In his presence the Lord would not open his lips, neither in order to answer his questions, nor in order to refute the accusations. Herod was altogether unworthy of hearing the truth, this being his greatest punishment and the punishment most to be dreaded by all the princes and

the powerful of this earth. Herod was much put out by
the silence and meekness of our Savior and was much
disappointed in his vain curiosity. But the unjust judge
tried to hide his confusion by mocking and ridiculing the
innocent Master with his whole cohort of soldiers and
ordering him to be sent back to Pilate. Having made
fun of the reserve of the Lord, the servants of Herod
joined in treating Him as a fool and as one deficient in
mind and they clothed Him in a white garment, in
order to mark Him as insane and to be avoided as dangerous. But by the hidden providence of the Most High
this dress signified the purity and innocence of the Savior,
and these ministers of wickedness were thus unwittingly
giving testimony of the truth, which they were trying to
obscure in deriding the miraculous power of the Lord.

607. Herod showed himself thankful to Pilate for the
courtesy of sending Jesus of Nazareth to be judged before his tribunal. He informed Pilate, that he found no
cause in Him, but held Him to be an ignorant man of
no consequence whatever. By the secret judgments of
divine Wisdom, Herod and Pilate were reconciled on
that day and thenceforward remained friends. Conducted by many soldiers, both of Herod and Pilate,
amid a still greater concourse, tumult, and excitement of
the people, Jesus returned from Herod to Pilate. For
the very ones who had some time before hailed and
venerated Him as the Savior and Messias, blessed of
the Lord (Matth. 21, 9), now perverted by the priests
and magistrates, had changed their minds, and they
despised and condemned the same Lord, whom they had
so shortly before reverenced and glorified. For of such
influence is usually the erroneous example of the chiefs
in misleading the people. In the midst of all this confusion and ignominy the Lord passed along, repeating

within Himself in unspeakable love, humility and patience, those words, which He had long before spoken by the mouth of David: "I am a worm and no man; the reproach of men and the outcast of people. All they that saw me have laughed me to scorn: they have spoken with their lips and wagged the head" (Ps. 21, 7). The Lord was a worm and no man, not only because He was not engendered like the rest of men, and because He was not merely and solely a man, being true God and man; but also because He was not treated like a man, but like a wretched and despised worm. Amid all the scorn with which He was overwhelmed and trodden under foot, He made no more outcry than an humble wormlet, which is despised and crushed as a most vile and despicable creature. All the innumerable multitudes that saw our Redeemer spoke of Him with wagging heads, as if retracting their previous conception and opinion of this Prophet of Nazareth.

608. Although his afflicted Mother was made interiorly aware of all that happened, She was not present in body when the priests advanced their insulting accusations before Herod, and when he sputtered forth his questions to the Author of life. She remained outside of the hall of judgment, whither they had taken the Lord. But when He came forth from the hall She met him and They looked upon each other in reciprocal sorrow of their souls, such as corresponded to the love between such a Son and Mother. The sight of the white vestment, by which they proclaimed Him fit to be treated only as an insane fool, pierced her heart with new sorrow; though She alone, of all mankind, recognized the mystery of his purity and innocence indicated by this vestment. She adored Him in it with deepest reverence and followed Him through the streets back to the house of Pilate; for

in this house was to be executed the divine decree for our salvation. On this way from Herod to Pilate it happened, that on account of the crush of the people and on account of the haste, they tripped Him up and threw Him on the ground several times. By their cruel pulling at the ropes with which He was bound, they caused the blood to flow from his sacred veins. His hands being tied, He could not easily help Himself to rise from his falls. Therefore the multitudes of the people, who followed and who were neither able, nor cared to stop in their onward rush, stepped upon the divine Lord, treading Him under foot and kicking Him. The blows and wounds He thus received, instead of stirring the compassion of the soldiers, only excited them to loud laughter; for, instigated by the demons, they had become devoid of all human compassion, no less than so many wild beasts.

609. At the sight of such unmeasured cruelty, the most sorrowful and loving Mother was moved to deepest compassion, and turning to her holy angels She commanded them to gather up the divine blood in order that it might not be trodden upon and dishonored by the feet of sinners. This the heavenly servants willingly fulfilled. She commanded also, that if her divine Son should again fall to the earth, they hasten to his assistance and prevent these evil-doers from injuring and stepping on his most sacred body. But She was the most prudent of all mortals, She did not wish them to execute her command, unless it met the approval of the Lord; and therefore She urged them to make this proposal themselves and ask his permission, representing to Him at the same time her anguish as his Mother in seeing Him thus irreverently subjected to the feet of sinners. In order to so much the sooner move the Lord to grant this petition, She begged Him through the holy angels, that He commute

this humiliation of being trodden upon and crushed by the rabble into an act of obedience in complying with the petition of his afflicted Mother, who at the same time acknowledged Herself as his slave and formed of the dust. All these petitions of his blessed Mother the angels presented to the Lord Christ in her name; not that He was ignorant of them, since He knew all things and was Himself the instigator of them through his divine grace, but the Lord desires in all these matters a regard for the due process of reason. The great Lady was aware of this desire and in her most exalted wisdom practiced virtues in diverse ways and by diverse activities, unimpeded by the foreknowledge of the Lord concerning all things.

610. Our Savior Jesus yielded to the desire and petitions of his most blessed Mother and gave the angels permission to execute her requests as her ministers. During the rest of the passage to the house of Pilate they would not permit the Lord to be tripped or cast to the ground, or to be stepped upon by the crowd as had happened before. But in regard to other injuries, He allowed the stupid wrath and blind malice of the servants of the law and of the populace to vent themselves freely and fully upon his divine Person. His most holy Mother heard and saw all with an unconquered but lacerated heart. In a proportionate manner this was also witnessed by the other Marys and saint John, who with ceaseless tears followed the Lord in company with his purest Mother. I do not stop to describe the sorrows of these and other pious women, who attended upon the Queen, because I would go too wide of my subject, especially if I were to describe the doings of Magdalen, most distinguished in her ardent love of Christ and most pleasing to the Savior. For to her we must apply, what Christ

himself said when He justified Her: that those love most to whom the greater sins are forgiven (Luke 7, 43).

611. Pilate was again confronted with Jesus in his palace and was bestormed anew by the Jews to condemn Him to death of the cross. Convinced of the innocence of Christ and of the mortal envy of the Jews, he was much put out at Herod's again referring the disagreeable decision to his own tribunal. Feeling himself obliged in his quality of judge to give this decision, he sought to placate the Jews in different ways. One of these was a private interview with some of the servants and friends of the highpriests and priests. He urged them to prevail upon their masters and friends, not any more to ask for the release of the malefactor Barabbas, but instead demand the release of our Redeemer; and to be satisfied with some punishment he was willing to administer before setting Him free. This measure Pilate had taken before they arrived a second time to press their demand for a sentence upon Jesus. The proposal to choose between freeing either Barabbas or Jesus was made to the Jews, not only once, but two or three times. The first time before sending Him to Herod and the second time after his return; this is related by the Evangelists with some variation, though not essentially contradicting truth (Matth. 27, 17). Pilate spoke to the Jews and said: "You have brought this Man before me, accusing Him of perverting the people by his doctrines; and having examined Him in your presence, I was not convinced of the truth of your accusations. And Herod, to whom I have sent Him and before whom you repeated your accusations, refused to condemn Him to death. It will be sufficient to correct and chastise Him for the present, in order that He may amend. As I am to release some malefactor for the feast of the Pasch, I will

release Christ, if you will have Him freed, and punish Barabbas." But the multitude of the Jews, thus informed how much Pilate desired to set Jesus free, shouted with one voice: "Enough, enough, not Christ, but Barabbas deliver unto us."

612. The custom of giving freedom to an imprisoned criminal at this great solemnity of the Pasch was introduced by the Jews in grateful remembrance of the release of their forefathers from servitude by their passage through the Red Sea, when the Almighty freed them from the power of Pharao by killing the first-born children of the Egyptians and afterwards annihilating him and his armies in the waters of the Red sea (Exodus 12, 29). In gratitude for this favor the Jews always sought out the greatest malefactor and pardoned him his crimes; while they refused such clemency to those who were less guilty. In their treaties with the Romans they expressly reserved this privilege; and the governors complied with it. But in the present instance they failed to follow out in their demands what they were so loudly proclaiming in regard to Jesus. According to law they were to demand the release of the greatest criminal and this they proclaimed Jesus to be; yet they persisted in demanding the punishment of Christ and the release of Barabbas, whom they judged less guilty. In such blindness and perversity had the wrath and envy of the demon cast them, that they lost the light of reason even in their own affairs and against their own selves.

613. While Pilate was thus disputing with the Jews in the pretorium, his wife, Procula, happened to hear of his doings and she sent him a message telling him: "What hast thou to do with this Man? Let him go free; for I warn thee that I have had this very day some visions in regard to Him!" This warning of Procula originated

through the activity of Lucifer and his demons. For they, observing all that was happening in regard to the person of Christ and the unchangeable patience with which He bore all injuries, were more and more confused and staggered in their rabid fury. Although the swollen pride of Lucifer could not explain how his Divinity could ever subject Itself to such great insults, nor how He could permit his body to suffer such ill-treatment, and although he could not come to any certain conviction, whether this Jesus was a Godman or not; yet the dragon was persuaded, that some great mystery was here transpiring among men which would be the cause of great damage and defeat to him and his malice if he did not succeed in arresting its progress in the world. Having come to this conclusion with his demons, he many times suggested to the pharisees the propriety of ceasing their persecutions of Christ. These suggestions, however, since they originated from malice and were void of any power for good, failed to move the obstinate and perverted hearts of the Jews. Despairing of success the demons betook themselves to the wife of Pilate and spoke to her in dreams, representing to her that this Man was just and without guilt, that if her husband should sentence Him he would be deprived of his rank and she herself would meet with great adversity. They urged her to advise Pilate to release Jesus and punish Barabbas, if she did not wish to draw misfortune upon their house and their persons.

614. Procula was filled with great fear and terror at these visions, and as soon as she heard what was passing between the Jews and her husband, she sent him the message mentioned by saint Matthew, not to meddle with this Man nor condemn One to death, whom she held to be just. The demon also injected similar misgivings

into the mind of Pilate and these warnings of his wife only increased them. Yet, as all his considerations rested upon worldly policy, and as he had not co-operated with the true helps given him by the Savior, all these fears retarded his unjust proceedings only so long as no other more powerful consideration arose, as will be seen in effect. But just now he began for the third time to argue (as saint Luke tells us), insisting upon the innocence of Christ our Lord and that he found no crime in Him nor any guilt worthy of death, and therefore he would punish and then dismiss Him (Luke 23, 22). As we shall see in the next chapter, he did really punish Christ in order to see whether the Jews would be satisfied. But the Jews, on the contrary, demanded that Christ be crucified. Thereupon Pilate asked for water and released Barabbas. Then he washed his hands in the presence of all the people, saying: "I have no share in the death of this just Man, whom you condemn. Look to yourselves in what you are doing, for I wash my hands in order that you may understand they are not sullied in the blood of the Innocent." Pilate thought that by this ceremony he could excuse himself entirely and that he thereby could put its blame upon the princes of the Jews and upon the people who demanded it. The wrath of the Jews was so blind and foolish that for the satisfaction of seeing Jesus crucified, they entered upon this agreement with Pilate and took upon themselves and upon their children the responsibility for this crime. Loudly proclaiming this terrible sentence and curse, they exclaimed: "His blood come upon us and upon our children" (Matth. 27, 25).

615. O most foolish and cruel blindness! O inconceivable rashness! The unjust condemnation of the Just and the blood of the Innocent, whom the judge himself is forced to proclaim guiltless, you wish to take upon

yourselves and upon your children, in order that his blood may call out against you to the end of the world! O perfidious and sacrilegious Jews! So lightly then weighs the blood of the Lamb, who bears the sins of the world, and the life of a Man, who is at the same time God! How is it possible you wish to load with it yourselves and your children? If He had been only your brother, your benefactor and master, your audacity would have been tremendous and your malice execrable. Justly indeed do you merit the punishment which you meet; and that the burden, which you have put upon yourselves and your children, allows you no rest or relief in all the world: it is just that this burden should rest upon you heavier than heaven and earth. But, alas! Though this divine Blood was intended to wash and cleanse all the children of Adam, and though it was in effect poured out upon all the children of the holy Church, yet there are many belonging to it who make themselves guilty of this blood by their works in the same manner as the Jews charged themselves with it, both by word and deed. They did not know or believe that it was the blood of the Savior, while Catholics both know and confess that it is their Redeemer's.

616. The sins and depraved lives of the Christians proclaim louder than tongues their abuse of the blood of Christ and their consent to the guilt in his death which they load upon themselves. Let Christ be affronted, spit upon, buffeted, stretched upon a cross, despised, let Him yield to Barabbas and die; let Him be tormented, scourged and crowned with thorns for our sins: let his blood interest us no more than that it flow copiously and be imputed to us for all eternity: let the incarnate God suffer and die; if only we are left free to enjoy the apparent goods of this world, to seize the

pleasing hour, to use creatures for our comfort, to be crowned with roses, live in joy; let our power be unrefrained, let no one seek preference before us; be we permitted to despise humility, abhor poverty, hoard up riches, engage in all deceits, forgive no injuries, entertain the delights of carnal pleasures, let our eyes see nothing that they shall not covet. Such be our rule in life without regard for aught else. And if by all this we crucify Christ, let his blood come upon us and upon our children.

617. Ask the damned in hell, whether these were not the sentiments expressed in their works as described by Solomon, and whether it was not because they spoke thus foolishly in their hearts, that they were called impious, and were so in reality. What else except damnation can they expect, who abuse the blood of Christ and waste it upon themselves, not as such who are seeking a remedy? Where do we find, among the children of the Church, any one that would willingly permit a thief and malefactor to be preferred to him? So little is this doctrine of humility practiced, that one excites surprise if he allows another just as good and honorable as himself, or even more honorable, to take precedence. Though it is certain that no one can be found as good as Christ or as bad as Barabbas, yet there are innumerable men who, in spite of this example, are offended and judge themselves disgraced, if they are not preferred and exalted by honors, riches and dignities, and in whatever pertains to the ostentation and applause of the world. These are sought after, contended for and solicited; in such things are consumed the thoughts and all the exertions and powers of men, almost from the time in which they can use their faculties until they lose them. The most lamentable misfortune is, that even those who, by their profession and their state, have renounced and turned

their backs upon such things, do not free themselves. While the Savior has commanded them to forget their people and the house of their parents (Ps. 44, 11), they devote to them the best part of their human existence, by giving them their attention and solicitude in the direction of their affairs, their best wishes and care in the augmentation of their worldly goods. It seems but a small matter to them to engage themselves in these vanities. Instead of forgetting the house of their father they forget the house of their God in which they live, and where they are divinely assisted to gain a salvation, an honor and esteem never possible in the world, and where they receive their sustenance without any anxiety or worry. They show themselves ungrateful for all these benefits by drifting away from the humility due to their state. Thus the humility of Christ our Savior, his patience, his injuries, the dishonor of the cross, the imitation of Christ's works, the following of his doctrines; all is left to the poor, to the lonely ones, to the weak and humble of this world; while the ways of Sion are deserted and full of wailing, because there are so few who will come to the solemn feast of the imitation of Christ our Lord (Thren. 1, 4).

618. Pilate was not conscious of the absurdity of his pretense, that to have washed his hands and to have charged the Jews with the blood of Christ, was sufficient to clear him before his conscience and before men; for by this ceremony, so full of hypocrisy and deceit, he tried to satisfy both. It is true that the Jews were the principal actors and more guilty in the condemnation of the innocent Godman, and that they themselves expressly charged themselves with its guilt. But Pilate was not on that account free from it; since, knowing the innocence of Christ our Lord, he should not have allowed a thief

and robber to be preferred before Christ; neither should he have chastised, nor pretended to correct Him, who showed nothing that could be corrected or amended (Luke 23, 25). Much less should he have condemned and delivered Him over to his mortal enemies, whose envy and cruelty was so evident. He is not a just judge who is aware of the truth and justice and places it in the balance with his own human respect and his own personal interest; for such a course drags down the right reason of men who are so cowardly of heart. Since they do not possess the strength and perfection of mind necessary to a judge, they cannot resist their greed, or their human respect. In their blind passions they forsake justice in order not to endanger their temporal advantages, as happened to Pilate.

619. In the house of Pilate, through the ministry of the holy angels, our Queen was placed in such a position that She could hear the disputes of the iniquitous judge with the scribes and priests concerning the innocence of Christ our Savior, and concerning the release of Barabbas in preference to Him. All the clamors of these human tigers She heard in silence and admirable meekness, as the living counterpart of her most holy Son. Although She preserved the unchanging propriety and modesty of her exterior, all the malicious words of the Jews pierced her sorrowful heart like a two-edged sword. But the voices of her unspoken sorrows resounded in the ears of the eternal Father more pleasantly and sweetly than the lamentation of the beautiful Rachel who, as Jeremias says, was beweeping her children because they cannot be restored (Jer. 31, 15). Our most beautiful Rachel the purest Mary, sought not revenge, but pardon for her enemies, who were depriving Her of the Only-begotten of the Father and her only Son. She imitated

all the actions of the most holy Soul of Christ and accompanied Him in the works of most exalted holiness and perfection; for neither could her torments hinder her charity, nor her affliction diminish her fervor, nor could the tumult distract her attention, nor the outrageous injuries of the multitudes prevent her interior recollection: under all circumstances She practiced the most exalted virtues in the most eminent degree.

INSTRUCTION WHICH THE GREAT MISTRESS OF HEAVEN, MOST BLESSED MARY, GAVE ME.

620. My daughter, in what thou hast written and understood, I see thee astonished to find, that Pilate and Herod exhibited less unkindness and cruelty in the death of my divine Son than the priests, highpriests and pharisees; and thou dwellest much upon the fact that those were secular and gentile judges, while these were teachers of the law and priests of the people of Israel, professing the true faith. In answer to thy thoughts I will remind thee of a doctrine not new, which thou hast understood on former occasions; but I wish that thou refresh it in thy mind and remember it for the rest of thy life. Know then, my dearest, that a fall from the highest position is extremely dangerous and the damage done is either irreparable, or very difficult of redress. Lucifer held an eminent position in heaven, as regards both natural gifts and gifts of grace; for in beauty he excelled all the creatures, and by his sin he fell to the deepest abyss of loathsomeness and misery and into a more hardened obstinacy than all his followers. The first parents of the human race, Adam and Eve, were exalted to the highest dignity and raised to exquisite favor, as coming forth from the hand of the Almighty: their fall caused perdition to themselves and to all their posterity, and

faith teaches what was the cost of their salvation. To restore them and their posterity was the work of an infinite mercy.

621. Many other souls have reached the heights of perfection and have thence fallen most unfortunately, arriving at a state in which they almost despaired or found themselves incapable of rising. This sad state in the creature originates from many causes. The first is the dismay and boundless confusion of one who feels that he has fallen from an exalted state of virtue; for he knows that he has not only lost great blessings, but he does not expect to obtain greater ones than those of the past and those he has lost; nor does he promise himself more firmness in keeping those he can obtain through renewed efforts, than he has shown in those acquired and now lost through his ingratitude. From this dangerous distrust originates lukewarmness, want of fervor and diligence, absence of zeal and devotion; since diffidence extinguishes all these in the soul, just as the sprightliness of ardent hope overcomes many difficulties, strengthens and vivifies weak human creatures to undertake great works. Another obstacle there is, not less formidable, namely: the souls accustomed to the blessings of God, either through their office, as the priests and religious, or by the exercise of virtues and the abundance of divine favors, as spiritual-minded persons, usually aggravate their sins by a certain contempt of these very blessings and a certain abuse of the divine things. For by the abundance of the divine favors they fall into a dangerous dullness of mind. They begin to think little of the divine favors and become irreverent. Thus failing to co-operate with God's grace, they hinder its effect. They lose the grace of holy fear of the Lord, which arouses and stimulates the will to obey the divine

commandments and to be alert in the avoidance of sin and pursuit of eternal life in the friendship of God. This is an evident danger for lukewarm priests, who frequent the holy Eucharist and other Sacraments, without fear and reverence; also for the learned and wise, and the powerful of this world, who so reluctantly correct and amend their lives. They have lost the appreciation and veneration of the remedial helps of the Church, namely, the Sacraments, preaching and instruction. Thus these medicines, which for other sinners are so salutary and counteract ignorance, weaken those who are the physicians of the spiritual life.

622. There are other reasons for this kind of danger, which must be referred to the Lord himself. For the sins of those souls who, by their state or by their advanced virtues, are more closely bound to their God, are weighed in the balance of God's justice in quite a different way from the sins of those who have been less favored by his mercy. Although the sins of all are more or less essentially the same, yet the circumstances of sin are very different. For the priests and teachers, the powerful and the dignitaries, and those who, on account of their station or by reputation, are supposed to be advanced in a holy life, cause great scandal by their fall or by any sins they commit. There is much more of bold disrespect in their presumption and temerity against God, whom they know better and to whom they owe much more, but whom they offend with more deliberation and knowledge than the ignorant. Hence, as is evident from the tenor of all the holy Scriptures, the sins of Catholics, and especially of those that are instructed and enlightened, are so displeasing to God. As the term of each man's life is preordained for each one as the time in which he is to gain the eternal reward,

so the measure or number of sins to be borne by the
patience or forbearance of the Lord is likewise pre-
ordained. This measure of divine justice is determined
not only by the number and quantity of the sins, but
also by their quality and weight. Thus it may happen,
that in the souls favored by greater enlightenment and
graces of heaven, the grievousness supplies what is wanting in the number of the sins, and that with fewer sins
they are forsaken sooner and chastised more severely than
others with many more sins. Nor can all expect for
themselves the same issue as David (II Reg. 12, 13) and
saint Peter; because not all of them have to their credit
as many good actions to be remembered by the Lord.
Besides the special privileges of some cannot be set up
as a rule for all others; because, according to the secret
judgments of the Lord, not all are destined for a special
office.

623. By this explanation, my dearest, thou wilt be
able to satisfy thy doubts and thou wilt understand what
a bitter evil so many souls incur, whom the Almighty
has redeemed by his blood, placed in the way of light
and drawn toward Himself; and how some persons can
fall from a more exalted state into more perverse obstinacy than others below them in station. This truth is
well illustrated in the mystery of my Son's Passion, in
which the priests, scribes and the whole people were
much more indebted to their God than the heathens, who
knew not of the true religion. I desire that this truth, as
exhibited by their example, convince thee of this terrible
danger and excite in thee holy fear. And with this fear
join humble thanks and an exalted esteem of the favors
of the Lord. In the days of abundance, be not unmind-
ful of the hour of want (Eccli. 13, 25). Ponder as well
the one as the other within thyself, and remember that

thou carriest thy treasure in a fragile vessel, which thou canst easily lose (II Cor. 4, 7). Know well, that the reception of such blessings argues not merit, and the possession of them is not due to thee in justice, but comes to thee by liberality and kindness. That the Most High has favored thee with so much familiar intercourse is no assurance that thou canst not fall, and no license to live carelessly and without reverence and fear. All things happen to thee according to the number and greatness of thy blessings; for the wrath of the serpent has increased toward thee in proportion, and is more alert against thee than against other souls. He has become aware that the Most High has not been so liberally loving to men of many generations as toward thee, and if thou meet so many blessings and mercies with ingratitude, thou shalt be most wretched and worthy of a rigorous punishment, against which thou canst make no objection.

CHAPTER XI

624. Pilate, aware of the obstinate hostility of the Jews against Jesus of Nazareth, and unwilling to condemn Him to death, of which he knew Him to be innocent, thought that a severe scourging of Jesus might placate the fury of the ungrateful people and soothe the envy of the priests and the scribes. If He should have failed in anything pertaining to their ceremonies and rites, they would probably consider Him sufficiently chastised and cease in their persecutions and in their clamors for his Death. Pilate was led to this belief by what they had told him in the course of his trial; for they had vainly and foolishly calumniated Christ of not observing the sabbath and other ceremonies, as is evident from his sermons reported by the Evangelists (John 9, 6). But Pilate was entirely wrong in his judgment and acted like an ignorant man; for neither could the Master of all holiness be guilty of any defect in the observance of that Law, which He had come not to abolish but to fulfill (Matth. 5, 7); nor even if the accusation had been true, would He have deserved such an outrageous punishment. For the laws of the Jews, far from demanding such an inhuman and cruel scourging, contained other regulations for atonement of the more common faults. In still greater error was this judge in expecting any mercy or natural kindness and compassion from the Jews. Their

174

anger and wrath against the most meek Master was not
human, not such as ordinarily is appeased by the overthrow and humiliation of the enemy.   For men have
hearts of flesh, and the love of their own kind is natural
and the source of at least some compassion.   But these
perfidious Jews were clothed in the guise of demons, or
rather transformed into demons, who exert the more
furious rage against those who are rendered more helpless and wretched; who, when they see any one most
helpless, say: let us pursue him now, since he has none to
defend nor free him from our hands.

625. Such was the implacable fury of the priests and
of their confederates, the pharisees, against the Author
of life.   For Lucifer, despairing of being able to hinder
his murder by the Jews, inspired them with his own
dreadful malice and outrageous cruelty.   Pilate, placed
between the known truth and his human and terrestrial
considerations, chose to follow the erroneous leading of
the latter, and order Jesus to be severely scourged, though
he had himself declared Him free from guilt (John 19,
1).   Thereupon those ministers of satan, with many
others, brought Jesus our Savior to the place of punishment, which was a courtyard or enclosure attached to
the house and set apart for the torture of criminals in
order to force them to confess their crimes.   It was
enclosed by a low, open building, surrounded by
columns, some of which supported the roof, while others
were lower and stood free.   To one of these columns,
which was of marble, they bound Jesus very securely;
for they still thought Him a magician and feared his
escape.

626. They first took off the white garment with not
less ignominy than when they clothed Him therein in
the house of the adulterous homicide Herod.   In loosen-

ing the ropes and chains, which He had borne since his capture in the garden, they cruelly widened the wounds which his bonds had made in his arms and wrists. Having freed his hands, they commanded Him with infamous blasphemies to despoil Himself of the seamless tunic which He wore. This was the identical garment with which his most blessed Mother had clothed Him in Egypt when He first began to walk, as I have related in its place. Our Lord at present had no other garment, since they had taken from Him his mantle, or cloak, when they seized Him in the garden. The Son of the eternal Father obeyed the executioners and began to unclothe Himself, ready to bear the shame of the exposure of his most sacred and modest body before such a multitude of people. But his tormentors, impatient at the delay which modesty required, tore away the tunic with violence in order to hasten his undressing and, as is said, flay the sheep with the wool. With the exception of a strip of cloth for a cincture, which He wore beneath the tunic and with which his Mother likewise had clothed Him in Egypt, the Lord stood now naked. These garments had grown with his sacred body, nor had He ever taken them off. The same is to be said of his shoes, which his Mother had placed on his feet. However, as I have said on a former occasion, He had many times walked barefooted during his preaching.

627. I understand that some of the doctors have said or have persuaded themselves, that our Savior Jesus at his scourging and at his crucifixion, for his greater humiliation, permitted the executioners to despoil Him of all his clothing. But having again been commanded under holy obedience to ascertain the truth in this matter, I was told that the divine Master was prepared to suffer all the insults compatible with decency; that the execu-

tioners attempted to subject his body to this shame of total nakedness, seeking to despoil Him of the cincture, which covered his loins; but in that they failed; because, on touching it, their arms became paralyzed and stiff, as had happened also in the house of Caiphas, when they attempted to take off his clothes (Chapt. XVII). All the six of his tormentors separately made the attempt with the same result. Yet afterwards, these ministers of evil, in order to scourge Him with greater effect, raised some of the coverings; for so much the Lord permitted, but not that He should be uncovered and despoiled of his garments entirely. The miracle of their being hindered and paralyzed in their brutal attempts did not, however, move or soften the hearts of these human beasts; but in their diabolical insanity they attributed it all to the supposed sorcery and witchcraft of the Author of truth and life.

628. Thus the Lord stood uncovered in the presence of a great multitude and the six torturers bound Him brutally to one of the columns in order to chastise Him so much the more at their ease. Then, two and two at a time, they began to scourge Him with such inhuman cruelty, as was possible only in men possessed by Lucifer, as were these executioners. The first two scourged the innocent Savior with hard and thick cords, full of rough knots, and in their sacrilegious fury strained all the powers of their body to inflict the blows. This first scourging raised in the deified body of the Lord great welts and livid tumors, so that the sacred blood gathered beneath the skin and disfigured his entire body. Already it began to ooze through the wounds. The first two having at length desisted, the second pair continued the scourging in still greater emulation; with hardened leather thongs they leveled their strokes upon the places already sore and caused the discolored tumors to break open

and shed forth the sacred blood until it bespattered and drenched the garments of the sacrilegious torturers, running down also in streams to the pavement. Those two gave way to the third pair of scourgers, who commenced to beat the Lord with extremely tough rawhides, dried hard like osier twigs. They scourged Him still more cruelly, because they were wounding, not so much his virginal body, as cutting into the wounds already produced by the previous scourging. Besides they had been secretly incited to greater fury by the demons, who were filled with new rage at the patience of Christ.

629. As the veins of the sacred body had now been opened and his whole Person seemed but one continued wound, the third pair found no more room for new wounds. Their ceaseless blows inhumanly tore the immaculate and virginal flesh of Christ our Redeemer and scattered many pieces of it about the pavement; so much so that a large portion of the shoulder-bones were exposed and showed red through the flowing blood; in other places also the bones were laid bare larger than the palm of the hand. In order to wipe out entirely that beauty, which exceeded that of all other men (Ps. 44, 3), they beat Him in the face and in the feet and hands, thus leaving unwounded not a single spot in which they could exert their fury and wrath against the most innocent Lamb. The divine blood flowed to the ground, gathering here and there in great abundance. The scourging in the face, and in the hands and feet, was unspeakably painful, because these parts are so full of sensitive and delicate nerves. His venerable countenance became so swollen and wounded that the blood and the swellings blinded Him. In addition to their blows the executioners spirted upon his Person their disgusting spittle and loaded Him with insulting epithets (Thren. 3, 30). The exact

number of blows dealt out to the Savior from head to
foot was 5,115.   The great Lord and Author of all creation who, by his divine nature was incapable of suffering,
was, in his human flesh and for our sake, reduced to a
man of sorrows as prophesied, and was made to experience our infirmities, becoming the last of men (Is. 53,
3), a man of sorrows and the outcast of the people.

630. The multitudes who had followed the Lord, filled
up the courtyard of Pilate's house and the surrounding
streets; for all of them waited for the issue of this event,
discussing and arguing about it according to each one's
views.   Amid all this confusion the Virgin Mother endured unheard of insults, and She was deeply afflicted by
the injuries and blasphemies heaped upon her divine Son
by the Jews and gentiles.   When they brought Jesus to
the scourging place She retired in the company of the
Marys and saint John to a corner of the courtyard.
Assisted by her divine visions, She there witnessed all
the scourging and the torments of our Savior.   Although
She did not see it with the eyes of her body nothing was
hidden to Her, no more than if She had been standing
quite near.   Human thoughts cannot comprehend how
great and how diverse were the afflictions and sorrows
of the great Queen and Mistress of the angels: together
with many other mysteries of the Divinity they shall
become manifest in the next life, for the glory of the
Son and Mother.   I have already mentioned in other
places of this history, and especially in that of the Passion, that the blessed Mother felt in her own body all
the torments of her Son.   This was true also of the
scourging, which She felt in all the parts of her virginal
body, in the same intensity as they were felt by Christ
in his body.   Although She shed no blood except what
flowed from her eyes with her tears, nor was lacerated

in her flesh; yet the bodily pains so changed and disfigured Her, that saint John and the holy women failed to find in Her any resemblance of Herself. Besides the tortures of the body She suffered ineffable sorrows of the soul; there sorrow was augmented in proportion to the immensity of her insight (Eccles. 1, 18). For her sorrows flowed not only from the natural love of a mother and a supreme love of Christ as her God, but it was proportioned to her power of judging more accurately than all creatures of the innocence of Christ, the dignity of his divine Person, the atrocity of the insults coming from the perfidious Jews and the children of Adam, whom He was freeing from eternal death.

631. Having at length executed the sentence of scourging, the executioners unbound the Lord from the column, and with imperious and blasphemous presumption commanded Him immediately to put on his garment. But while they had scourged the most meek Master, one of his tormentors, instigated by the devil, had hidden his clothes out of sight, in order to prolong the nakedness and exposure of his divine Person for their derision and sport. This evil purpose suggested by the devil, was well known to the Mother of the Lord. She therefore, making use of her power as Queen, commanded Lucifer and all his demons to leave the neighborhood, and immediately, compelled by her sovereign power and virtue, they fled. She gave orders that the tunic be brought by the holy angels within reach of her most holy Son, so that He could again cover his sacred and lacerated body. All this was immediately attended to, although the sacrilegious executioners understood not the miracle, nor how it had been wrought; they attributed it all to the sorcery and magic of the demon. During this protracted nakedness our Savior had, in addition to his wounds,

suffered greatly from the cold of that morning as mentioned by the Evangelists (Mark 14, 55; Luke 22, 35;
John 18, 18). His sacred blood had frozen and com-
pressed the wounds, which had become inflamed and
extremely painful; the cold had diminished his powers
of resistance, although the fire of his infinite charity
strained them to the utmost in order to suffer more and
more. Though compassion is so natural in rational creatures, there was none for Him in his affliction and necessity, except that of his sorrowful Mother, who tearfully
bewailed and pitied Him in the name of the whole human
race.

632. Among other divine mysteries, hidden to the
wise of this world, this also causes great astonishment,
that the wrath of the Jews, who were men of flesh and
blood like ourselves, should not have been appeased at
their seeing Christ torn and wounded by 5,115 lashes;
that the sight of a person so lacerated should not have
moved their natural compassion, but should arouse their
envy to inflict new and unheard of tortures upon the
Victim. Their implacable fury at once planned another
outrageous cruelty. They went to Pilate and in the
presence of his counselors said: "This seducer and de-
ceiver of the people, Jesus of Nazareth, in his boasting
and vanity, has sought to be recognized by all as the king
of the Jews. In order that his pride may be humbled
and his presumption be confounded, we desire your permission to place upon Him the royal insignia merited by
his fantastic pretensions." Pilate yielded to the unjust
demand of the Jews, permitting them to proceed according to their intentions.

633. Thereupon they took Jesus to the pretorium,
where, with the same cruelty and contempt, they again
despoiled him of his garments and in order to deride

Him before all the people as a counterfeit king, clothed Him in a much torn and soiled mantle of purple color. They placed also upon his sacred head a cap made of woven thorns, to serve Him as a crown (John 19, 2). This cap was woven of thorn branches and in such a manner that many of the hard and sharp thorns would penetrate into the skull, some of them to the ears and others to the eyes. Hence one of the greatest tortures suffered by the Lord was that of the crown of thorns. Instead of a sceptre they placed into his hands a contemptible reed. They also threw over His shoulders a violet colored mantle, something of the style of capes worn in churches; for such a garment belonged to the vestiture of a king. In this array of a mock-king the perfidious Jews decked out Him, who by his nature and by every right was the King of kings and the Lord of lords (Apoc. 19, 16). Then all the soldiers, in the presence of the priests and pharisees, gathered around Him and heaped upon Him their blasphemous mockery and derision. Some of them bent their knees and mockingly said to Him: God save Thee, King of the Jews. Others buffeted Him; others snatched the cane from his hands and struck Him on his crowned head; others ejected their disgusting spittle upon Him; all of them, instigated by furious demons, insulted and affronted Him in different manners.

634. O charity incomprehensible and exceeding all measure! O patience never seen or imagined among mortals! Who, O my Lord and God, since Thou art the true and mighty God both in essence and in thy works, who could oblige Thee to suffer the humiliation of such unheard of torments, insults and blasphemies? On the contrary, O my God, who among men has not done many things which offend Thee and which should have caused

Thee to refuse suffering and to deny them thy favor? Who could ever believe all this, if we knew not of thy infinite goodness. But now, since we see it and in firm faith look upon such admirable blessings and miracles of love, where is our judgment? what effect upon us has the light of truth? What enchantment is this that we suffer, since at the very sight of thy sorrows, scourges, thorns, insults and affronts, we seek for ourselves, without the least shame or fear, the delights, the riches, the ease, the preferments and vanities of this world? Truly, great is the number of fools (Eccles. 1, 15), since the greatest foolishness and dishonesty is to recognize a debt and be unwilling to pay it; to receive blessings and never give thanks for them; to have before one's eyes the greater good, and despise it; to claim it for ourselves and make no use of it; to turn away and fly from life, and seek eternal death. The most innocent Jesus opened not his mouth in those great and many injuries. Nor was the furious wrath of the Jews appeased, either by the mockery and derision of the divine Master, or by the torments added to the contempt of his most exalted Person.

635. It seemed to Pilate that the spectacle of a man so illtreated as Jesus of Nazareth would move and fill with shame the hearts of that ungrateful people. He therefore commanded Jesus to be brought from the pretorium to an open window, where all could see Him crowned with thorns, disfigured by the scourging and the ignominious vestiture of a mock-king. Pilate himself spoke to the people, calling out to them: "Ecce Homo," "Behold, what a man!" (John 19, 5). See this Man, whom you hold as your enemy! What more can I do with Him than to have punished Him in this severe manner? You certainly have nothing more to fear from Him. I do not find any cause of death in

Him. What this judge said was certainly the full truth; but in his own words he condemned his outrageous injustice, since, knowing and confessing that this Man was just and not guilty of death, he had nevertheless ordered Him to be tormented and punished in such a way that, according to the natural course, he should have been killed many times over. O blindness of self-love! O hellish malice of estimating only the influence of those, who can confer or take away mere earthly dignities! How deeply do such motives obscure the reason, how much do they twist the course of justice, how completely do they pervert the greatest truths in judging of the just by the standards of the unjust! Tremble, ye judges of the earth (Ps. 2, 10), look to it that the sentences you render are not full of deceit; for you yourselves shall be judged and condemned by your unjust judgments! As the priests and pharisees, in their eager and insatiable hostility, were irrevocably bent upon taking away the life of Christ our Savior, nothing but his Death would content or satisfy them; therefore they answered Pilate: "Crucify Him, Crucify Him!" (John 19, 6.)

636. When the Blessed among women, most holy Mary, saw her divine Son as Pilate showed Him to the people and heard him say: "Ecce homo!" She fell upon her knees and openly adored Him as the true Godman. The same was also done by saint John and the holy women, together with all the holy angels of the Queen and Lady; for they saw that not only Mary, as the Mother of the Savior, but that God himself desired them thus to act. The most prudent Lady spoke to the eternal Father, to the angels and especially to her most beloved Son precious words of sorrow, compassion and profound reverence, possible to be conceived only in her chaste

and love inflamed bosom. In her exalted wisdom She pondered also the ways and means by which the evidences of his innocence could be made most opportunely manifest at a time when He was so insulted, mocked and despised by the Jews. With this most proper intention She renewed the petitions above mentioned, namely, that Pilate, in his quality of judge, continue to maintain the innocence of Jesus our Redeemer and that all the world should understand, that Jesus was not guilty of death nor of any of the crimes imputed to Him by the Jews.

637. On account of these prayers of the most blessed Mother Pilate was made to feel great compassion at seeing Jesus so horribly scourged and illtreated and regret at having punished Him so severely. Although he was naturally disposed to such emotions by his soft and compassionate disposition; yet they were principally caused by the light he received through the intercession of the Queen and Mother of grace. This same light moved the unjust judge after the crowning of thorns to prolong his parley with the Jews for the release of Christ, as is recorded in the nineteenth chapter of the Gospel of saint John. When they again asked him to crucify the Lord, he answered: "Take Him yourselves and crucify Him, for I do not find any cause for doing it." They replied: "According to our law He is guilty of death, for He claims to be the Son of God." This reply threw Pilate into greater consternation, for he conceived it might be true, that Jesus was the Son of God according to his heathen notions of the Divinity. Therefore he withdrew with Jesus into the pretorium, where, speaking with Him alone, he asked whence He was? The Lord did not answer this question; for Pilate was not in a state of mind either to understand or to merit a reply. Never-

theless he insisted and said to the King of heaven: "Dost Thou then not speak to me? Dost Thou not know, that I have power to crucify Thee and power to dismiss Thee?" Pilate sought to move Him to defend Himself and tell what he wanted to know. It seemed to Pilate that a man so wretched and tormented would gladly accept any offer of favor from a judge.

638. But the Master of truth answered Pilate without defending Himself but with unexpected dignity; for He said: "Thou shouldst not have any power against Me, unless it were given thee from above. Therefore, he that hath delivered Me to thee, hath the greater sin." This answer by itself made the condemnation of Christ inexcusable in Pilate; since he could have understood therefrom, that neither he nor Cæsar had any power of jurisdiction over this man Jesus; that by a much higher decree He had been so unreasonably and unjustly delivered over to his judgment; that therefore Judas and the priests had committed a greater sin than he in not releasing Him; and that nevertheless He too was guilty of the same crime, though not in such high degree. Pilate failed to arrive at these mysterious truths; but he was struck with still greater consternation at the words of Christ our Lord, and therefore made still more strenuous efforts to liberate Him. The priests, who were now abundantly aware of his intentions, threatened him with the displeasure of the emperor, which he would incur, if he permitted this One, who had aspired to be king, to escape death. They said: "If thou freest this Man, thou art no friend of Cæsar; since he who makes a king of himself rises up against his orders and commands." They urged this because the Roman emperors never permitted anyone in the whole empire to assume the title or insignia of a King without their consent and order; if therefore

Pilate should permit it, he would contravene the decrees of Cæsar. He was much disturbed at this malicious and threatening intimation of the Jews, and seating himself in his tribunal at the sixth hour in order to pass sentence upon the Lord, he once more turned to plead with the Jews, saying: "See there your King!" And all of them answered: "Away with Him, away with Him, crucify Him!" He replied: "Shall I crucify your King?" Whereupon they shouted unanimously: "We have no other king than Cæsar."

639. Pilate permitted himself to be overcome by the obstinacy and malice of the Jews. On the day of Parasceve then, seated in his tribunal, which in Greek was called lithostratos, and in Hebrew gabatha, he pronounced the sentence of death against the Author of life, as I shall relate in the following chapter. The Jews departed from the hall in great exultation and joy, proclaiming the sentence of the most innocent Lamb. That they did not realize whom they thus sought to annihilate was the occasion of our Redemption. All this was well known to the sorrowful Mother, who, though outside of the hall of judgment, saw all the proceedings by exalted vision. When the priests and pharisees rushed forth exulting in the condemnation of Christ to the death of the Cross, the pure heart of this most blessed Mother was filled with new sorrow and was pierced and transfixed with the sword of unalleviated bitterness. Since the sorrow of most holy Mary on this occasion surpassed all that can enter the thoughts of man, it is useless to speak more of it, and it must be referred to the pious meditation of Christians. Just as impossible is it to enumerate her interior acts of adoration, worship, reverence, love, compassion, sorrow and resignation.

640. My daughter, thou reflectest with wonder upon the hardness and malice of the Jews, the weakness of Pilate, who knew of their evil dispositions and permitted himself to be overcome, though fully convinced of the innocence of my Son and Lord. I wish to relieve thee of this astonishment by furnishing thee with instructions and warnings suitable for making thee careful on the path to eternal life. Know then that the ancient prophecies concerning the mysteries of the Redemption and all the holy Scriptures were to be infallibly fulfilled; for sooner shall heaven and earth fall to pieces, than that their words fail of their effect as determined in the divine Mind (Matth. 24, 35; Acts 3, 18). In order that the most ignominious death foretold for my Lord should be brought about (Sap. 2, 20; Jer. 11, 19) it was necessary that He should be persecuted by men. But that these men should happen to be the Jews, the priests and the unjust Pilate, was their own misfortune, not the choice of the Almighty, who wishes to save all (I Tim. 2, 4). Their own wickedness and malice brought them to their ruin; for they resisted the great grace of having in their midst their Redeemer and Master, of knowing Him, of conversing with Him, of hearing his doctrine and preaching, of witnessing his miracles; and they had received such great favors, as none of the ancient Patriarchs had attained by all their longings (Matth. 13, 7). Hence the cause of the Savior was justified. He manifestly had cultivated his vineyard by his own hands and showered his favors upon it (Matth. 21, 33). But it brought Him only thorns and briars, and its keepers took away his life, refusing to recognize Him, as was their opportunity and their duty before all other men.

641. This same, which happened in the head Christ the Lord and Son of God, must happen to all the members of his mystical body, that is, to the just and predestined to the end of the world. For it would be monstrous to see the members incongruous with the Head, the children show no relation with the Father, or the disciples unlike their Master. Although sinners must always exist (Matth. 18, 7), since in this world the just shall always be mingled with the unjust, the predestined with the reprobate, the persecutors with the persecuted, the murderers with the murdered, the afflicting with the afflicted; yet these lots are decided by the malice and the goodness of men. Unhappy shall be he, through whom scandal comes into the world and who thus makes himself an instrument of the demon. This kind of activity was begun in the new Church by the priests and pharisees, and by Pilate, who all persecuted the Head of this mystic body and, in the further course of the world, by all those who persecute its members, the saints and the predestined, imitating and following the Jews and the devil in their evil work.

642. Think well, then, my dearest, which of these lots thou wishest to choose in the sight of my Son and me. If thou seest thy Redeemer, thy Spouse and thy Chief tormented, afflicted, crowned with thorns and saturated with reproaches and at the same time desirest to have a part in Him and be a member of his mystical body, it is not becoming, or even possible, that thou live steeped in the pleasures of the flesh. Thou must be the persecuted and not a persecutor, the oppressed and not the oppressor; the one that bears the cross, that encounters the scandal, and not that gives it; the one that suffers, and at the same time makes none of the neighbors suffer. On the contrary, thou must exert thyself for their conversion and

salvation in as far as is compatible with the perfection of thy state and vocation. This is the portion of the friends of God and the inheritance of his children in mortal life; in this consists the participation in grace and glory, which by his torments and reproaches and by his death of the Cross my Son and Lord has purchased for them. I too have co-operated in this work and have paid the sorrows and afflictions, which thou hast understood and which I wish thou shalt never allow to be blotted out from my inmost memory. The Almighty would indeed have been powerful enough to exalt his predestined in this world, to give them riches and favors beyond those of others, to make them strong as lions for reducing the rest of mankind to their invincible power. But it was inopportune to exalt them in this manner, in order that men might not be led into the error of thinking that greatness consists in what is visible and happiness in earthly goods; lest, being induced to forsake virtues and obscure the glory of the Lord, they fail to experience the efficacy of divine grace and cease to aspire toward spiritual and eternal things. This is the science which I wish thee to study continually and in which thou must advance day by day, putting into practice all that thou learnest to understand and know.

CHAPTER XII

643. To the great satisfaction and joy of the priests and pharisees Pilate then decreed the sentence of death on the Cross against Life itself, Jesus our Savior. Hav· ing announced it to the One they had thus condemned in spite of his innocence, they brought Him to another part of the house of Pilate, where they stripped Him of the purple mantle, in which they had derided Him as mock-king. All happened by the mysterious dispensation of God; though on their part it was due to the concerted malice of the Jews; for they wished to see Him undergo the punishment of the Cross in his own clothes so that in them He might be recognized by all. Only by his garments could He now be recognized by the people, since his face had been disfigured beyond recognition by the scourging, the impure spittle, and the crown of thorns. They again clothed Him with the seamless tunic, which at the command of the Queen was brought to Him by the angels; for the executioners had thrown it into a corner of another room in the house, where they left it to place upon Him the mocking and scandalous purple cloak. But the Jews neither understood nor noticed any of these circumstances, since they

191

were too much taken up with the desire of hastening his Death.

644. Through the diligence of the Jews in spreading the news of the sentence decreed against Jesus of Nazareth, the people hastened in multitudes to the house of Pilate in order to see Him brought forth to execution. Since the ordinary number of inhabitants was increased by the gathering of numerous strangers from different parts to celebrate the Pasch, the city was full of people. All of them were stirred by the news and filled the streets up to the very palace of Pilate. It was a Friday, the day of the Parasceve, which in Greek signifies preparation, or getting ready; for on that day the Jews prepared themselves, or got ready, for the ensuing Sabbath, their greatest feast, on which no servile work was to be performed, not even such as cooking meals; all this had to be done on this Friday. In the sight of all these multitudes they brought forth our Savior in his own garments and with a countenance so disfigured by wounds, blood and spittle, that no one would have again recognized Him as the One they had seen or known before. At the command of his afflicted Mother the holy angels had a few times wiped off some of the impure spittle; but his enemies had so persistently continued in their disgusting insults, that now He appeared altogether covered by their vile expectorations. At the sight of such a sorrowful spectacle a confused shouting and clamor arose from the people, so that nothing could be understood, but all formed one uproar and confusion of voices. But above all the rest were heard the shouts of the priests and pharisees, who in their unrestrained joy and exultation harangued the people to become quiet and clear the streets through which the divine Victim was to pass, in order that they might hear the

sentence of death proclaimed against Him. The people
were divided and confused in their opinions, according
to the suggestions of their own hearts. At this spectacle
were present different kinds of people, who had been
benefited and succored by the miracles and the kindness
of Jesus, and such as had heard and accepted his teachings and had become his followers and friends. These
now showed their sympathy, some in bitter tears, others
by asking what this Man had done to deserve such punishment; others were dumbfounded and began to be
troubled and confused by this universal confusion and
tumult.

645. Of the eleven Apostles saint John alone was
present. He with the sorrowful Mother and the three
Marys stood within sight of the Lord, though in a
retired corner. When the holy Apostle saw his divine
Master brought forth, the thought of whose love toward
himself now shot through his mind, he was so filled with
grief, that his blood congealed in his veins and his face
took on the appearance of death. The three Marys fell
away into a prolonged swoon. But the Queen of virtues
remained unconquered and her magnanimous heart,
though overwhelmed by a grief beyond all conception of
man, never fainted or swooned; She did not share the
imperfections or weaknesses of the others. In all her
actions She was most prudent, courageous and admirable; calmly She comforted saint John and the pious
women. She besought the Lord to strengthen them, in
order that She might have their company to the end
of the Passion. In virtue of this prayer the Apostle and
the holy women were consoled and encouraged, so that
they regained their senses and could speak to the Mistress of heaven. Amid all this bitterness and confusion
She did nothing unbecoming or inconsiderate, but shed

forth incessant tears with the dignity of a Queen. Her attention was riveted upon Her Son, the true God; She prayed to the eternal Father and offered to Him his sorrows and torments, imitating in her actions all that was done by our Savior. She recognized the malice of sin, penetrated the mysteries of the Redemption, appealed to the angels and interceded for friends and enemies. While giving way to her maternal love and to the sorrows corresponding to it, She at the same time practiced all the virtues, exciting the highest admiration of all heaven and delighting in the highest degree the eternal Godhead. Since it is not possible for me to describe the sentiments filling the heart of this Mother of wisdom, nor those at times also uttered by her lips, I leave them to be imagined by Christian piety.

646. The servants and priests sought to quiet the multitudes, in order that they might be able to hear the sentence pronounced against Jesus of Nazareth; for after it had been made known to Him in person, they desired to have it read before the people and in his presence. When the people had quieted down, they began to read it in a loud voice, so that all could hear it, while Jesus was standing in full view as a criminal. The sentence was proclaimed also in the different streets and at the foot of the Cross; and it was afterwards published and spread in many copies. According to the understanding given to me, the copies were a faithful reproduction, excepting some words which have been added. I will not discuss them, for the exact words of this sentence have been shown me and I give them here without change.

LITERAL RENDERING OF THE SENTENCE OF DEATH PRONOUNCED AGAINST JESUS OF NAZARETH, OUR SAVIOR.

647. "I Pontius Pilate, presiding over lower Galilee and governing Jerusalem, in fealty to the Roman Empire, and being within the executive mansion, judge, decide, and proclaim, that I condemn to death, Jesus, of the Nazarean people and a Galileean by birth, a man seditious and opposed to our laws, to our senate, and to the great emperor Tiberius Cæsar. For the execution of this sentence I decree, that his death be upon the cross and that He shall be fastened thereto with nails as is customary with criminals; because, in this very place, gathering around Him every day many men, poor and rich, He has continued to raise tumults throughout Judea, proclaiming Himself the Son of God and King of Israel, at the same time threatening the ruin of this renowned city of Jerusalem and its temple, and of the sacred Empire, refusing tribute to Cæsar; and because He dared to enter in triumph this city of Jerusalem and the temple of Solomon, accompanied by a great multitude of the people carrying branches of palms. I command the first centurion, called Quintus Cornelius, to lead Him for his greater shame through the said city of Jerusalem, bound as He is, and scourged by my orders. Let Him also wear his own garments, that He may be known to all, and let Him carry the Cross on which He is to be crucified. Let Him walk through all the public streets between two other thieves, who are likewise condemned to death for their robberies and murders, so that this punishment be an example to all the people and to all malefactors."

"I desire also and command in this my sentence, that this malefactor, having been thus led through the public streets, be brought outside the city through the pagora gate, now called the Antonian portal, and under the proclamations of the herald, who shall mention all the crimes pointed out in my sentence, He shall be conducted to the summit of the mountain called Calvary, where justice is wont to be executed upon wicked transgressors. There, fastened and crucified upon the Cross, which He shall carry as decreed above, his body shall remain between the aforesaid thieves. Above the Cross, that is, at its top, He shall have placed for Him his name and title in the three languages; namely in Hebrew, Greek and Latin; and in all and each one of them shall be written: THIS IS JESUS OF NAZARETH, KING OF THE JEWS, so that it may be understood by all and become universally known."

"At the same time I command, that no one, no matter of what condition, under pain of the loss of his goods and life, and under punishment for rebellion against the Roman empire, presume audaciously to impede the execution of this just sentence ordered by me to be executed with all rigor according to the decrees and laws of the Romans and Hebrews. Year of the creation of the world 5233, the twenty-fifth day of March."

Pontius Pilatus Judex et Gubernator Galilaeae inferioris
    pro Romano Imperio qui supra propria manu.

(Pontius Pilate, Judge and Governor of lower Galilee
    for the Roman Empire, who signed the above with
    his own hand.)

648. According to the above reckoning the creation of

the world happened in March; and from the day on
which Adam was created until the Incarnation of the
Word 5199 years; adding the nine months, during which
He remained in the virginal womb of his most holy
Mother, and the thirty-three years of his life, we complete the 5233 years and three months, which according
to the reckoning of the Romans intervened between the
anniversary of his birth and the 25th of March, the day
of his death. According to the reckoning of the Roman
Church there are not more than nine months and seven
days to the first year, since it begins its count of years
with the first of January of the second year of the world.
Of all the opinions of the teachers of the Church I have
understood the one which corresponds to the reckoning
of the Roman Church in the Roman martyrology to be
the correct one. This I have also stated in the chapter of
the Incarnation of Christ our Lord in the first book of
the second part, chapter eleventh.

649. The sentence of Pilate against our Savior having
been published in a loud voice before all the people, the
executioners loaded the heavy Cross, on which He was
to be crucified, upon his tender and wounded shoulders.
In order that He might carry it they loosened the bonds
holding his hands, but not the others, since they wished
to drag Him along by the loose ends of the ropes that
bound his body. In order to torment Him the more
they drew two loops around his throat. The Cross was
fifteen feet long, of thick and heavy timbers. The herald
began to proclaim the sentence and the whole confused
and turbulent multitude of the people, the executioners
and soldiers, with great noise, uproar and disorder began
to move from the house of Pilate to mount Calvary
through the streets of Jerusalem. The Master and Redeemer of the world, Jesus, before receiving the Cross,

looked upon it with a countenance full of extreme joy and exultation such as would be shown by a bridegroom looking at the rich adornments of his bride, and on receiving it, He addressed it as follows:

650. "O Cross, beloved of my soul, now prepared and ready to still my longings, come to Me, that I may be received in thy arms, and that, attached to them as on an altar, I may be accepted by the eternal Father as the sacrifice of his everlasting reconciliation with the human race. In order to die upon thee, I have descended from heaven and assumed mortal and passible flesh; for thou art to be the sceptre with which I shall triumph over all my enemies, the key with which I shall open the gates of heaven for all the predestined (Is. 22, 22), the sanctuary in which the guilty sons of Adam shall find mercy, and the treasurehouse for the enrichment of their poverty. Upon thee I desire to exalt and recommend dishonor and reproach among men, in order that my friends may embrace them with joy, seek them with anxious longings, and follow Me on the path which I through thee shall open up before them. My Father and eternal God, I confess Thee as the Lord of heaven and earth (Matth. 11, 25), subjecting Myself to thy power and to thy divine wishes, I take upon my shoulders the wood for the sacrifice of my innocent and passible humanity and I accept it willingly for the salvation of men. Receive Thou, eternal Father, this sacrifice as acceptable to thy justice, in order that from today on they may not any more be servants, but sons and heirs of thy kingdom together with Me" (Rom. 8, 17).

651. None of these sacred mysteries and happenings were hidden from the great Lady of the world, Mary; for She had a most intimate knowledge and understanding of them, far beyond that of all the angels. The

events, which She could not see with the eyes of her body, She perceived by her intelligence and revealed science, which manifested to Her the interior operation of her most holy Son. By this divine light She recognized the infinite value of the wood of the Cross after once it had come in contact with the deified humanity of Jesus our Redeemer. Immediately She venerated and adored it in a manner befitting it. The same was also done by the heavenly spirits attending upon the Queen. She imitated her divine Son in the tokens of affections, with which He received the Cross, addressing it in the words suited to her office as Coadjutrix of the Redeemer. By her prayers to the eternal Father She followed Him in his exalted sentiments as the living original and exemplar, without failing in the least point. When She heard the voice of the herald publishing and rehearsing the sentence through the streets, the heavenly Mother, in protest against the accusations contained in the sentence and in the form of comments on the glory and honor of the Lord, composed a canticle of praise and worship of the innocence and sinlessness of her all-holy Son and God. In the composing of this canticle the holy angels helped Her, conjointly with them She arranged and repeated it, while the inhabitants of Jerusalem were blaspheming their own Creator and Savior.

652. As all the faith, knowledge and love of creatures, during this time of the Passion, was enshrined in its highest essence in the magnanimous soul of the Mother of wisdom, She alone had the most proper conception and correct judgment of the suffering and Death of God for men. Without for a moment failing in the attention necessary to exterior actions, her wisdom penetrated all the mysteries of the Redemption and the manner in which it was to be accomplished through the ignorance

of the very men who were to be redeemed.   She entered into the deepest consideration of the dignity of the One, who was suffering, of what He was suffering, from and for whom He was suffering.   Of the dignity of the person of Christ our Redeemer, uniting within Himself the divine and the human natures, of their perfections and attributes, the most blessed Mary alone possessed the highest and intuitive knowledge outside of the Lord himself.   On this account She alone among all mere creatures attached sufficient importance to the Passion and Death of her Son and of the true God.   Of what He suffered, She was not only an eye-witness, but She experienced it personally within Herself, occasioning the holy envy not only of men, but of the angels themselves, who were not thus favored.   But they well knew that their great Queen and Mistress felt and suffered in soul and body the same torments and sorrows as her most holy Son and that the holy Trinity was inexpressibly pleased with Her; and therefore they sought to make up by their praise and worship for the pains which they could not share.   Sometimes, when the sorrowful Mother could not personally witness the sufferings of her Son, She was made to feel in her virginal body and in her spirit the effects of his torments before her intelligence made Her aware of them.   Thus surprised She would say: "Ah! what new martyrdom have they devised for my sweetest Lord and Master?"   And then She would receive the clearest knowledge of what the Lord was enduring.   The most loving Mother was so admirably faithful in her sufferings and in imitating the example of Christ our God, that She never permitted Herself any easement either of her bodily pains, such as rest, or nourishment, or sleep; nor any relaxation of the spirit, such as any consoling thoughts or considerations, except when She was visited from on high by divine influence. Then only would She humbly and thankfully accept relief, in order that She might recover strength to attend still more fervently to the object of her sorrows and to the cause of his sufferings. The same wise consideration She applied to the malicious behavior of the Jews and their servants, to the needs of the human race, to their threatening ruin, and to the ingratitude of men, for whom He suffered. Thus She perfectly and intimately knew of all these things and felt it more deeply than all the creatures.

653. Another hidden and astonishing miracle was wrought by the right hand of God through the instrumentality of the blessed Mary against Lucifer and his infernal spirits. It took place in the following manner: The dragon and his associates, though they could not understand the humiliation of the Lord, were most attentive to all that happened in the Passion of the Lord. Now, when He took upon Himself the Cross, all these enemies felt a new and mysterious tremor and weakness, which caused in them great consternation and confused distress. Conscious of these unwonted and invincible feelings the prince of darkness feared, that in the Passion and Death of Christ our Lord some dire and irreparable destruction of his reign was imminent. In order not to be overtaken by it in the presence of Christ our God, the dragon resolved to retire and fly with all his followers to the caverns of hell. But when he sought to execute this resolve, he was prevented by the great Queen and Mistress of all creation; for the Most High, enlightening Her and intimating to Her what She was to do, at the same time invested Her with his power. The heavenly Mother, turning toward Lucifer and his squadrons, by her imperial command hindered them

from flying; ordering them to await and witness the Passion to the end on mount Calvary. The demons could not resist the command of the mighty Queen; for they recognized and felt the divine power operating in Her. Subject to her sway they followed Christ as so many prisoners dragged along in chains to Calvary, where the eternal wisdom had decreed to triumph over them from the throne of the Cross, as we shall see later on. There is nothing which can exemplify the discouragement and dismay, which from that moment began to oppress Lucifer and his demons. According to our way of speaking, they walked along to Calvary like criminals condemned to a terrible death, and seized by the dismay and consternation of an inevitable punishment. This punishment of the demon was in conformity with his malicious nature and proportioned to the evil committed by him in introducing death and sin into the world, to remedy which, God himself was now undergoing Death.

654. Our Savior proceeded on the way to Calvary bearing upon his shoulders, according to the saying of Isaias, his own government and principality (Is. 9, 6), which was none else than his Cross, from whence He was to subject and govern the world, meriting thereby that his name should be exalted above all other names and rescuing the human race from the tyrannical power of the demon over the sons of Adam (Col. 2, 15). The same Isaias calls it the yoke and sceptre of the oppressor and executor, who was imperiously exacting the tribute of the first guilt. In order to destroy this tyrant and break the sceptre of his reign and the yoke of our servitude, Christ our Savior placed the Cross upon his shoulders; namely, upon that place, where are borne both the yoke of slavery and the sceptre of royal power.

He wished to intimate thereby, that He despoiled the
demon of this power and transferred it to his own
shoulders, in order that thenceforward the captive children of Adam should recognize Him for their legitimate
Lord and true King. All mortals were to follow Him in
the way of the Cross (Matth. 14, 24) and learn, that
by this Cross they were subjected to his power (John 12,
32) and now become his vassals and servants, bought
by his own life-blood (I Cor. 4, 20).

655. But alas, the pity of our most ungrateful forgetfulness! That the Jews and ministers of the Passion
should be ignorant of this mystery hidden to princes of
this world, and that they should not dare touch the
Cross of the Savior, because they considered it the
wood of ignominy and shame, was their own fault and
a very great one. Yet not so great as our own, since
its mystery being already revealed to us, we spend our
indignation only on the blindness of those who were
persecuting our Lord and God. For, if we blame them
for being ignorant of what they ought to have known,
how much should we blame ourselves, who, knowing and
confessing Christ the Redeemer, persecute and crucify
Him by our offenses (Heb. 6, 6)? O my sweetest Love,
Jesus, light of my intellect and glory of my soul! Do
not, O my Lord, trust in my sluggish torpidity to follow
Thee with my Cross on thy way! Take it upon Thee
to do me this favor; draw me after Thee, to run after
the fragrance of thy sweetest love (Cant. 1, 3) of thy
ineffable patience, of thy deepest humility, that I may
desire for contempt and anguish, and seek after participation in thy ignominy, insults and sorrows. Let this
be my portion and my inheritance in this mortal and
oppressing life, let this be my glory and my repose;
and outside of the Cross and its ignominy, I desire not

to live or be consoled or to partake of any rest or enjoyment. As the Jews and all of that blind multitude avoided the touch of the Cross of Him, who was so innocently sentenced to die upon it, He opened with it a passage and cleared for Himself a way. His perfidious persecutors looked upon his glorious dishonor as a contagion and they fled from its approach, though all the rest of the streets were full of shouting and clamoring people, who crowded aside as the herald advanced proclaiming the sentence.

656. The executioners, bare of all human compassion and kindness, dragged our Savior Jesus along with incredible cruelty and insults. Some of them jerked Him forward by the ropes in order to accelerate his passage, while others pulled from behind in order to retard it. On account of this jerking and the weight of the Cross they caused Him to sway to and fro and often to fall to the ground. By the hard knocks He thus received on the rough stones great wounds were opened, especially on the two knees and they were widened at each repeated fall. The heavy Cross also inflicted a wound on the shoulder on which it was carried. The unsteadiness caused the Cross sometimes to knock against his sacred head, and sometimes the head against the Cross; thus the thorns of his crown penetrated deeper and wounded the parts, which they had not yet reached. To these torments of the body the ministers of evil added many insulting words and execrable affronts, ejecting their impure spittle and throwing the dirt of the pavement into his face so mercilessly, that they blinded the eyes that looked upon them with such divine mercy. Thus they of their own account condemned themselves to the loss of the graces, with which his very looks were fraught. By the haste with which they dragged Him

along in their eagerness to see Him die, they did not allow Him to catch his breath; for his most innocent body, having been in so few hours overwhelmed with such a storm of torments, was so weakened and bruised, that to all appearances He was ready to yield up life under his pains and sorrows.

657. From the house of Pilate the sorrowful and stricken Mother followed with the multitudes on the way of her divine Son, accompanied by saint John and the pious women. As the surging crowds hindered Her from getting very near to the Lord, She asked the eternal Father to be permitted to stand at the foot of the Cross of her blessed Son and see Him die with her own eyes. With the divine consent She ordered her holy angels to manage things in such a way as to make it possible for Her to execute her wishes. The holy angels obeyed Her with great reverence; and they speedily led the Queen through some bystreet, in order that She might meet her Son. Thus it came that both of Them met face to face in sweetest recognition of each Other and in mutual renewal of each other's interior sorrows. Yet They did not speak to one another, nor would the fierce cruelty of the executioners have permitted such an intercourse. But the most prudent Mother adored her divine Son and true God, laden with the Cross; and interiorly besought Him, that, since She could not relieve Him of the weight of the Cross and since She was not permitted to command her holy angels to lighten it, He would inspire these ministers of cruelty to procure some one for his assistance. This prayer was heard by the Lord Christ; and so it happened, that Simon of Cyrene was afterwards impressed to carry the Cross with the Lord (Matth. 27, 32). The pharisees and the executioners were moved to this meas-

ure, some of them out of natural compassion, others for fear lest Christ, the Author of life, should lose his life by exhaustion before it could be taken from Him on the Cross.

658. Beyond all human thought and estimation was the sorrow of the most sincere Dove and Virgin Mother while She thus witnessed with her own eyes her Son carrying the Cross to Mount Calvary; for She alone could fittingly know and love Him according to his true worth. It would have been impossible for Her to live through this ordeal, if the divine power had not strengthened Her and preserved Her life. With bitterest sorrow She addressed the Lord and spoke to Him in her heart: "My Son and eternal God, light of my eyes and life of my soul, receive, O Lord, the sacrifice of my not being able to relieve Thee of the burden of the Cross and carry it myself, who am a daughter of Adam; for it is I who should die upon it in love of Thee, as Thou now wishest to die in most ardent love of the human race. O most loving Mediator between guilt and justice! How dost Thou cherish mercy in the midst of so great injuries and such heinous offenses! O charity without measure or bounds, which permits such torments and affronts in order to afford it a wider scope for its ardor and efficacy! O infinite and sweetest love, would that the hearts and the wills of men were all mine, so that they could give no such thankless return for all that Thou endurest! O who will speak to the hearts of the mortals to teach them what they owe to Thee, since Thou hast paid so dearly for their salvation from ruin!" Other most prudent and exalted sentiments besides these were conceived by the great Lady, so that I cannot express them by words of mine.

659. As the Evangelist tells us, there were other

women among the crowds, who followed the Savior in bitter tears and lamentations (Luke 23, 27). The sweetest Jesus turning toward them, addressed them and said: "Daughters of Jerusalem, weep not over Me; but weep for yourselves and for your children. For behold, the days shall come, wherein they shall say: Blessed are the barren, and the wombs that have not borne, and the paps that have not given suck. Then shall they begin to say to the mountains: Fall upon us, and to the hills: Cover us. For if in the green wood they do these things, what shall be done in the dry?" By these mysterious words the Lord acknowledged the tears shed on account of his Passion, and to a certain extent, by showing his appreciation of them, He approved of them. In these women He wished to teach us for what purpose our tears should be shed so that they may attain their end. These compassionate disciples of the Lord were at that time ignorant of the true reason for their tears, since they wept over his sufferings and injuries, and not over the cause of these sufferings; and therefore they merited to be instructed and admonished of the truth. It was as if the Savior had said to them: Weep over your sins and over the sins of your children, and attribute what I suffer to those sins. I suffer not for my sins, for I am guilty of none and it is not even possible that I be guilty of any. If I approve of your compassion for Me as good and just, much more do I desire you to weep over your sins, for which I suffer, and by this manner of weeping you shall acquire for yourselves and your children the price of my blood and of my Redemption, ignored by this blind people. For there shall come days, namely the days of universal judgment and chastisement, in which those shall be held fortunate, who have not begotten children; and the foreknown shall call upon the mountains and the hills to shield them against my wrath. For if their sins, now only assumed by Me, have such effects on me, who am innocent, what horrible punishments will they draw upon those, who are so barren and without any fruits of grace and merits?

660. As a reward for their tears and their compassion these women were enlightened so as to understand this doctrine. In fulfillment of the prayerful wish of the blessed Mother the pharisees and ministers were inspired with the resolve to engage some man to help Jesus our Savior in carrying the Cross to mount Calvary. At this juncture, Simon, of Cyrene, the father of the disciples Alexander and Rufus (Mark 15, 21), happened to come along. He was called by this name because he was a native of Cyrene, a city of Lybia, and had come to Jerusalem. This Simon was now forced by the Jews to carry the Cross a part of the way. They themselves would not touch it, yea would not even come near it, as being the instrument of punishment for One whom they held to be a notorious malefactor. By this pretended caution and avoidance of his Cross they sought to impress the people with a horror for Jesus. The Cyrenean took hold of the Cross and Jesus was made to follow between the two thieves, in order that all might believe Him to be a criminal and malefactor like to them. The Virgin Mother walked very closely behind Jesus, as She had desired and asked from the eternal Father. To his divine will She so conformed Herself in all the labors and torments of her Son that, witnessing with her own eyes and partaking of all the sufferings of her Son in her blessed soul and in her body, She never allowed any sentiment or wish to arise interiorly or exteriorly, which could be interpreted as regret for the sacrifice She

had made in offering her Son for the death of the Cross and its sufferings. Her charity and love of men, and her grace and holiness, were so great, that She vanquished all these movements of her human nature.

INSTRUCTION WHICH THE GREAT QUEEN AND LADY GAVE ME.

661. I desire that the fruit of the obedience with which thou writest the history of my life shall be, that thou become a true disciple of my most holy Son and of myself. The main purpose of the exalted and venerable mysteries, which are made known to thee, and of the teachings, which I so often repeat to thee, is that thou deny and strip thyself, estranging thy heart from all affection to creatures, neither wishing to possess them nor accept them for other uses. By this precaution thou wilt overcome the impediments, which the devils seek to place in the way of the dangerous softness of thy nature. I who know thee, thus advise and lead thee by the way of instruction and correction as thy Mother and Instructress. By the divine teaching thou knowest the mysteries of the Passion and Death of Christ and the one true way of life, which is the Cross; and thou knowest that not all who are called, are chosen. Many there are who wish to follow Christ and very few who truly dispose themselves to imitate Him; for as soon as they feel the sufferings of the Cross they cast it aside. Laborious exertions are very painful and averse to human nature according to the flesh; and the fruits of the spirit are more hidden and few guide themselves by the light. On this account there are so many among mortals, who, forgetful of the eternal truths, seek the flesh and the continual indulgence of its pleasures. They ardently seek honors and fly from injuries: they strive

after riches, and contemn poverty; they long after pleasure and dread mortification. All these are enemies of the Cross of Christ (Phil. 3, 18), and with dreadful aversion they fly from it, deeming it sheer ignominy, just like those who crucified Christ, the Lord.

662. Another deceit has spread through the world: many imagine that they are following Christ their Master, though they neither suffer affliction nor engage in any exertion or labor. They are content with avoiding boldness in committing sins, and place all their perfection in a certain prudence or hollow self-love, which prevents them from denying anything to their will and from practicing any virtues at the cost of their flesh. They would easily escape this deception, if they would consider that my Son was not only the Redeemer, but their Teacher; and that He left in this world the treasures of his Redemption not only as a remedy against its eternal ruin, but as a necessary medicine for the sickness of sin in human nature. No one knew so much as my Son and Lord; no one could better understand the quality of love than the divine Lord, who was and is wisdom and charity itself; and no one was more able to fulfill all his wishes (I John 4, 16). Nevertheless, although He well could do it, He chose not a life of softness and ease for the flesh, but one full of labors and pains; for He judged his instructions to be incomplete and insufficient to redeem man, if He failed to teach them how to overcome the demon, the flesh and their own self. He wished to inculcate, that this magnificent victory is gained by the Cross, by labors, penances, mortifications and the acceptance of contempt: all of which are the trade-marks and evidences of true love and the special watchwords of the predestined.

663. Thou, my daughter, knowest the value of the

holy Cross and the honor which it confers upon ignominies and tribulations; do thou embrace the Cross and
bear it with joy in imitation of my Son and thy Master
(Matth. 16, 24). In this mortal life let thy glory be
in tribulations, persecutions (Rom. 5, 3), contempt, infirmities, poverty, humiliation and in whatever is painful
and averse to mortal flesh. And in order that in all
thy exercises thou mayest imitate me and give me pleasure, I wish that thou seek no rest or consolation in any
earthly thing. Thou must not dwell in thy thoughts
upon what thou bearest, nor seek to relieve thyself by
enlisting the compassion of others. Much less must
thou make much of, or try to impress others with the
recital of the persecutions or molestations of creatures,
nor should it ever be heard from thy lips, how much
thou endurest, nor shouldst thou compare thy sufferings
with those of others. I do not wish to say, that it is a
sin to accept of some reasonable and moderate alleviation, or to mention thy afflictions. But in thee, my dearest, much alleviation, if not a sin, would be an infidelity
to thy Spouse and Lord; for He has put thee personally
under more obligation than many generations of men
and thy response in suffering and love will be defective
and wanting, if it is not complete and loyal in all respects.
So faithful does the Lord wish thy correspondence to be,
that thou must allow thy weak nature not even one sigh
for mere natural relief and consolation. If love alone
impels thee, thou wilt allow thyself to be carried along
by its sweet force and rest in it alone; and the love of
the Cross would immediately dispense with such natural
relief, in the same way as thou knowest I have done in
my total self-sacrifice. Let this be to thee a general
rule: that all human consolation is an imperfection and
a danger, and that thou shouldst welcome only that,

which the Most High sends to thee Himself or through his holy angels. And even these favors of the divine right hand thou must accept only in so far as they strengthen thee to suffer more constantly and to withdraw thee from all that ministers to the senses.

CHAPTER XIII

HOW OUR SAVIOR JESUS WAS CRUCIFIED ON MOUNT
CALVARY; THE SEVEN WORDS SPOKEN BY HIM ON
THE CROSS AND THE ATTENDANCE OF HIS SORROW-
FUL MOTHER AT HIS SUFFERINGS.

664. Our Savior then, the new and true Isaac, the
Son of the eternal Father, reached the mountain of
sacrifice, which is the same one to which his prototype
and figure, Isaac, was brought by the patriarch Abraham (Gen. 22, 9). Upon the most innocent Lamb of
God was to be executed the rigor of the sentence, which
had been suspended in favor of the son of the Patriarch.
Mount Calvary was held to be a place of defilement and
ignominy, as being reserved for the chastisement of condemned criminals, whose cadavers spread around it their
stench and attached to it a still more evil fame. Our
most loving Jesus arrived at its summit so worn out,
wounded, torn and disfigured, that He seemed altogether transformed into an object of pain and sorrows.
The power of the Divinity, which deified his most holy
humanity by its hypostatical union, helped Him, not to
lighten his pains, but to strengthen Him against death;
so that, still retaining life until death should be permitted
to take it away on the Cross, He might satiate his love
to the fullest extent. The sorrowful and afflicted Mother,
in the bitterness of her soul, also arrived at the summit
of the mount and remained very close to her divine Son;
but in the sorrows of her soul She was as it were beside
Herself, being entirely transformed by her love and by

the pains which She saw Jesus suffer. Near her were saint John and the three Marys; for they alone, through her intercession and the favor of the eternal Father, had obtained the privilege of remaining so constantly near to the Savior and to his Cross.

665. When the most prudent Mother perceived that now the mysteries of the Redemption were to be fulfilled and that the executioners were about to strip Jesus of his clothes for crucifixion, She turned in spirit to the eternal Father and prayed as follows: "My Lord and eternal God, Thou art the Father of thy only-begotten Son. By eternal generation He is engendered, God of the true God, namely Thyself, and as man He was born of my womb and received from me this human nature, in which He now suffers. I have nursed and sustained Him at my own breast; and as the best of sons that ever can be born of any creature, I love Him with maternal love. As his Mother I have a natural right in the Person of his most holy humanity and thy Providence will never infringe upon any rights held by thy creatures. This right of a Mother then, I now yield to Thee and once more place in thy hands thy and my Son as a sacrifice for the Redemption of man. Accept, my Lord, this pleasing offering, since this is more than I can ever offer by submitting my own self as a victim or to suffering. This sacrifice is greater, not only because my Son is the true God and of thy own substance, but because this sacrifice costs me a much greater sorrow and pain. For if the lots were changed and I should be permitted to die in order to preserve his most holy life, I would consider it a great relief and the fulfillment of my dearest wishes." The eternal Father received this prayer of the exalted Queen with ineffable pleasure and complacency. The patriarch Abraham was permitted

to go no further than to prefigure and attempt the sacrifice of a son, because the real execution of such a sacrifice God reserved to Himself and to his Onlybegotten. Nor was Sara, the mother of Isaac, informed of the mystical ceremony, this being prevented not only by the promptness of Abraham's obedience, but also because he mistrusted, lest the maternal love of Sara, though she was a just and holy woman, should impel her to prevent the execution of the divine command. But not so was it with most holy Mary, to whom the eternal Father could fearlessly manifest his unchangeable will in order that She might, as far as her powers were concerned, unite with Him in the sacrifice of his Onlybegotten.

666. The invincible Mother finished her prayer and She perceived that the impious ministers were preparing to give to the Lord the drink of wine, myrrh and gall, of which saint Matthew and saint Mark speak (Matth. 27, 34; Mark 15, 23). Taking occasion from the words of Solomon: Give strong drink to the sorrowful and wine to those that suffer bitterness of heart, the Jews were accustomed to give to those about to be executed a drink of strong and aromatic wine in order to raise their vital spirits and to help them to bear their torments with greater fortitude. This custom they now perverted in order to augment the sufferings of the Savior (Prov. 3, 6). The drink, which was intended to assist and strengthen other criminals, by the perfidy of the Jews was now mixed with gall, so that it should have no other effect than to torment his sense of taste by its bitterness. The blessed Mother was aware of their intentions and in her maternal tenderness and compassion asked the Lord not to drink of it. Jesus in deference to the petition of his Mother, without rejecting entirely this new suffering, tasted of the mixture, but would not drink it entirely (Matth. 27, 34).

667. It was already the sixth hour, which corresponds to our noontime, and the executioners, intending to crucify the Savior naked, despoiled Him of the seamless tunic and of his garments. As the tunic was large and without opening in front, they pulled it over the head of Jesus without taking off the crown of thorns; but on account of the rudeness with which they proceeded, they inhumanly tore off the crown with the tunic. Thus they opened anew all the wounds of his head, and in some of them remained the thorns, which, in spite of their being so hard and sharp, were wrenched off by the violence with which the executioners despoiled Him of his tunic and, with it, of the crown. With heartless cruelty they again forced it down upon his sacred head, opening up wounds upon wounds. By the rude tearing off of the tunic were renewed also the wounds of his whole body, since the tunic had dried into the open places and its removal was, as David says, adding new pains to his wounds (Ps. 68, 27). Four times during the Passion did they despoil Jesus of his garments and again vest Him. The first time in order to scourge Him at the pillar; the second time in order to clothe Him in the mock purple; the third, when they took this off in order to clothe Him in his tunic; the fourth, when they finally took away his clothes. This last was the most painful, because his wounds were more numerous, his holy humanity was much weakened, and there was less shelter against the sharp wind on mount Calvary; for also this element was permitted to increase the sufferings of his death-struggle by sending its cold blasts across the mount.

668. To all these sufferings was added the confusion of being bereft of his garments in the presence of his most blessed Mother, of her pious companions, and in full sight of the multitudes gathered around. By his

divine power He, however, reserved for Himself the nether garment which his Mother had wound around his loins in Egypt; for neither at the scourging, nor at the crucifixion could the executioners remove it, and He was laid in the sepulchre still covered with this cloth. That this really happened, has been revealed to me many times. Certainly, He desired to die in the greatest poverty and to take with Him nothing of all that He created and possessed in this world. He would gladly have died entirely despoiled and bereft of even this covering, if it had not been for the desires and the prayers of his blessed Mother, to which Christ wished to yield. On her account He substituted this most perfect obedience of a Son toward his Mother for extreme poverty at his Death. The holy Cross was lying on the ground and the executioners were busy making the necessary preparations for crucifying Him and the two thieves. In the meanwhile our Redeemer and Master prayed to the Father in the following terms:

669. "Eternal Father and my Lord God, to the incomprehensible Majesty of thy infinite goodness and justice I offer my entire humanity and all that according to thy will it has accomplished in descending from thy bosom to assume passible and mortal flesh for the Redemption of men, my brethren. I offer Thee, Lord, with Myself, also my most loving Mother, her love, her most perfect works, her sorrows, her sufferings, her anxious and prudent solicitude in serving Me, imitating Me and accompanying Me unto death. I offer Thee the little flock of my Apostles, the holy Church and congregation of the faithful, such as it is now and as it shall be to the end of the world; and with it I offer to Thee all the mortal children of Adam. All this I place in thy hands as the true and almighty Lord and God. As far as my

wishes are concerned, I suffer and die for all, and I desire that all shall be saved, under the condition that all follow Me and profit of my Redemption. Thus may they pass from the slavery of the devil to be thy children, my brethren and co-heirs of the grace merited by Me. Especially, O my Lord, do I offer to Thee the poor, the despised and afflicted, who are my friends and who follow Me on the way to the Cross. I desire that the just and the predestined be written in thy eternal memory. I beseech Thee, my Father, to withhold thy chastisement and not to raise the scourge of thy justice over men; let them not be punished as they merit for their sins. Be Thou from now on their Father as Thou art mine. I beseech Thee also, that they may be helped to ponder upon my Death in pious affection and be enlightened from above; and I pray for those who are persecuting Me, in order that they may be converted to the truth. Above all do I ask Thee for the exaltation of thy ineffable and most holy name."

670. This prayer and supplication of our Savior Jesus were known to the most blessed Mother, and She imitated Him and made the same petitions to the eternal Father in as far as She was concerned. The most prudent Virgin never forgot or disregarded the first word which She had heard from the mouth of her divine Son as an infant: "Become like unto Me, my Beloved." His promise, that in return for the new human existence which She had given Him in her virginal womb, He would, by his almighty power, give Her a new existence of divine and eminent grace above all other creatures, was continually fulfilled. To this favor was due also her deep science and enlightenment concerning all the operations of the sacred humanity of her Son, none of which ever escaped her knowledge and attention. Whatever

She thus perceived She imitated; so that She was always anxious to study and penetrate them with deep understanding, to put them promptly into action, and to practice them courageously and zealously during all her life. In this neither sorrow could disturb Her, nor anguish hinder Her, nor persecution detain Her, nor the bitterness of her suffering weaken Her. If the great Queen had assisted at the Passion with the same sentiments as the rest of the just, it would indeed have been admirable; but not so admirable as the way in which She suffered. She was singular and extraordinary in all her sufferings; for, as I have said above, She felt in her own virginal body all the torments of Christ our Lord, both interior and exterior. On account of this conformity we can say, that also the heavenly Mother was scourged, crowned, spit upon, buffeted, laden with the Cross and nailed upon it; for She felt these pains and all the rest in her purest body. Although She felt them in a different manner, yet She felt them with such conformity that the Mother was altogether a faithful likeness of her Son. Besides the greatness of her dignity, which in most holy Mary must, on this account, have corresponded in the highest possible degree with that of Christ, there was concealed therein another mystery. This was, that the desire of Christ to see his exalted love and benignity as exhibited in his Passion copied in all its magnitude in a mere creature, was fulfilled in Her, and no one possessed a greater right to this favor than his own Mother.

671. In order to find the places for the auger-holes on the Cross, the executioners haughtily commanded the Creator of the universe. (O dreadful temerity!), to stretch Himself out upon it. The Teacher of humility obeyed without hesitation. But they, following their inhuman instinct of cruelty, marked the places for the holes,

not according to the size of his body, but larger, having in mind a new torture for their Victim. This inhuman intent was known to the Mother of light, and the knowledge of it was one of the greatest afflictions of her chastest heart during the whole Passion. She saw through the intentions of these ministers of sin and She anticipated the torments to be endured by her beloved Son when his limbs should be wrenched from their sockets in being nailed to the Cross. But She could not do anything to prevent it, as it was the will of the Lord to suffer these pains for men. When He rose from the Cross, and they set about boring the holes, the great Lady approached and took hold of one of his hands, adoring Him and kissing it with greatest reverence. The executioners allowed this because they thought that the sight of his Mother would cause so much the greater affliction to the Lord; for they wished to spare Him no sorrow they could cause Him. But they were ignorant of the hidden mysteries; for the Lord during his Passion had no greater source of consolation and interior joy than to see in the soul of his most blessed Mother, the beautiful likeness of Himself and the full fruits of his Passion and Death. This joy, to a certain extent, comforted Christ our Lord also in that hour.

672. Having bored the three holes into the Cross, the executioners again commanded Christ the Lord to stretch Himself out upon it in order to be nailed to it. The supreme and almighty King, as the Author of patience, obeyed, and at the will of the hangmen, placed Himself with outstretched arms upon the blessed wood. The Lord was so weakened, disfigured and exhausted, that if the ferocious cruelty of those men had left the least room for natural reason and kindness, they could not have brought themselves to inflict further torments

upon the innocent and meek Lamb, humbly suffering such nameless sorrows and pains. But not so with them; for the judges and their executioners (O terrible and most hidden judgments of the Lord!) were transformed in their malice and deathly hatred into demons, void of the feelings of sensible and earthly men and urged on only by diabolical wrath and fury.

673. Presently one of the executioners seized the hand of Jesus our Savior and placed it upon the auger-hole, while another hammered a large and rough nail through the palm. The veins and sinews were torn, and the bones of the sacred hand, which made the heavens and all that exists, were forced apart. When they stretched out the other hand, they found that it did not reach up to the auger-hole; for the sinews of the other arm had been shortened and the executioners had maliciously set the holes too far apart, as I have mentioned above. In order to overcome the difficulty, they took the chain, with which the Savior had been bound in the garden, and looping one end through a ring around his wrist, they, with unheard of cruelty, pulled the hand over the hole and fastened it with another nail. Thereupon they seized his feet, and placing them one above the other, they tied the same chain around both and stretched them with barbarous ferocity down to the third hole. Then they drove through both feet a large nail into the Cross. Thus the sacred body, in which dwelled the Divinity, was nailed motionless to the holy Cross, and the handiwork of his deified members, formed by the Holy Ghost, was so stretched and torn asunder, that the bones of his body, dislocated and forced from their natural position, could all be counted. The bones of his breast, of his shoulders and arms, and of his whole body yielded to the cruel violence and were torn from their sinews.

674. It is impossible for human tongue or words of mouth to describe the torments of our Savior Jesus and what He suffered on this occasion. On the last day alone more will be known, in order that his cause may be justified before sinners and the praise and exaltation of the saints may be so much the greater. But at present, while our faith in this truth gives us occasion and obliges us to apply our reason (if such we possess), I ask, implore and beseech the children of the holy Church, each one for himself, to study this most venerable sacrament. Let us contemplate it and weigh it with all its circumstances, and we shall find powerful motives to abhor and firmly resolve to avoid sin, as the cause of all this suffering to the Author of life. Let us contemplate and look upon his Virgin Mother, so afflicted in spirit and overwhelmed by the torments of her purest body, in order that through this gate of light we may enter to see the Sun that illumines our heart. O Mistress and Queen of virtues! O true Mother of the immortal King of ages become man! It is true, O my Lady, that the hardness of our ungrateful hearts makes us very unfit and unworthy of suffering thy pains and those of thy most holy Son our Lord; but through thy clemency make us partakers of this favor, which we do not deserve. Purify and free us from this deadening lukewarmness and gross neglect. If we are the cause of these sufferings, what propriety or what justice can there be in visiting them only on Thee and on thy Beloved? Let the chalice pass from the lips of the Innocent, in order that it may be tasted by the guilty who deserve it. But alas! Where is our good sense? Where wisdom and knowledge? Where is the light of our eyes? Who has so entirely deprived us of our understanding? Who has robbed us of our human and sensible hearts? If I, O Lord, had not re-

ceived from Thee this being according to thy image and likeness; if Thou hadst not given me life and motion; if all the elements and creatures, formed by thy hand for my service (Eccli. 39, 30), were not giving me continual notice of thy immense love: at least thy being nailed so outrageously to the Cross, and all thy torments and sorrows for my salvation, should have sufficed to draw me to Thee with the bonds of compassion and gratitude, of love and confidence in thy ineffable kindness. But if so many voices cannot awaken me, if such love does not enkindle mine, if thy Passion and Death do not move me, if such great benefits cannot oblige me, what end shall I expect as the result of my foolishness?

675. After the Savior was nailed to the Cross, the executioners judged it necessary to bend the points of the nails which projected through the back of the wood, in order that they might not be loosened and drawn out by the weight of the body. For this purpose they raised up the Cross in order to turn it over, so that the body of the Lord would rest face downward upon the ground with the weight of the Cross upon Him. This new cruelty appalled all the bystanders and a shout of pity arose in the crowd. But the sorrowful and compassionate Mother intervened by her prayers, and asked the eternal Father not to permit this boundless outrage to happen in the way the executioners had intended. She commanded her holy angels to come to the assistance of their Creator. When, therefore, the executioners raised up the Cross to let it fall, with the crucified Lord face downward upon the ground, the holy angels supported Him and the Cross above the stony and fetid ground, so that his divine countenance did not come in contact with the rocks and pebbles. Thus altogether ignorant of the miracle the executioners bent over the points of the nails;

for the sacred body was so near to the ground and the Cross was so firmly held by the angels, that the Jews thought it rested upon the hard rock.

676. Then they dragged the lower end of the Cross with the crucified God near to the hole, wherein it was to be planted. Some of them getting under the upper part of the Cross with their shoulders, others pushing upward with their halberds and lances, they raised the Savior on his Cross and fastened its foot in the hole they had drilled into the ground. Thus our true life and salvation now hung in the air upon the sacred wood in full view of the innumerable multitudes of different nations and countries. I must not omit mentioning another barbarity inflicted upon the Lord as they raised Him: for some of them placed the sharp points of their lances and halberds to his body and fearfully lacerating Him under the armpits in helping to push the Cross into position. At this spectacle new cries of protest arose with still more vehemence and confusion from the multitude of people. The Jews blasphemed, the kind-hearted lamented, the strangers were astounded, some of them called the attention of the bystanders to the proceedings, others turned away their heads in horror and pity; others took to themselves a warning from this spectacle of suffering, and still others proclaimed Him a just Man. All these different sentiments were like arrows piercing the heart of the afflicted Mother. The sacred body now shed much blood from the nail wounds, which, by its weight and the shock of the Cross falling into the hole, had widened. They were the fountains, now opened up, to which Isaias invites us to hasten with joy to quench our thirst and wash off the stains of our sins (Is. 12, 3). No one shall be excused who does not quickly approach to drink of them; since the waters are sold without ex-

change of silver or gold, and they are given freely to those who will but receive them (Is. 54, 1).

677. Then they crucified also the two thieves and planted their crosses to the right and the left of the Savior; for thereby they wished to indicate that He deserved the most conspicuous place as being the greatest malefactor. The pharisees and priests, forgetting the two thieves, turned all the venom of their fury against the sinless and holy One by nature. Wagging their heads in scorn and mockery (Matth. 27, 39) they threw stones and dirt at the Cross of the Lord and his royal Person, saying: "Ah Thou, who destroyest the temple and in three days rebuildest it, save now Thyself; others He has made whole, Himself He cannot save; if this be the Son of God let Him descend from the Cross, and we will believe in Him" (Matth. 27, 42). The two thieves in the beginning also mocked the Lord and said: "If Thou art the Son of God, save Thyself and us." These blasphemies of the two thieves caused special sorrow to our Lord, since they were so near to death and were losing the fruit of their death-pains, by which they could have satisfied in part for their justly punished crimes. Soon after, however, one of them availed himself of the greatest opportunity that a sinner ever had in this world, and was converted from his sins.

678. When the great Queen of the angels, most holy Mary, perceived that the Jews in their perfidy and obstinate envy vied in dishonoring Him, in blaspheming Him as the most wicked of men and in desiring to blot out his name from the land of the living, as Jeremias had prophesied (Jer. 11, 19), She was inflamed with a new zeal for the honor of her Son and true God. Prostrate before the person of the Crucified, and adoring Him, She besought the eternal Father to see to the honor of

his Onlybegotten and manifest it by such evident signs that the perfidy of the Jews might be confounded and their malice frustrated of its intent. Having presented this petition to the Father, She, with the zeal and authority of the Queen of the universe, addressed all the irrational creatures and said: "Insensible creatures, created by the hand of the Almighty, do you manifest your compassion, which in deadly foolishness is denied to Him by men capable of reason. Ye heavens, thou sun, moon and ye stars and planets, stop in your course and suspend your activity in regard to mortals. Ye elements, change your condition, earth lose thy stability, let your rocks and cliffs be rent. Ye sepulchres and monuments of the dead, open and send forth your contents for the confusion of the living. Thou mystical and figurative veil of the temple, divide into two parts and by thy separation threaten the unbelievers with chastisement, give witness to the truth and to the glory of their Creator and Redeemer, which they are trying to obscure."

679. In virtue of this prayer and of the commands of Mary, the Mother of the Crucified, the Omnipotence of God had provided for all that was to happen at the death of his Onlybegotten. The Lord enlightened and moved the hearts of many of the bystanders at the time of these happenings on earth, and even before that time, in order that they might confess Jesus crucified as holy, just and as the true Son of God. This happened, for instance, with the centurion and many others mentioned in the Gospels, who went away from Calvary striking their breasts in sorrow. Among them were not only those who previously had heard and believed his doctrine, but also a great number of such as had never seen Him or witnessed his miracles. For the same reason Pilate was also inspired not to change the title of the Cross which

they had placed over the head of the Savior in Hebrew, Greek and Latin. For when the Jews protested and asked Him not to write: Jesus of Nazareth, King of the Jews; but: This one says, He is King of the Jews; Pilate answered: What is written, is written, and I do not wish it to be changed. All the inanimate creatures, by divine will, obeyed the command of the most holy Mary. From the noon hour until three o'clock in the afternoon, which was called the ninth hour, when the Lord expired, they exhibited the great disturbances and changes mentioned in the Gospels. The sun hid its light, the planets showed great alterations, the earth quaked, many mountains were rent; the rocks shook one against the other, the graves opened and sent forth some of the dead alive. The changes in the elements and in the whole universe were so notable and extraordinary that they were evident on the whole earth. All the Jews of Jerusalem were dismayed and astonished; although their outrageous perfidy and malice made them unworthy of the truth and hindered them from accepting what all the insensible creatures preached to them.

680. The soldiers who had crucified Jesus our Savior, according to a custom permitting the executioners to take possession of the property of those whom they executed, now proceeded to divide the garments of the innocent Lamb. The cloak or outside mantle, which by divine disposition they had brought to mount Calvary and which was the one Christ had laid aside at the washing of the feet, they divided among themselves, cutting it into four parts (John 19, 23). But the seamless tunic, by a mysterious decree of Providence, they did not divide, but they drew lots and assigned it entirely to the one who drew the lot for it; thus fulfilling the prophecy in the twenty-first Psalm. The mysterious signification of the

undivided tunic is variously explained by the saints and doctors; one of these explanations being, that though the Jews lacerated and tore with wounds the sacred humanity of Christ our Lord, yet they could not touch or injure the Divinity which was enclosed in the sacred humanity; and whoever should draw the lot of justification by partaking of his Divinity, should thenceforward possess and enjoy it entirely.

681. As the wood of the Cross was the throne of his majesty and the chair of the doctrine of life, and as He was now raised upon it, confirming his doctrine by his example, Christ now uttered those words of highest charity and perfection: "Father, forgive them, for they know not what they do!" (Luke 23, 34.) This principle of charity and fraternal love the divine Teacher had appropriated to Himself and proclaimed by his own lips (John 15, 12; Matth. 15, 44). He now confirmed and executed it upon the Cross, not only pardoning and loving his enemies, but excusing those under the plea of ignorance whose malice had reached the highest point possible to men in persecuting, blaspheming and crucifying their God and Redeemer. Such was the difference between the behavior of ungrateful men favored with so great enlightenment, instruction and blessing; and the behavior of Jesus in his most burning charity while suffering the crown of thorns, the nails, and the Cross and unheard of blasphemy at the hands of men. O incomprehensible love! O ineffable sweetness! O patience inconceivable to man, admirable to the angels and fearful to the devils! One of the two thieves, called Dismas, became aware of some of the mysteries. Being assisted at the same time by the prayers and intercession of most holy Mary, he was interiorly enlightened concerning his Rescuer and Master by the first word on the Cross.

Moved by true sorrow and contrition for his sins, he turned to his companion and said: "Neither dost thou fear God, seeing that thou art under the same condemnation? And we indeed justly, for we receive the due reward of our deeds; but this Man hath done no evil." And thereupon speaking to Jesus, he said: "Lord, remember me when Thou shalt come into thy kingdom!" (Luke 23, 40.)

682. In this happiest of thieves, in the centurion, and in the others who confessed Jesus Christ on the Cross, began to appear the results of the Redemption. But the one most favored was this Dismas, who merited to hear the second word of the Savior on the Cross: "Amen, I say to thee, this day shalt thou be with Me in Paradise." O fortunate thief, who, of all others, heard those words so much desired by all the saints and just of the earth! Such a word the ancient Patriarchs and Prophets did not hear; they had judged themselves very happy to be allowed to descend into limbo and wait through the long ages for paradise, which thou, in changing so happily thy condition, didst acquire in one moment. Thou hast now ceased to rob earthly possessions of thy neighbor, and immediately snatchest heaven from the hands of thy Master. Thou seizest it in justice and He yields it to thee in grace, since thou wast the last disciple of his doctrine on earth and the most alert of all in practicing it after having heard it from his mouth. Thou hast lovingly corrected thy brother, confessed thy Creator, reprehended those who blasphemed Him, imitated Him in patient suffering, asked Him humbly as thy Redeemer not to forget thy miseries; and He, as thy Exalter, has at once fulfilled thy desires without delaying the guerdon merited for thee and all the mortals.

683. Having thus justified the good thief, Jesus turned

his loving gaze upon his afflicted Mother, who with saint John was standing at the foot of the Cross. Speaking to both, he first addressed his Mother, saying: "Woman, behold thy son!" and then to the Apostle: "Behold thy Mother!" (John 19, 26.) The Lord called Her Woman and not Mother, because this name of Mother had in it something of sweetness and consolation, the very pronouncing of which would have been a sensible relief. During his Passion He would admit of no exterior consolation, having renounced for that time all exterior alleviation and easement, as I have mentioned above. By this word "woman" he tacitly and by implication wished to say: Woman blessed among all women, the most prudent among all the daughters of Adam, Woman, strong and constant, unconquered by any fault of thy own, unfailing in my service and most faithful in thy love toward Me, which even the mighty waters of my Passion could not extinguish or resist (Cant. 8, 7), I am going to my Father and cannot accompany Thee further; my beloved disciple will attend upon Thee and serve Thee as his Mother, and he will be thy son. All this the heavenly Queen understood. The holy Apostle on his part received Her as his own from that hour on; for he was enlightened anew in order to understand and appreciate the greatest treasure of the Divinity in the whole creation next to the humanity of Christ our Savior. In this light He reverenced and served Her for the rest of her life, as I will relate farther on. Our Lady also accepted him as her son in humble subjection and obedience. Always practicing the highest possible perfection and holiness without failing on any occasion, and not permitting even the immensity of her present suffering to weigh down her magnanimous and most prudent heart, She promised then and there that

She would show him this obedience during her whole
life.

684. Already the ninth hour of the day was approaching, although the darkness and confusion of nature made
it appear to be rather a chaotic night. Our Savior spoke
the fourth word from the Cross in a loud and strong
voice, so that all the bystanders could hear it: "My God,
my God, why hast thou forsaken Me?" (Matth. 27, 46.)
Although the Lord had uttered these words in his own
Hebrew language, they were not understood by all.
Since they began with: "Eli, eli," some of them thought
He was calling upon Elias, and a number of them mocked
Him saying: "Let us see whether Elias shall come to
free Him from our hands?" But the mystery concealed
beneath these words was just as profound as it was un-
intelligible to the Jews and gentiles; and they have been
interpreted in many ways by the doctors of the Church.
I shall give the interpretation which has been manifested
to me. The dereliction of which Christ speaks, was not
one in which the Divinity separated from the humanity,
dissolving the hypostatic union, nor including a cessa-
tion of the beatific vision in his soul; for both of these
He enjoyed from the first moment of his conception by
the Holy Ghost in the virginal womb and could never
lose. But certainly the sacred humanity was in so far
forsaken by the Divinity as it did not ward off death or
the most bitter sorrows of his Passion; though, on the
other hand, the eternal Father did not forsake Him
entirely, since He showed his concern by causing the
changes in the visible creation in order to give witness
for his honor at his Death. Christ our Savior intimated
quite a different dereliction by these words of complaint,
one which originated from his immense love for men;
namely, from his love of the foreknown as lost and the

reprobate, which during his last hour caused in Him the same anguish as it did during his prayer in the garden. He grieved that his copious and superabundant Redemption, offered for the whole human race, should not be efficacious in the reprobate and that He should find Himself deprived of them in the eternal happiness, for which He had created and redeemed them. As this was to happen in consequence of the decree of his Father's eternal will, He lovingly and sorrowfully complained of it in the words: "My God, my God, why hast Thou forsaken Me?" that is, in so far as God deprived Him of the salvation of the reprobate.

685. In confirmation of this sorrow the Lord added: "I thirst!" The sufferings of the Lord and his anguish could easily cause a natural thirst. But for Him this was not a time to complain of this thirst or to quench it; and therefore Jesus would not have spoken of it so near to its expiration, unless in order to give expression to a most exalted mystery. He was thirsting to see the captive children of Adam make use of the liberty, which He merited for them and offered to them, and which so many were abusing. He was athirst with the anxious desire that all should correspond with Him in the faith and love due to Him, that they profit by his merits and sufferings, accept his friendship and grace now acquired for them, and that they should not lose the eternal happiness which He was to leave as an inheritance to those that wished to merit and accept it. This was the thirst of our Savior and Master; and the most blessed Mary alone understood it perfectly and began, with ardent affection and charity, to invite and interiorly to call upon all the poor, the afflicted, the humble, the despised and downtrodden to approach their Savior and thus quench, at least in part, his thirst which they could not quench

entirely. But the perfidious Jews and the executioners, evidencing their unhappy hard-heartedness, fastened a sponge soaked in gall and vinegar to a reed and mockingly raised it to his mouth, in order that He might drink of it. Thus was fulfilled the prophecy of David: "In my thirst they gave me vinegar to drink" (John 16, 28; Ps. 68, 22). Our most patient Savior tasted of it, partaking of this drink in mysterious submission to the condemnation of the reprobate. But at the instance of his blessed Mother He immediately desisted; because the Mother of grace was to be the portal and Mediatrix of those who were to profit of the Passion and the Redemption of mankind.

686. In connection with this same mystery the Savior then pronounced the sixth word: "Consummatum est," "It is consummated" (John 19, 29). Now is consummated this work of my coming from heaven and I have obeyed the command of my eternal Father, who sent Me to suffer and die for the salvation of mankind. Now are fulfilled the holy Scriptures, the prophecies and figures of the old Testament, and the course of my earthly and mortal life assumed in the womb of my Mother. Now are established on earth my example, my doctrines, my Sacraments and my remedies for the sickness of sin. Now is appeased the justice of my eternal Father in regard to the debt of the children of Adam. Now is my holy Church enriched with the remedies for the sins committed by men; the whole work of my coming into the world is perfected in so far as concerns Me, its Restorer; the secure foundation of the triumphant Church is now laid in the Church militant, so that nothing can overthrow or change it. These are the mysteries contained in the few words: "Consummatum est."

687. Having finished and established the work of Re-

demption in all its perfection, it was becoming that the incarnate Word, just as He came forth from the Father to enter mortal life (John 16, 8), should enter into immortal life of the Father through death. Therefore Christ our Savior added the last words uttered by Him: "Father, into thy hands I commend my spirit." The Lord spoke these words in a loud and strong voice, so that the bystanders heard them. In pronouncing them He raised his eyes to heaven, as one speaking with the eternal Father, and with the last accent He gave up his spirit and inclined his head. By the divine force of these words Lucifer with all his demons were hurled into the deepest caverns of hell, there they lay motionless, as I shall relate in the next chapter. The invincible Queen and Mistress of all virtues understood these mysteries beyond the understanding of all creatures, as She was the Mother of the Savior and the Coadjutrix of his Passion. In order that She might participate in it to the end, just as She had felt in her own body the other torments of her Son, She now, though remaining alive, felt and suffered the pangs and agony of his death. She did not die in reality; but this was because God miraculously preserved her life, when according to the natural course death should have followed. This miraculous aid was more wonderful than all the other favors She received during the Passion. For this last pain was more intense and penetrating; and all that the martyrs and the men sentenced to death have suffered from the beginning of the world cannot equal what the blessed Mary suffered during the Passion. The great Lady remained at the foot of the Cross until evening, when the sacred body (as I shall relate) was interred. But in return for this last anguish of death, all that was still of this mortal life in the virginal body of the purest Mother, was more than ever exalted and spiritualized.

688. Of many of the sacraments and mysteries connected with the doings of Christ our Savior on the Cross the Evangelists make no mention; and we as Catholics can only form prudent conjectures founded upon the infallible certainty of our faith. But among those which have been manifested to me in this history, and concerning this part of the Passion, is a prayer, which Christ addressed to his eternal Father before speaking the seven words on the Cross recorded by the Evangelists. I call it a prayer because it was addressed to the Father; but in reality it was a last bequest or testament, which He made as a true and most wise Father in order to consign his possessions to his family, that is, to the whole human race. Even natural reason teaches us, that he who is the head of a family or the lord over many or few possessions, would not be a prudent dispenser of his goods, and inattentive to his office or dignity, if at the hour of his death he would not make known his will in regard to the disposition of his goods and his estate, in order that each one of his family may know what belongs to him and may possess it justly and peacefully without recourse to lawsuits. For this very reason, and in order that they may set their minds at ease in preparation for the hour of death, men of the world make their last testaments. And even the religious resign the things permitted them for daily use, because in that hour earthly matters are apt to fill the mind with anxieties and prevent them from rising toward their Creator. Although earthly things could not disturb our Savior, since He neither possessed them, nor, if He had possessed any, could He be embarrassed by them in his infinite power; yet it was fitting, that He should in that hour dispose of the spiritual riches and treasures which He had amassed for mankind in the course of his pilgrimage.

689. Of these eternal goods the Savior made his last disposition on the Cross, distributing them and pointing out those who should be legitimate heirs and those who should be disinherited, and mentioning the reasons for the one as well as the other. All this He did in conference with his eternal Father, as the supreme Lord and most just Judge of all creatures; for in this testament are rehearsed the mysteries of the predestination of the saints and of the reprobation of the wicked. It was a testament hidden and sealed for mankind; only the blessed Mary understood it, because, in addition to her being informed of the operations of the divine Soul of Christ, She was also to be the universal Heiress of all creation. As She was the Coadjutrix of salvation, She was also to be the testamentary Executrix. For the Son placed all things in her hands, just as the Father had assigned the whole creation to Him. She was to execute his will and she was to distribute all the treasures acquired and due to her Son as God on account of his infinite merits. This understanding has been given me as part of this history for the exaltation of our Queen and in order that sinners might approach Her as the Custodian of all the treasures gained by her Son and our Redeemer in the sight of his eternal Father. All help and assistance is in the hands of most holy Mary and She is to distribute it according to her most sweet kindness and liberality.

TESTAMENT MADE BY CHRIST OUR LORD ON THE CROSS
IN HIS PRAYER TO THE ETERNAL FATHER.

690. When the holy wood of the Cross had been raised on mount Calvary, bearing aloft with it the incarnate Word crucified before speaking any of the seven

words, Christ prayed interiorly to his heavenly Father and said: "My Father and eternal God, I confess and magnify Thee from this tree of the Cross, and I offer Thee a sacrifice of praise in my Passion and Death; for, by the hypostatic union with the divine nature, Thou hast raised my humanity to the highest dignity, that of Christ, the Godman, anointed with thy own Divinity. I confess Thee on account of the plenitude of the highest possible graces and glory, which from the first instant of my Incarnation Thou hast communicated to my humanity, and because from all eternity up to this present hour Thou hast consigned to me full dominion of the universe both in the order of grace and of nature. Thou hast made Me the Lord of the heavens and of the elements (Matth. 28, 18), of the sun, the moon and the stars; of fire and air, of the earth and the sea, of all the animate and inanimate creatures therein; Thou hast made Me the Disposer of the seasons, of the days and nights, with full lordship and possession according to my free will, and Thou hast set Me as the Head, the King and Lord of all angels and men (Ephes. 1, 21), to govern and command them, to punish the wicked and to reward the good (John 5, 22); Thou hast given Me the dominion and power of disposing all things from highest heavens to deepest abysses of hell (Apoc. 20, 1). Thou hast placed in my hands the eternal justification of men, the empires, kingdoms and principalities, the great and the little, the rich and the poor; and of all that are capable of thy grace and glory, Thou hast made Me the Justifier, the Redeemer and Glorifier, the universal Lord of all the human race, of life and death, of the holy Church, its treasures, laws and blessings of grace: all hast Thou, my Father, consigned to my hands, subjected to my will and my decrees, and for this I confess, exalt and magnify thy holy name."

691. "Now, at this moment, my Lord and eternal Father, when I am returning from this world to thy right hand through this death on the Cross, by which I completed the task of the Redemption of men assigned to Me, I desire that this same Cross shall be the tribunal of our justice and mercy. Nailed to it, I desire to judge those for whom I give my life. Having justified my cause, I wish to dispense the treasures of my coming into the world and of my Passion and Death to the just and the reprobate according as each one merits by his works of love or hatred. I have sought to gain all mortals and invited them to partake of my friendship and grace; from the first moment of my Incarnation I have ceaselessly labored for them; I have borne inconveniences, fatigues, insults, ignominies, reproaches, scourges, a crown of thorns, and now suffer the bitter death of the Cross; I have implored thy vast kindness upon all of them; I have watched in prayer, fasted and wandered about teaching them the way of eternal life. As far as in Me lay I have sought to secure eternal happiness for all men, just as I merited it for all, without excluding any one. I have established and built up the law of grace and have firmly and forever established the Church in which all human beings can be saved."

692. "But in our knowledge and foresight We are aware, my God and Father, that on account of their malice and rebellious obstinacy not all men desire to accept our eternal salvation, nor avail themselves of our mercy and of the way I have opened to them by my labors, life and death; but that many will prefer to follow their sinful ways unto perdition. Thou art just, my Lord and Father, and most equitable are thy judgments (Ps. 68, 137); and therefore it is right, since Thou hast made Me the Judge of the living and the dead,

of the good and the bad (Act 10, 3), that I give to the good the reward of having served and followed Me, and to sinners the chastisement of their perverse obstinacy; that the just should share in my goods, and the wicked be deprived of the inheritance, which they refuse to accept. Now then, my eternal Father, in my and thy name and for thy glorification, I make my last bequest according to my human will, which is conformable to thy eternal and divine will. First shall be mentioned my most pure Mother, who gave Me human existence; Her I constitute my sole and universal Heiress of all the gifts of nature, of grace and of glory that are mine. She shall be Mistress and Possessor of them all. The gifts of grace, of which as a mere creature She is capable, She shall actually receive now, while those of glory I promise to confer upon Her in their time. I desire that She shall be Mistress of angels and men, claim over them full possession and dominion and command the service and obedience of all. The demons shall fear Her and be subject to Her. All the irrational creatures, the heavens, the stars, the planets, the elements with all the living beings, the birds, the fishes and the animals contained in them, shall likewise be subject to Her and acknowledge Her as Mistress, exalting and glorifying Her with Me. I wish also that She be the Treasurer and Dispenser of all the goods in heaven and on earth. Whatever She ordains and disposes in my Church for my children, the sons of men, shall be confirmed by the three divine Persons; and whatever She shall ask for mortals now, afterwards and forever, We shall concede according to her will and wishes."

693. "To the holy angels, who have obeyed thy holy and just will, I assign as habitation the highest heavens as their proper and eternal abode, and with it the joys

of eternal vision and fruition of our Divinity. I desire that they enjoy its everlasting possession together with our company and friendship. I decree, that they recognize my Mother as their legitimate Queen and Lady, that they serve Her, accompany and attend upon Her, bear Her up in their hands in all places and times, obeying Her in all that She wishes to ordain and command. The demons, rebellious to our perfect and holy will, I cast out and deprive of our vision and company; again do I condemn them to our abhorrence, to eternal loss of our friendship and glory, to privation of the vision of my Mother, of the saints and of my friends, the just. I appoint and assign to them as their eternal dwelling the place most remote from our royal throne, namely the infernal caverns, the centre of the earth, deprived of light and full of the horrors of sensible darkness (Jude 6). I decree this to be their portion and inheritance, as chosen by them in their pride and obstinacy against the divine Being and decrees. In those eternal dungeons of darkness they shall be tormented by everlasting and inextinguishable fire."

694. "From the multitudes of men, in the fulness of my good will, I call, select and separate all the just and the predestined, who through my grace save themselves by imitating Me, doing my will and obeying my holy law. These, next to my most pure Mother, I appoint as the inheritors of all my mysteries, my blessings, my sacramental treasures, of the mysteries concealed in the holy Scriptures; of my humility, meekness of heart; of the virtues of faith, hope, and charity; of prudence, justice, fortitude and temperance; of my divine gifts and favors; of my Cross, labors, contempt, poverty and nakedness. This shall be their portion and inheritance in this present and mortal life.

Since they must choose these in order to labor profitably, I assign to them the trials I have chosen for Myself in this life, as a pledge of my friendship, in order that they may undergo them with joy. I offer them my protection and defense, my holy inspirations, my favors and powerful assistance, my blessings and my justification, according to each one's disposition and degree of love. I promise to be to them a Father, a Brother and a Friend, and they shall be my chosen and beloved children, and as such I appoint them as the inheritors of all my merits and treasures without limitation. I desire that all who dispose themselves, shall partake of the goods of my holy Church and of the Sacraments; that, if they should lose my friendship, they shall be able to restore themselves and recover my graces and blessings through my cleansing blood. For all of them shall be open the intercession of my Mother and of the saints, and She shall recognize them as her children, shielding them and holding them as her own. My angels shall defend them, guide them, protect them and bear them up in their hands lest they stumble, and if they fall, they shall help them to rise" (Ps. 90, 11, 12).

695. "Likewise it is my will that my just and chosen ones shall stand high above the reprobate and the demons, that they shall be feared and obeyed by my enemies; that all the rational and irrational creatures shall serve them; that all the influences of the heavens, the planets and the stars shall favor them and give them life; that the earth, its elements and animals, shall sustain them; all the creatures, that are mine and serve Me, shall be theirs, and shall serve also them as my children and friends (I Cor. 3, 22; Wis. 16, 24), and their blessing shall be in the dew of heaven and in the fruits of the earth (Genes. 27, 28). I wish to hold

with them my delights (Pros. 8, 31), communicate to them my secrets, converse with them intimately and live with them in the militant Church in the species of bread and wine, as an earnest and an infallible pledge of the eternal happiness and glory promised to them; of it, I make them partakers and heirs, in order that they may enjoy it with Me in heaven by perpetual right and in unfailing beatitude."

696. "I consent that the foreknown and reprobate (though they were created for another and much higher end), shall be permitted to possess as their portion and inheritance the concupiscence of the flesh and the eyes (John 1, 2-16), pride in all its effects; that they eat and be satisfied with the dust of the earth, namely, with riches; with the fumes and the corruption of the flesh and its delights, and with the vanity and presumption of the world. For such possessions have they labored, and applied all the diligence of their mind and body; in such occupations have they consumed their powers, their gifts and blessings bestowed upon them by Us, and they have of their own free will chosen deceit, despising the truth I have taught them in the holy law (Rom. 2, 8). They have rejected the law which I have written in their hearts and the one inspired by my grace; they have despised my teachings and my blessings, and listened to my and their own enemies; they have accepted their deceits, have loved vanity (Ps. 4, 3), wrought injustice, followed their ambitions, sought their delight in vengeance, persecuted the poor, humiliated the just, mocked the simple and the innocent, strove to exalt themselves and desired to be raised above all the cedars of Lebanon in following the laws of injustice" (Ps. 36, 35).

697. "Since they have done all this in opposition to

our divine goodness and remained obstinate in their malice, and since they have renounced the rights of sonship merited for them by Me, I disinherit them of my friendship and glory. Just as Abraham separated the children of the slave, setting aside some possessions for them and reserving the principal heritage for Isaac, the son of the freedwoman Sarah (Gen. 25, 5), thus I set aside their claims on my inheritance by giving them the transitory goods, which they themselves have chosen. Separating them from our company and from that of my Mother, of the angels and saints, I condemn them to the eternal dungeons and the fire of hell in the company of Lucifer and his demons, whom they have freely served, I deprive them forever of all hope of relief. This is, O my Father, the sentence which I pronounce as the Head and the Judge of men and angels (Eph. 4, 15; Col. 2, 10), and this is the testament made at my Death, this is the effect of my Redemption, whereby each one is rewarded with that which he has justly merited according to his works and according to thy incomprehensible wisdom in the equity of thy strictest justice" (II Tim. 4, 8). Such was the prayer of Christ our Savior on the Cross to his eternal Father. It was sealed and deposited in the heart of the most holy Mary as the mysterious and sacramental testament, in order that through her intercession and solicitous care it might at its time, and even from that moment, be executed in the Church, just as it had before this time been prepared and perfected by the wise providence of God, in whom all the past and the future is always one with the present.

698. My daughter, seek with all the powers of thy mind during thy whole life to remember the mysteries manifested to thee in this chapter. I, as thy Mother and thy Instructress, shall ask the Lord by his divine power to impress in thy heart the knowledge, which I have vouchsafed thee, in order that it may remain fixed and ever present to thee as long as thou livest. In virtue of this blessing keep in thy memory Christ crucified, who is my divine Son and thy Spouse, and never forget the sufferings of the Cross and the doctrine taught by Him upon it. This is the mirror by which thou must arrange all thy adornments and the source from which thou art to draw thy interior beauty, like a true daughter of the Prince (Ps. 44, 14), in order that thou mayest be prepared, proceed and reign as the spouse of the supreme King. As this honorable title obliges thee to seek with all thy power to imitate Him as far as is becoming thy station and possible to thee by his grace, and as this is to be the true fruit of my doctrine, I wish that from today on thou live crucified with Christ, entirely assimilated to thy exemplar and model and dead to this earthly life (II Cor. 5, 15). I desire that in thee shall vanish the effects of the first sin, that thou live only for the operations and movements of divine virtue, and that thou renounce thy inheritance as a daughter of the first Adam, in order that in thee may bear fruit the inheritance of the second Adam, who is Jesus Christ, thy Redeemer and Teacher.

699. Thy state of life must be for thee a most rigid

cross on which thou must remain crucified, and thou must not widen thy path by seeking for dispensation and weakening interpretation of thy rules to make it easy and comfortable, but at the same time, insecure and full of imperfections. This is the deception into which the children of Babylon and of Adam fall, that each one according to his state seeks to find ease in the work commanded by the law of God. They set aside the salvation of their soul in their efforts to buy heaven very cheaply, or risk losing it by dreading the restrictions and entire subjection necessary to observe rigorously the divine law and its precepts. Hence arises the desire to find explanations and opinions, which smooth the paths and highways of eternal life, without heeding the doctrine of my divine Son, that the path of life is very narrow (Matth. 7, 14). They forget that the Lord himself has walked these narrow paths, in order that no one might imagine he can reach eternal life over paths more spacious and comfortable to the flesh and to the inclinations vitiated by sins. This danger is greater for ecclesiastics and religious, who by their very state must follow the Master and must accommodate themselves to his life of poverty and must choose for this purpose the way of the Cross. Some of them however are apt to seek the dignities attached to the religious state for their temporal advantage, for the increase of their own honor and praise. In order to secure it they lighten the Cross they have promised to bear, so that they live a carnal life, little restricted and much eased by deceptive dispensations and vain excuses. In their time they shall recognize the truth and that saying of the Holy Ghost: Each one thinks his path secure, but the Lord weighs in his hands the hearts of men (Prov. 21, 2).

700. So far from this deceit, do I wish thee to be, my daughter, that thou must live strictly up to the most rigorous demands of thy profession; in such a way that thou canst not stretch thyself in any way, being nailed immovably to the Cross with Christ. Thou must set aside all temporal advantages, for the least point pertaining to the utmost perfection of thy state. Thy right hand, my daughter, must be nailed to the Cross by obedience, and reserve not for thyself the least movement, the least activity, or word, or thought not controlled by this virtue. Thou must not maintain any position that is of thy own choice, but only such as is willed by others; thou must not appear wise in thy own conceit in anything, but ignorant and blind, in order to follow entirely the guidance of thy superiors (Prov. 3, 7). He that promises, says the wise man (Prov. 6, 1), binds his hands, and by his words shall he be bound and chained. Thou hast bound thy hand by the vow of obedience and hast thereby lost thy liberty and thy right of wishing or not wishing. Thy left hand thou hast nailed to the Cross by the vow of poverty, depriving thee of all right to follow any inclination toward the objects usually coveted by the eyes; for both in the use and in the desire for such creatures thou must rigorously imitate Christ impoverished and despoiled upon the Cross. By the third vow, that of chastity, thy feet are nailed to the Cross, in order that all thy steps and movements may be pure, chaste and beautiful. For this thou must not permit in thy presence the least word offensive to purity, nor, by looking upon or touching any human creature, allow any sensual image or impression within thee; thy eyes and all thy senses are to remain consecrated to chastity, without making more use of them than to fix them upon Jesus crucified. The

fourth vow, of perpetual enclosure, thou wilt maintain
in the bosom of my divine Son, to which I consign thee.
In order that this doctrine may appear to thee sweet,
and this path less narrow, contemplate and consider
in thy heart the image of my Son and Lord full of
blood, torments, sorrows, and at last nailed to the Cross,
no part of his sacred body being exempt from wounds
and excruciating pains. The Lord and I were most solicitous and compassionate toward all the children of
men; for them We suffered and endured such bitter
sorrows, in order that they might be encouraged not to
refuse less severe sufferings for their own eternal good
and in return for so obliging a love. Therefore let
mortals show themselves thankful, willingly entering
upon the rough and thorny path and accepting the Cross,
to bear it after Christ. Thus will they walk upon the
direct path toward heaven and gain an eternal happiness
(Matth. 16, 24).

CHAPTER XIV

701. The hidden and venerable mysteries of this chapter correspond to many others scattered through the whole extent of this history. One of them is, that Lucifer and his demons in the course of the life and miracles of our Savior, never could ascertain fully whether the Lord was true God and Redeemer of the world, and consequently what was the dignity of the most holy Mary. This was so disposed by divine Providence, in order that the whole mystery of the Incarnation and the Redemption of the human race might be more fittingly accomplished. Lucifer, although knowing that God was to assume human flesh, nevertheless knew nothing of the manner and the circumstances of the Incarnation. As he was permitted to form an opinion of this mystery in accordance with his pride, he was full of hallucinations, sometimes believing Christ to be God on account of his miracles, sometimes rejecting such an opinion on account of seeing Him poor, humiliated, afflicted and fatigued. Harassed by these contradicting evidences, he remained in doubt and continued his inquiries until the predestined hour of Christ's Death on the Cross, where, in virtue of the Passion and Death of the sacred humanity, which he had himself brought about, he was to be both undeceived and vanquished by the full solution of these mysteries.

702. This triumph of Christ our Savior was accomplished in such an exalted and miraculous manner, that I feel the sluggishness and insufficiency of my powers to describe it. It took place in a manner too spiritual and too far removed from the perception of the senses, according to which I must describe its process. In order to manifest it, I should wish we were able to speak and understand one another by means of the simple intercourse and vision peculiar to the angels; for such would be necessary in order to describe and understand correctly this great miracle of the omnipotence of God. I shall say what I can and leave the understanding of it more to the enlightenment of faith than to the signification of my words.

703. In the preceding chapter I have said that Lucifer and his demons, as soon as they saw the Lord taking the Cross upon his sacred shoulders, wished to fly and cast themselves into hell; for at that moment they began to feel with greater force the operations of his divine power. By divine intervention this new torment made them aware that the Death of this innocent Man, whose destruction they had plotted and who could not be a mere man, threatened great ruin to themselves. They therefore desired to withdraw and they ceased to incite the Jews and the executioners, as they had done hitherto. But the command of the most blessed Mary, enforced by the divine power, detained them and, enchained like fiercest dragons, compelled them to accompany Christ to Calvary. The ends of the mysterious chain that bound them were placed into the hands of Mary, the great Queen, who, by the power of her divine Son, held them all in subjection and bondage. Although they many times sought to break away and raged in helpless fury, they could not overcome the power of the heavenly

Lady. She forced them to come to Calvary and stand around the Cross, where She commanded them to remain motionless and witness the end of the great mysteries there enacted for the salvation of men and the ruin of themselves.

704. Lucifer and his infernal hosts were so overwhelmed with pains and torments by the presence of the Lord and his blessed Mother, and with the fear of their impending ruin, that they would have felt greatly relieved to be allowed to cast themselves into the darkness of hell. As this was not permitted them, they fell upon one another and furiously fought with each other like hornets disturbed in their nest, or like a brood of vermin confusedly seeking some dark shelter. But their rabid fury was not that of animals, but that of demons more cruel than dragons. Then the haughty pride of Lucifer saw itself entirely vanquished and all his proud thoughts of setting his throne above the stars of heaven and drinking dry the waters of the Jordan put to shame (Is. 14, 13; Job 40, 18). How weak and annihilated was now he, who so often had presumed to overturn the whole earth! How downcast and confounded he, who had deceived so many souls by false promises and vain threats! How dismayed this unhappy one at the sight of the gibbet, where he had sought to place Mardocheus! (Esther 7, 9). What horrid shame to see the true Esther, most holy Mary, asking for the rescue of her people and the downfall of the traitor and the chastisement of his pride! There our invincible Judith beheaded him (Judith 13, 10); there She trod upon his haughty neck. From now on, O Lucifer, I know that thy arrogance and pride is much greater than thy strength (Is. 16, 6). Instead of splendor now worms clothe thee about (Is. 14, 11), and rottenness envelops and consumes

thy carrion corpse! Thou, who hast afflicted the nations, art now more wounded, bound and oppressed than all the world. Thenceforward I do not fear thy counterfeit threats; I will no longer listen to thy wiles; for I see thee reduced, weakened and entirely helpless.

705. The time had now come for this ancient dragon to be vanquished by the Master of life. As this was to be the hour of his disillusionment, and as this poisonous asp was not to escape it by stopping his ears to the voice of the Enchanter (Ps. 57, 5), the Lord began to speak the seven words from his Cross, at the same time providing that Lucifer and his demons should understand the mysteries therein contained. For it was by this disclosure that the Lord wished to triumph over them, over sin and death, and despoil them of their tyrannous power over the human race. The Savior then pronounced the first word: "Father, forgive them, for they know not what they do!" (Luke 23, 34). By these words the princes of darkness came to the full conviction, that Christ our Lord was speaking to the eternal Father, that He was his natural Son and the true God with Him and the Holy Ghost, that He had permitted death in his most sacred and perfect humanity, united to the Divinity for the salvation of the whole human race; that now He offered his infinitely precious merits for the pardon of the sins of all those children of Adam, who should avail themselves thereof for their rescue, not excepting even the wretches that crucified Him. At this discovery Lucifer and his demons were thrown into such fury and despair that they instantly wished to hurl themselves impetuously to the depths of hell and strained all their powers to accomplish it in spite of the powerful Queen.

706. In the second word spoken by the Lord to the fortunate thief: "Amen I say to thee, today thou shalt

be with Me in paradise," the demons understood that the fruits of the Redemption in the justification of sinners ended in the glorification of the just. They were made aware that from this hour the merits of Christ would commence to act with a new force and strength, that through them should be opened the gates of Paradise, which had been closed by the first sin, and that from now on men would enter upon eternal happiness and occupy their destined heavenly seats, which until now had been impossible for them. They perceived the power of Christ to call sinners, justify and beautify them, and they felt the triumphs gained over themselves by the exalted virtues, the humility, patience, meekness and all the virtues of his life. The confusion and torment of Lucifer at seeing this cannot be explained by human tongue; but it was so great, that he humiliated himself so far as to beg the most blessed Virgin to permit them to descend into hell and be cast out from her presence; but the great Queen would not consent, as the time had not yet arrived.

707. At the third word spoken by the Lord to his Mother: "Woman, behold thy son!" the demons discovered that this heavenly Lady was the true Mother of the Godman, the same Woman whose likeness and prophetic sign had been shown to them in the heavens at their creation, and who was to crush their head as announced by the Lord in the terrestrial paradise. They were informed of the dignity and excellence of this great Lady over all creatures, and of her power which they were even now experiencing. As they had from the beginning of the world and from the creation of the first woman, used all their astuteness to find out who this great woman that was announced in the heavens could be, and as they now discovered Her in Mary, whom

they had until now overlooked, these dragons were seized with inexpressible fury; their having been thus mistaken crushed their arrogance beyond all their other torments, and in their fury they raged against their own selves like bloodthirsty lions, while their helpless wrath against the heavenly Lady was increased a thousandfold. Moreover, they discerned that saint John was appointed by Christ our Lord as the angel guardian of his Mother, endowed with the powers of the priesthood. This they understood to be in the nature of a threat against their own wrath, which was well known to saint John. Lucifer saw not only the power of the Evangelist, but that given to all the priests in virtue of their participation in the dignity and power of our Redeemer; and that the rest of the just, even though no priests, were placed under the special protection of the Lord and made powerful against hell. All this paralyzed the strength of Lucifer and his demons.

708. The fourth word of Christ was addressed to the eternal Father: "God, my God, why hast Thou forsaken Me?" The evil spirits discovered in these words that the charity of God toward men was boundless and everlasting; that, in order to satisfy it, He had mysteriously suspended the influence of the Divinity over his most sacred humanity, thus permitting his sufferings to reach the highest degree and drawing from them the most abundant fruits; that He was aware and lovingly complained of his being deprived of the salvation of a part of the human race; how ready He was to suffer more, if such would be ordained by the eternal Father. Man's good fortune in being so beloved by God increased the envy of Lucifer and his demons, and they foresaw the divine Omnipotence following out this immense love without limitation. This knowledge crushed the haughty

malice of the enemies and they were made well aware of their own weakness and helplessness in opposing this love, if men themselves should not choose to neglect its influence.

709. The fifth word of Christ, "I thirst," confirmed Christ's triumph over the devil and his followers; they were filled with wrath and fury because the Lord clearly let them see their total overthrow. By these words they understood Him to say to them: If what I suffer for men and my love for them seem great to you, be assured that my love for them is still unsatiated, that it continues to long for their eternal salvation, and that the mighty waters of torments and sufferings have not extinguished it (Cant. 8, 7). Much more would I suffer for them, if it were necessary, in order to deliver them from your tyranny and make them powerful and strong against your malice and pride.

710. In the sixth word of the Lord: "It is consummated!" Lucifer and his hordes were informed that the mystery of the Incarnation and Redemption was now accomplished and entirely perfected according to the decree of divine wisdom. For they were made to feel that Christ our Redeemer had obediently fulfilled the will of the eternal Father; that He had accomplished all the promises and prophecies made to the world by the ancient Fathers; that his humility and obedience had compensated for their own pride and disobedience in heaven in not having subjected themselves and acknowledged Him as their Superior in human flesh; and that they were now through the wisdom of God justly humbled and vanquished by the very Lord whom they despised. The great dignity and the infinite merits of Christ demanded that in this very hour He should exercise his office and power of Judge over angels and men, such as had been

conceded to Him by the eternal Father. He now applied this power by hurling this sentence at Lucifer and all his followers, that, being condemned to eternal fire, they instantly depart into the deepest dungeons of hell. This very sentence was included in the pronouncing of the seventh word: "Father, into thy hands I commend my spirit!" (Luke 23, 46.) The mighty Queen and Mother concurred with the will of her Son Jesus and united with his her command that Lucifer and all demons depart to the infernal depths. In virtue of these decrees of the supreme King and of the Queen, the evil spirits were routed from Calvary and precipitated to deepest hell more violently and suddenly than a flash of light through the riven clouds.

711. Christ our Savior, as the triumphant Conqueror having vanquished the great enemy, now yielded up his spirit to the Father and permitted death to approach by inclining his head (John 19, 30). By this permission He also vanquished death, which had been equally deceived in Him with the demons. For death could not attack men, or had any jurisdiction of them, except through the first sin, of which it was a punishment. On this account the Apostle says that the weapon or the sting of death is sin, which opens up the wounds by which death enters into the world of humanity (Rom. 5, 12); and as our Savior paid the debt of sin which He could not commit, therefore, when death took away his life without the shadow of justice, it lost the power which it had over the other sons of Adam (I Cor. 15, 55). Thenceforward neither death nor the devil could attack men, unless they, failing to avail themselves of the victory of Christ, should again subject themselves of their own free will. If our first Father Adam had not sinned and we ourselves in him, we would not suffer the punishment of death, but

merely pass over to the happiness of the eternal father-
land. But sin has made us its subjects and slaves of the
devil. He avails himself of death to deprive us first of
the grace, the blessings and the friendship of God.
Thereby he also prevents us from reaching eternal life
and we remain in the slavery of sin and the devil, subject to his tyrannous power (I John 3, 8). Our Savior
Christ despoiled the demon of all these advantages and,
in dying without sin and satisfying for our own,
merited that our death should be a death of the body only,
and not of the soul; that it should have power to take
away our temporal life, but not our eternal; the natural,
not the spiritual; and that it should thenceforward be
merely the portal to the eternal happiness, if we ourselves
did not renounce that blessing. Thus the Lord satisfied
for the chastisements due to the first sin, at the same
time furnishing us a means of offering a compensation
in our own name by accepting our natural and bodily
death for the love of God. Christ absorbed death (I
Cor. 15, 51) and offered his own as a bait for deceiving
death (Osee. 13, 14). By his Death He put an end of
its power, overcame it, and was the Death of death itself.

712. In this triumph the Savior fulfilled the prophecy
contained in the canticle and prayer of Habbacuc, of
which I shall select some passages necessary for my purpose. The prophet was informed of the mystery and
the power of Christ over death and the devil. In
prophetic foresight he prayed that the Lord vivify the
work of his hands, that is, man; that in his greatest
wrath He remember his mercy. He prophesied that the
glory of this miracle should fill the heavens and the
praise of it, the earth; that its splendor shall be as that
of light; that in his hands He shall embrace the horns,
which are the arms of the Cross and wherein is hidden

his strength; that death should fly from Him captive and vanquished; that before his feet the devil should be routed and measure the earth (Habac. 3, 2-5). All this was fulfilled to the letter; for Lucifer departed having his head crushed under the feet of Christ and his blessed Mother, who subdued Him by their sufferings and by their power. Since the devil was forced to cast himself to lowest hell, which is the middle of the earth and farthest removed from its surface, he is said to measure the earth. The rest of the canticle pertains to the triumph of Christ our Lord in the succeeding ages of the Church; but that need not be rehearsed here. It is, however, proper for men to understand that Lucifer and his demons were restricted, lamed and weakened in their power of tempting the rational creatures, unless their sins and their own free will do not again unbind them and encourage them to return for the destruction of the world. All this will be better understood from the proceedings of the infernal council held in hell and from what I shall say further in the course of this history.

COUNCIL HELD BY LUCIFER AND HIS DEMONS IN HELL AFTER THE DEATH OF CHRIST OUR LORD.

713. The rout of Lucifer and his angels from Calvary to the abyss of hell was more violent and disastrous than their first expulsion from heaven. Though, as holy Job says (Job 10, 21), that place is a land of darkness, covered with the shades of death, full of gloomy disorder, misery, torments and confusion; yet on this occasion the chaos and disorder was a thousandfold increased; because the damned were made to feel new horror and additional punishments at the sudden meeting of the ferocious demons in their rabid fury. It is certain that

the devils have not the power of assigning the damned
to a place of greater or lesser torment; for all their torments are decreed by divine justice according to the measure of the demerits of each of the condemned.   But,
besides this essential punishment, the just Judge allows
them to suffer other accidental punishments from time
to time according to occasion; for their sins have left
roots in the world and cause much damage to others,
who are damned on their account, and the new effects still
arising from former sins cause such accidental punishments in the damned.   Thus the demons devised new
torments for Judas, for having sold and brought about
the death of Christ.   They also understood then that this
place of dreadful punishments, where they had thrown
him and of which I have spoken above, was destined for
the chastisement of those who damned themselves by
refusing to practice their faith in their lives and for those
who purposely refuse to believe and avail themselves of
the fruits of the Redemption.   Against these the devils
execute a more furious wrath, similar to the one they
have conceived against Jesus and Mary.

714. As soon as Lucifer was permitted to proceed in
these matters and arise from the consternation in which
he remained for some time, he set about proposing to
his fellow-demons new plans of his pride.   For this purpose he called them all together and placing himself in
an elevated position, he spoke to them: "To you, who
have for so many ages followed and still follow my
standards for the vengeance of my wrongs, is known the
injury which I have now sustained at the hands of this
Mangod, and how for thirty-three years He has led me
about in deceit, hiding his Divinity and concealing the
operations of his soul, and how He has now triumphed
over us by the very Death which we have brought upon

Him. Before He assumed flesh I hated Him and refused to acknowledge Him as being more worthy than I to be adored by the rest of creation. Although on account of this resistance I was cast out from heaven with you and was degraded to this abominable condition so unworthy of my greatness and former beauty, I am even more tormented to see myself thus vanquished and oppressed by this Man and by his Mother. From the day on which the first man was created I have sleeplessly sought to find Them and destroy Them; or if I should not be able to destroy Them, I at least wished to bring destruction upon all his creatures and induce them not to acknowledge Him as their God, and that none of them should ever draw any benefit from his works. This has been my intent, to this all my solicitude and efforts were directed. But in vain, since He has overcome me by his humility and poverty, crushed me by his patience, and at last has despoiled me of the sovereignty of the world by his Passion and frightful Death. This causes me such an excruciating pain, that, even if I succeeded in hurling Him from the right hand of his Father, where He sits triumphant, and if I should draw all the souls redeemed down into this hell, my wrath would not be satiated or my fury placated."

715. "Is it possible that the human nature, so inferior to my own, shall be exalted above all the creatures! That it should be so loved and favored, as to be united to the Creator in the person of the eternal Word! That He should first make war upon me before executing this work, and afterwards overwhelm me with such confusion! From the beginning I have held this humanity as my greatest enemy; it has always filled me with intolerable abhorrence. O men, so favored and gifted by your God, whom I abhor, and so ardently loved by Him! How shall

I hinder your good fortune? How shall I bring upon you my unhappiness, since I cannot destroy the existence you have received? What shall we now begin, O my followers? How shall we restore our reign? How shall we recover our power over men? How shall we overcome them? For if men from now on shall not be most senseless and ungrateful, if they are not worse disposed than we ourselves toward this Godman, who has redeemed them with so much love, it is clear that all of them will eagerly follow Him; none will take notice of our deceits; they will abhor the honors which we insidiously offer them, and will love contempt; they will seek the mortification of the flesh and will discover the danger of carnal pleasure and ease; they will despise riches and treasures, and love the poverty so much honored by their Master; and all that we can offer to their appetites they will abhor in imitation of their true Redeemer. Thus will our reign be destroyed, since no one will be added to our number in this place of confusion and torments; all will reach the happiness which we have lost, all will humiliate themselves to the dust and suffer with patience; and my wrath and haughtiness will avail me nothing."

716. "Ah, woe is me, what torment does this mistake cause me! When I tempted Him in the desert, the only result was to afford Him a chance to leave the example of this victory, by following which men can overcome me so much the more easily. My persecutions only brought out more clearly his doctrine of humility and patience. In persuading Judas to betray Him, and the Jews to subject Him to the deadly torture of the Cross, I merely hastened my ruin and the salvation of men, while the doctrine I sought to blot out was only the more firmly implanted. How could One who is God humiliate Himself to such an extent? How could He bear so much

from men who are evil? How could I myself have been led to assist so much in making this salvation so copious and wonderful? O how godlike is the power of that Man which could torment and weaken me so? And how can this Woman, his Mother and my Enemy, be so mighty and invincible in her opposition to me? New is such power in a mere creature, and no doubt She derived it from the divine Word, whom She clothed in human flesh. Through this Woman the Almighty has ceaselessly waged war against me, though I have hated Her in my pride from the moment I recognized Her in her image or heavenly sign. But if my proud indignation is not to be assuaged, I benefit nothing by my perpetual war against this Redeemer, against his Mother and against men. Now then, ye demons who follow me, now is the time to give way to our wrath against God. Come all of ye to take counsel what we are to do; for I desire to hear your opinions."

717. Some of the principal demons gave their answers to this dreadful proposal, encouraging Lucifer by suggesting diverse schemes for hindering the fruit of the Redemption among men. They all agreed that it was not possible to injure the person of Christ, to diminish the immense value of his merits, to destroy the efficacy of the Sacraments, to falsify or abolish the doctrine which Christ had preached; yet they resolved that, in accordance with the new order of assistance and favor established by God for the salvation of men, they should now seek new ways of hindering and preventing the work of God by so much the greater deceits and temptations. In reference to these plans some of the astute and malicious demons said: "It is true, that men now have at their disposal a new and very powerful doctrine and law, new and efficacious Sacraments, a new Model and In-

structor of virtues, a powerful Intercessor and Advocate in this Woman; yet the natural inclinations and passions of the flesh remain just the same, and the sensible and delectable creatures have not changed their nature. Let us then, making use of this situation with increased astuteness, foil as far as in us lies the effects of what this Godman has wrought for men. Let us begin strenuous warfare against mankind by suggesting new attractions, exciting them to follow their passions in forgetfulness of all else. Thus men, being taken up with these dangerous things, cannot attend to the contrary."

718. Acting upon this counsel they redistributed the spheres of work among themselves, in order that each squadron of demons might, with a specialized astuteness, tempt men to different vices. They resolved to continue to propagate idolatry in the world, so that men might not come to the knowledge of the true God and the Redemption. Wherever idolatry would fail, they concluded to establish sects and heresies, for which they would select the most perverse and depraved of the human race as leaders and teachers of error. Then and there was concocted among these malignant spirits the sect of Mahomet, the heresies of Arius, Pelagius, Nestorius, and whatever other heresies have been started in the world from the first ages of the Church until now, together with those which they have in readiness, but which it is neither necessary nor proper to mention here. Lucifer showed himself content with these infernal counsels as being opposed to divine truth and destructive of the very foundation of man's rescue, namely divine faith. He lavished flattering praise and high offices upon those demons, who showed themselves willing and who undertook to find the impious originators of these errors.

719. Some of the devils charged themselves with perverting the inclinations of children at their conception

and birth; others to induce parents to be negligent in the education and instruction of their children, either through an inordinate love or aversion, and to cause a hatred of parents among the children. Some offered to create hatred between husbands and wives, to place them in the way of adultery, or to think little of the fidelity promised to their conjugal partners. All agreed to sow among men the seeds of discord, hatred and vengeance, proud and sensual thoughts, desire of riches or honors, and by suggesting sophistical reasons against all the virtues Christ has taught; above all they intended to weaken the remembrance of his Passion and Death, of the means of salvation, and of the eternal pains of hell. By these means the demons hoped to burden all the powers and the faculties of men with solicitude for earthly affairs and sensual pleasures, leaving them little time for spiritual thoughts and their own salvation.

720. Lucifer heard these different suggestions of the demons, and answering them, he said: "I am much beholden to you for your opinions: I approve of them and adopt them all; it will be easy to put them into practice with those, who do not profess the law given by this Redeemer to men, though with those who accept and embrace these laws, it will be a difficult enterprise. But against this law and against those that follow it, I intend to direct all my wrath and fury and I shall most bitterly persecute those who hear the doctrine of this Redeemer and become his disciples; against these must our most relentless battle be waged to the end of the world. In this new Church I must strive to sow my cockle (Matth. 14, 25), the ambitions, the avarice, the sensuality, and the deadly hatreds, with all the other vices, of which I am the head. For if once these sins multiply and increase among the faithful, they will, with

their concomitant malice and ingratitude, irritate God and justly deprive men of the helps of grace left to them by the merits of the Redeemer. If once they have thus despoiled themselves of these means of salvation, we shall have assured victory over them. We must also exert ourselves to weaken piety and all that is spiritual and divine; so that they do not realize the power of the Sacraments and receive them in mortal sin, or at least without fervor and devotion. For since these Sacraments are spiritual, it is necessary to receive them with well-disposed will, in order to reap their fruits. If once they despise the medicine, they shall languish in their sickness and be less able to withstand our temptations; they will not see through our deceits, they will let the memory of their Redeemer and of the intercession of his Mother slip from their minds. Thus will their foul ingratitude make them unworthy of grace and so irritate their God and Savior, as to deprive them of his helps. In all this I wish, that all of you assist me strenuously, losing neither time nor occasion for executing my commands."

721. It is not possible to rehearse all the schemes of this dragon and his allies concocted at that time against the holy Church and her children, in order that these waters of Jordan might be swallowed up in his throat (Job 40, 18). It is enough to state that they spent nearly a full year after the Death of Christ in conferring and considering among themselves the state of the world up to that time and the changes wrought by Christ our God and Master through his Death and after having manifested the light of his faith by so many miracles, blessings and examples of holy men. If all these labors have not sufficed to draw all men to the way of salvation, it can be easily understood, that

Lucifer should have prevailed and that his wrath should be so great, as to cause us justly to say with saint John: "Woe to the earth, for satan is come down to you full of wrath and fury!" But alas! that truths so infallible and so much to be dreaded and avoided by men, should in our days be blotted from the minds of mortals to the irreparable danger of the whole world! Our enemy is astute, cruel and watchful: we sleepy, lukewarm and careless! What wonder that Lucifer has intrenched himself so firmly in the world, when so many listen to him, accept and follow his deceits, so few resist him, and entirely forget the eternal death, which he so furiously and maliciously seeks to draw upon them? I beseech those, who read this, not to forget this dreadful danger. If they are not convinced of this danger through the evil condition of the world and through the evils each one experiences himself, let them at least learn of this danger by the vast and powerful remedies and helps, which the Savior thought it necessary to leave behind in his Church. For He would not have provided such antidotes if our ailment and danger of eternal death were not so great and formidable.

INSTRUCTION WHICH THE QUEEN OF HEAVEN GAVE ME.

722. My daughter, by divine enlightenment thou hast received a deep understanding of the glorious triumph of my Son and Lord on the Cross over the demons and of their rout and vanquishment. But thou must remember that thou art yet ignorant of much more than what thou knowest concerning these ineffable mysteries. For in mortal flesh the creature cannot comprehend them in their reality, and divine Providence reserves the full understanding of them as a reward of the saints in

heaven and for the beatific vision, in which these mysteries will be comprehended clearly. This insight will also be given to the reprobate, to each one according to his degree, for their confusion and punishment at the end of their career. But what thou hast learned will suffice to apprise thee of the dangers of this mortal life and to enliven thy hope of overcoming thy enemies. I wish also to warn thee of the new wrath, which the dragon has conceived especially against thee for what thou hast written in this chapter. He has ceaselessly pursued thee with his wrath and has sought to hinder thee from writing my life, as thou hast experienced continually in this work. But now his haughty pride is incensed against thee especially, because thou hast revealed his humiliation, his crushing ruin at the Death of my most blessed Son, the condition in which it left him and the secret counsels for revenging himself upon the children of Adam and especially upon the members of the holy church. All this has excited and disturbed him anew, seeing that these secrets will be revealed to those yet ignorant of them. Thou wilt feel his wrath in the difficulties he will place in thy way, the temptations and persecutions thou hast already encountered. Therefore I warn thee to be wary and circumspect against the rabid fury and cruelty of thy enemy.

723. Thou art astonished, and justly, to see, on the one hand, the power of my Son's merits and of his Redemption, the ruin and weakness caused by the demons in men; and, on the other hand, to see the power of the devil lording it over the world in haughty presumption. Although the light given to thee in writing this history is equal to this astonishment, I wish to add still another point of information, in order that thou mayest guard thyself so much the more carefully against ene-

mies so full of malice. It is certain, that when hell came to the full knowledge of the sacrament of the Incarnation and Redemption, and of the poverty, humility and lowliness of the birth of Jesus, of his life and miracles, ending in the mysterious Passion and Death, and of all the rest of his labors to draw men to Him, Lucifer and his demons were weakened and disabled and they saw that they could not tempt the faithful in the same way as the rest of men and as they ceaselessly desire to do. In the primitive Church this terror and fear of the baptized, and of the followers of Christ our Lord, continued many years; for the divine virtues shone forth brightly in their imitation of Christ, in their zeal in confessing the faith, in following the teachings of the Gospel, in practicing heroic virtues and most fervent love, humility, patience and contempt of the vanities and deceits of the world. Many shed their blood and gave their life for Christ the Lord; they performed many admirable and exalted deeds for the glory of his name. This invincible fortitude resulted from their living at a time so near to the Passion and Death of their Redeemer and so close to the prodigious example of his patience and humility; but also because they were less tempted by the devils, who could not so soon rise from the crushing defeat brought upon them by the triumph of the crucified God.

724. This close imitation and living reproduction of Christ, confronting the demons in the first children of the Church, they feared so much, that they dared not approach and they precipitously fled from the Apostles and the just ones imbued with the doctrines of my divine Son. In them were offered up to the Almighty the first fruits of grace, and of Redemption. What is seen in the saints and in perfect Christians in those

times, would happen in the present times with all the
Catholics if they would accept grace and work with it
instead of permitting it to go to waste, and if they would
seek the way of the Cross; for Lucifer fears it just
as much now as in the times thou hast been writing of.
But soon the charity, zeal and devotion in many of the
faithful began to grow cold and they forgot the blessings of the Redemption; they yielded to their carnal inclinations and desires, they loved vanity and avarice,
and permitted themselves to be fascinated and deceived
by the false pretenses of Lucifer, obscuring the glory
of their Savior and inveigling them into the meshes of
their mortal enemies. This foul ingratitude has thrown
the world into the present state and has encouraged the
demons to rise up in their pride against God, audaciously
presuming to possess themselves of all the children of
Adam on account of this forgetfulness and carelessness
of Catholics. They presume to plot the destruction of
the whole Church by the perversion of so many who
have fallen away from it; and by inducing those who
are in it, to think little of it, or by hindering them from
producing the fruits of the blood and death of their
Redeemer. The greatest misfortune is, that many Catholics fail to recognize this great damage and do not seri-
ously think of a remedy, although they can presume that
the times, of which Jesus forewarned the women of Jerusalem, have arrived; namely, those in which the sterile
should be happy, and in which many would call upon
the mountains and the hills to cover and fall upon them,
in order not to see the devastation of wickedness cutting
down the sons of perdition, the dried trees, barren of
all the fruits of virtue. In these evil times dost thou
live, my dearest; and in order that thou mayest not be
included in the perdition of so many souls, do thou be-

wail it in the bitterness of thy heart, never forgetting the mysteries of the Incarnation, Passion and Death of my Divine Son. I desire thee to give thanks in compensation for the great number of those, who forget it, and I assure thee that the mere memory and contemplation of these mysteries are terrible to hell, torment and drive away the demons, and that they avoid and fly those who thankfully remember the life and passion of my divine Son.

CHAPTER XV

725. The Evangelist saint John tells us that near
the Cross stood Mary, the most holy Mother of Jesus,
with Mary Cleophas and Mary Magdalen. Although
this is said of the time before Jesus expired, it must
be understood, that the unconquerable Queen remained
also afterwards, always standing beneath the Cross and
adoring her dead Jesus and his divinity inseparably
united to his sacred body. Amid the impetuous floods
of sorrow, that penetrated to the inmost recesses of her
chastest heart, the great Lady remained immovably constant in the exercise of ineffable virtues, while contemplating within Her the mysteries of man's Redemption and the order in which divine Wisdom disposed of
all these sacraments. The greatest affliction of the
Mother of mercy was the traitorous ingratitude, which
men, to their own great loss, would show toward this
extraordinary blessing, so worthy of eternal thanksgiving. But now She was especially solicitous for the
burial of the sacred body of her divine Son and how to
procure some one to take it down from the Cross.
Full of this sorrowful anxiety, keeping her heavenly
eyes riveted upon it, She turned to her holy angels
around Her and spoke to them: "Ministers of the Most

High, my friends in tribulation, you know that there is
no sorrow like unto my sorrow; tell me then, how shall
I take down from the Cross, whom my soul loves; how
and where shall I give Him honorable burial, since this
duty pertains to me as his Mother? Tell me what to
do, and assist me on this occasion by your diligence."

726. The holy angels answered: "Our Queen and
Mistress, let thy afflicted heart be dilated for what is still
to be borne. The omnipotent Lord has concealed his
glory and power from mortals in order to subject Himself to the cruelty of man's impious malice and has
always permitted the laws established for the course
of human events to be fulfilled. One of them is, that
the condemned shall not leave the cross without the
consent of the judge. We are ready and able to obey
Thee and to defend our true God and Creator, but his
will restrains us, because He wishes to justify his cause
to the end and to shed the rest of the blood still in
Him for the benefit of mankind and in order that He
may bind them still more firmly to make a return for
his copious and redeeming love (Ps. 79, 7). If they
do not avail themselves of this blessing as they ought,
their punishment shall be deplorable and its severity
shall make amends for the long-suffering of God in delaying his vengeance." This answer of the angels increased the sorrow of the afflicted Mother; for it had
not been as yet revealed to Her, that her divine Son
should be wounded by the lance, and the fear of what
should happen to the sacred body renewed her tribulation and anxiety.

727. She soon saw an armed band approaching Calvary; and in her dread of some new outrage against
the deceased Savior, She spoke to saint John and the
pious women: "Alas, now shall my affliction reach its

utmost and transfix my heart! Is it possible, that the executioners and the Jews are not yet satisfied with having put to death my Son and Lord? Shall they now heap more injury upon his dead body?" It was the evening of the great Sabbath of the Jews, and in order to celebrate it with unburdened minds, they had asked Pilate for permission to shatter the limbs of the three men sentenced, so that, their death being hastened, they might be taken from the crosses and not left on them for the following day. With this intent the company of soldiers, which Mary now saw, had come to mount Calvary. As they perceived the two thieves still alive, they broke their limbs and so hastened their end (John 19, 31). But when they examined Jesus they found Him already dead, and therefore did not break his bones, thus fulfilling the mysterious prophecy in Exodus (Ex. 12, 46), commanding that no bones be broken in the figurative lamb to be eaten for the Pasch. But a soldier, by the name of Longinus, approaching the Cross of Christ, thrust his lance through the side of the Savior. Immediately water and blood flowed from the wound, as saint John, who saw it and who gives testimony of the truth, assures us (John 19, 34).

728. This wounding of the lance, which could not be felt by the sacred and dead body of the Lord, was felt by the most blessed Mother in his stead and in the same manner as if her chaste bosom had been pierced. But even this pain was exceeded by the affliction of her most holy soul, in witnessing the cruel laceration of the breast of her dead Son. At the same time, moved by compassion and love and in forgetfulness of her own sorrow, She said to Longinus: "The Almighty look upon thee with eyes of mercy for the pain thou hast caused to my soul!" So far and no farther went her

indignation (or more properly, her most merciful meekness), for the instruction of all of us who are ever injured. For to the mind of this sincerest Dove, this injury to the dead Christ weighed most heavily; and the retribution sought by Her for the delinquent was one of the greatest blessings, namely that God should look upon him with eyes of mercy and return blessings and gifts of grace for the offense. Thus it also happened; for the Savior, moved by the prayer of his blessed Mother, ordained that some of the blood and water from his sacred side should drop upon the face of Longinus and restore to him his eyesight, which he had almost lost. At the same time sight was given to his soul, so that he recognized in the Crucified his Savior, whom he had so inhumanly mutilated. Through this enlightenment Longinus was converted; weeping over his sins and having washed them in the blood and water of the side of Christ, he openly acknowledged and confessed Him as the true God and Savior of the world. He proclaimed Him as such in the presence of the Jews, confounding by his testimony their perfidy and hardness of heart.

729. The most prudent Queen then perceived the mystery of this lance-thrust, namely, that in this last pouring forth of the blood and water issued forth the new Church, cleansed and washed by the Passion and Death of Jesus, and that from his sacred side, as from the roots, should now spread out through the whole world the fruits of life eternal. She conferred within Herself also upon the mystery of that rock struck by the rod of divine justice (Exod. 17, 6), in order that the living waters might issue forth, quenching the thirst of all the human race and recreating and refreshing all who betook themselves to drink therefrom. She con-

sidered the coincidence of the five fountains from the wounds of his hands, feet and sides, which opened up the new paradise of the most holy humanity of our Savior, and which were more copious and powerful to fertilize the earth than those of the terrestrial paradise divided into four streams over the surface of the globe (Gen. 2, 10). These and other mysteries the great Lady rehearsed in a canticle of praise, which She composed in honor of her divine Son after his being wounded by the lance. Together with this canticle She poured forth a most fervent prayer, that all these mysteries of the Redemption be verified in the blessings spread over the whole human race.

730. The evening of that day of the parasceve was already approaching, and the loving Mother had as yet no solution of the difficulty of the burial of her dead Son, which She desired so much; but the Lord ordained, that the tribulations of his tenderest Mother should be relieved by Joseph of Arimathea and Nikodemus, whom he had inspired with the thought of caring for the burial of their Master. They were both just men and disciples of the Lord, although not of the seventy-two; for they had not as yet openly confessed themselves as disciples for fear of the Jews, who suspected and hated as enemies all those that followed Christ and acknowledged Him as Teacher. The dispositions of divine Providence concerning the burial of her Son had not been made known to the most prudent Virgin and thus her painful anxiety increased to such an extent, that She saw no way out of the difficulty. In her affliction She raised her eyes to heaven and said: "Eternal Father and my Lord, by the condescension of thy goodness and infinite wisdom I was raised to the exalted dignity of being the Mother of thy Son; and by that same bounty

of an immense God Thou hast permitted me to nurse
Him at my breast, nourish Him and accompany Him to
his death.   Now it behooves me as his Mother to give
honorable burial to his sacred body, though I can go no
farther than to desire it and deeply grieve, because I
am unable to fulfill my wishes.   I beseech thy divine
Majesty to provide some way for accomplishing my
desires."

731. This prayer the loving Mother offered up after
the sacred body of the Lord was perforated by the
lance. Soon after She saw another group of men coming toward Calvary with ladders and other apparatus
seemingly for the purpose of taking from the Cross her
priceless Treasure; but as She did not know their intentions, She was tortured by new fears of the cruelty of
the Jews, and turning to saint John, She said: "My Son,
what may be the object of these people in coming with
all these instruments?"   The apostle answered: "Do
not fear them that are coming, my Lady; for they
are Joseph and Nikodemus with some of their servants,
all of them friends and servants of thy divine Son and
my Lord."   Joseph was just in the eyes of the Most
High (John 19, 38), a noble decurion in the employ-
ment of the government, a member of the council, who
as is given us to understand in the Gospel, had not consented to the resolves and the proceedings of the murderers of Christ and who had recognized Jesus as the
true Messias.   Although Joseph had been a secret disciple of the Lord, yet at his death, in consequence of the
efficacious influence of the Redemption, he openly confessed his adherence.   Setting aside all fear of the envy
of the Jews and caring nothing for the power of the
Romans, he went boldly to Pilate and asked for the
body of Jesus (Mark 15, 43), in order to take Him

down from the Cross and give Him honorable burial. He openly maintained that he was innocent and the true Son of God, as witnessed by the miracles of his life and death.

732. Pilate dared not refuse the request of Joseph, but gave him full permission to dispose of the dead body of Jesus as he thought fit. With this permission Joseph left the house of the judge and called upon Nikodemus. He too was a just man, learned in divine and human letters and in the holy Scriptures, as is evident in what saint John related of him when he visited Christ at Night in order to hear the doctrine of Jesus Christ (John 3, 2). Joseph provided the winding sheets and burial cloths for the body of Jesus, while Nikodemus bought about one hundred pounds of the spices, which the Jews were accustomed to use in the burial of distinguished men (Matth. 27, 59). Provided with these and with other necessaries they took their way to Calvary. They were accompanied by their servants and some other pious and devout persons, in whom likewise the blood shed for all by the crucified God had produced its salutary effects.

733. They approached most Holy Mary, who, in the company of saint John and the holy women, stood in inconceivable sorrow at the foot of the Cross. Instead of a salute, their sorrow at the sight of so painful a spectacle as that of the divine Crucified, was roused to such vehemence and bitterness, that Joseph and Nikodemus remained for a time prostrate at the feet of the Queen and all of them at the foot of the Cross without speaking a word. All of them wept and sighed most bitterly until the invincible Queen raised them from the ground and animated and consoled them; whereupon they saluted Her in humble compassion. The most ob-

servant Mother thanked them kindly, especially for the
service they were about to render to their God and
Savior, and promised them the reward in the name of
Him whose body they were to lay in the tomb. Joseph
of Arimathea answered: "Even now, our Lady, do we
feel in the secret of our hearts the sweet delight of
the divine Spirit, who has moved us to such love, that
we never could merit it or succeed in explaining it."
Then they divested themselves of their mantles and with
their own hands Joseph and Nikodemus placed the ladders to the holy Cross.   On these they ascended in order to detach the sacred body, while the glorious Mother
stood closely by leaning on the arms of saint John and
Mary Magdalen.   It seemed to Joseph, that the sorrow
of the heavenly Lady would be renewed, when the sacred
body should be lowered and She should touch it, and
therefore He advised the Apostle to take Her aside in
order to draw away her attention.   But saint John,
who knew better the invincible heart of the Queen, answered that from the beginning She had stood by to witness the torments of the Lord and that She would not
leave him whom She venerated as her God and loved
as the Son of her Womb.

734. Nevertheless they continued to urge the expe-
diency of her retiring for a short time, until they should
lower their Master from the Cross.   But the great Lady
responded: "My dearest masters, since I was present,
when my sweetest Son was nailed to the Cross, fear not
to allow me to be present at his taking down; for this
act of piety, though it shall affect my heart with new
sorrow, will, in its very performance, afford a great relief."   Thereupon they began to arrange for the taking
down of the body.   First they detached the crown from
the head, laying bare the lacerations and deep wounds

it had caused. They handed it down with great reverence and amid abundant tears, placing it in the hands of the sweetest Mother. She received it prostrate on her knees, in deepest adoration bathed it with her tears, permitting the sharp thorns to wound her virginal countenance in pressing it to her face. She asked the eternal Father to inspire due veneration toward the sacred thorns in those Christians, who should obtain possession of them in future times.

735. In imitation of the Mother, saint John with the pious women and the other faithful there present, also adored it; and this they also did with the nails, handing them first to most holy Mary for veneration and afterward showing their own reverence. Then the great Lady placed Herself on her knees and held the unfolded cloth in her outstretched arms ready to receive the dead body of her Son. In order to assist Joseph and Nikodemus, saint John supported the head, and Mary Magdalen the feet, of Christ and thus they tearfully and reverently placed Him into the arms of his sweetest Mother. This was to Her an event of mixed sorrow and consolation; for in seeing Him thus wounded and all his beauty disfigured beyond all children of men (Ps. 44, 3), the sorrows of her most chaste heart were again renewed; and in holding Him in her arms and at her breast, her incomparable sorrow was rejoiced and her love satiated by the possession of her Treasure. She looked upon Him with supreme worship and reverence, shedding tears of blood. In union with Her, as He rested in her arms, all the multitude of her attendant angels worshipped Him, although unseen by all others except Mary. Then saint John first, and after him all those present in their turn, adored the sacred Body. The most prudent Mother, seated on the ground,

in the meanwhile held Him in her arms in order that
they might satisfy their devotion.

736. In all these proceedings our great Queen acted
with such heavenly wisdom and prudence, that She excited the admiration of the angels and men; for all her
words were full of the deepest significance, the most
winning affection and compassion for her deceased Son,
full of tenderness in her lamenting, and full of mystery in sentiment and meaning. Her sorrow exceeded
all that could ever be felt by mortals. She moved the
hearts to compassion and tears. She enlightened all in
the understanding of the sacrament now transpiring
under their hands. Above all, without failing in the
least of her duties, She preserved her humble dignity
and serenity of countenance in the midst of her heart-
rending affliction. With uniform adaptation to the circumstances She spoke to her beloved Son, to the eternal
Father, to the angels, to the bystanders, and to the whole
human race, for whose Redemption the Lord had undergone his Passion and Death. I will not detain myself
in particularizing the most prudent and sorrowful words
of the Lady on this occasion; for Christian piety will
be able to conceive many of them, and I cannot stay to
enumerate all these mysteries.

737. Some time passed during which the sorrowful
Mother held at her breast the dead Jesus, and as evening
was far advancing, saint John and Joseph besought Her
to allow the burial of her Son and God to proceed. The
most prudent Mother yielded; and they now embalmed
the sacred body, using all the hundred pounds of the
spices and the aromatic ointments brought by Nikodemus. Thus anointed the deified body was placed on
a bier, in order to be carried to the sepulchre. The heavenly Queen, most attentive in her zealous love, called

from heaven many choirs of angels, who, together with those of her guard, should accompany the burial of their Creator. Immediately they descended from on high in shapes visible to their Queen and Lady, though not to the rest. A procession of heavenly spirits was formed and another of men, and the sacred body was borne along by saint John, Joseph, Nikodemus and the centurion, who had confessed the Lord and now assisted at his burial. They were followed by the blessed Mother, by Mary Magdalen and the rest of the women disciples. Besides these a large number of the faithful assisted, for many had been moved by the divine light and had come to Calvary after the lance-thrust. All of them, in silence and in tears, joined the procession. They proceeded toward a nearby garden, where Joseph had hewn into the rock a new grave, in which nobody had as yet been buried or deposited (John 19, 41). In this most blessed sepulchre they placed the sacred body of Jesus. Before they closed it up with the heavy stone, the devout and prudent Mother adored Christ anew, causing the admiration of men and angels. They imitated Her, all of them adoring the crucified Savior now resting in his grave; thereupon they closed the sepulchre with the stone, which, according to the Evangelist, was very heavy (Matth. 27, 60).

738. At the same time the graves, which had opened at the Death of Christ, were again closed; for among other mysteries of their opening up, was this, that these graves as it were unsealed themselves in order to receive Him, whom the Jews had repudiated, when He was alive and their Benefactor. At the command of the Queen many angels remained to guard the sepulchre, where She had left her heart. In the same order and silence, in which they had come, they now returned to

Calvary. The heavenly Mistress of all virtues approached the holy Cross and worshipped it in deepest reverence. In this Joseph and all the rest of the mourners followed Her. It was already late and the sun had sunk, when the great Lady betook Herself from Calvary to the house of the Cenacle in the company of the faithful. Having brought Her to the Cenacle, saint John, the Marys and the others took leave of Her with many tears and sighs and asked for her benediction. The most humble and prudent Lady thanked them for their service to her divine Son and the consolation afforded Her; She permitted them to depart with many hidden and interior favors and with the blessing of her most amiable and kindest heart.

739. The Jews, confused and disturbed by the events, went to Pilate on the morning of the sabbath and asked him for soldiers to guard the sepulchre; for Christ, this seducer, they said, had openly announced, that after three days He would arise; hence his disciples might steal the body and then say that He had arisen. Pilate yielded to this malicious measure and gave them the guard they desired, which they stationed at the sepulchre (Matth. 28, 12). But the perfidious priests merely wished to palliate the event, which they feared would really happen, as was manifest afterwards, when they bribed the soldiers of the guard to testify, that Jesus had not arisen, but had been stolen by the disciples. As no counsel will prevail against God (Prov. 21, 30), the Resurrection of Christ became only so much the more public and was the more fully confirmed.

INSTRUCTION WHICH THE QUEEN OF HEAVEN GAVE ME.

740. My daughter, the lance-thrust which my blessed Son received in his side, was cruel and very painful only

to me; but its effects and mysteries are most sweet to those souls who know how to taste its sweetness. It was a great affliction to me; but whoever meets with this mysterious favor will find it a great relief and consolation in his sorrows. In order that thou mayest understand this and participate in it, thou must know, that my Son and Lord, on account of his most ardent love for men, in addition to the wounds of the feet and hands, wished to open the wound of his heart, the seat of love, in order that through this port the souls might enter and there receive refuge and relief. This is the only retreat which I wish thee to seek during the time of thy banishment, and which thou must consider as thy habitation upon earth. There thou wilt find the conditions and laws of love for imitating me and learn how for injuries thou must return blessings to all who commit them against thee and thine, just as thou hast seen me do, when I was grieved by the wounding of the side of my dead Son. I assure thee, my dearest, that thou canst not do anything more adapted to the obtaining of the efficacious graces from the Almighty. The prayer, which thou offerest in a forgiving spirit, is powerful not only for thy own good, but for the good of the one that offends thee; for the kind heart of my Son is easily moved, when He sees that creatures imitate Him in pardoning offenders and in praying for them; for they thereby participate in his most ardent charity manifested on the Cross. Write this doctrine in thy heart and in imitation of me practice this virtue, of which I thought so highly. Through this wound look upon the heart of Christ thy Spouse and upon me, sweetly and ardently loving in it thy enemies and all creatures.

741. Consider also the anxious and ever ready provi-

dence of the Most High in coming to the aid of the creatures, that call to Him in true confidence. This thou hast seen in my behalf, when I found myself afflicted and at a loss concerning the proper burial of my divine Son. In order to come to my assistance in this plight, the Lord showed his sweet love by moving the hearts of Joseph and Nikodemus and of the other faithful to assist me in burying Him. By their opportune help I was so much consoled in this tribulation, that on account of their behavior and my prayer the Most High filled them with wonderful influences of the Divinity, by which they were regaled during the time of taking Jesus from the Cross and his burial; and from that time on these faithful were enlightened and filled with the mysteries of the Redemption. This is the admirable disposition of the sweet and powerful providence of God, that in order to bind Himself to do good to some of his creatures, He sends affliction upon others, thus giving an occasion for the practice of benevolence, so that at the same time those in necessity may be benefited. Thus the benefactor, on account of the good work he does and on account of the prayer of the poor, is rewarded by receiving graces of which he otherwise would not be worthy. The Father of mercies, who inspires and assists the good work done, afterwards pays for it as if it were due in justice. For we can correspond to his inspirations merely according to our insignificant abilities, while all that is really good, comes entirely from his hands (James 1, 17).

742. Consider also the equity maintained by this Providence in compensating the injuries received in patient suffering. For after my divine Son had suffered death amid the contempt, dishonor and blasphemies of men, the Most High at once provided for an honorable

burial and moved many to confess Him as the true God and Redeemer, to proclaim Him as holy, innocent and just, and, at the very time when they had finished their frightful crucifixion, to adore Him as the Son of God. Even his enemies were made to feel within themselves the horror and confusion of their sin in persecuting Him. Although these benefits availed not all men, yet all of them were effects of the innocent Death of the Lord. I also concurred in my prayers, in order that the Lord might be acknowledged and honored by those known to me.

— NOTES —

— NOTES —

— *NOTES* —

— NOTES —

— *NOTES* —